queer
d i s b e l i e f

Why LGBTQ Equality Is an Atheist Issue

by **Camille Beredjick**

queer
disbelief

Why LGBTQ Equality Is an Atheist Issue

Camille Beredjick

Friendly Atheist Press

2017

Published by Friendly Atheist Press

December 2017 printing

Trademarks: All trademarks are the property of their respective owners. The publisher is not associated with any product or vendor mentioned in this book.

Typeset in 10 pt/12.5 pt Spectral
DTP services provided by Toon Media Publishing

Layout designed by Arthur Weber
Cover designed by Tracey Moody

Queer Disbelief: Why LGBTQ Equality Is an Atheist Issue

ISBN: 978-0-692-98964-7

For Peter, who made the world kinder.

Contents

Foreword

WHEN Richard Dawkins' *The God Delusion* came out in 2006, he made very clear what his goal was: "If this book works as I intend, religious readers who open it will be atheists when they put it down." It was an audacious goal, to say the least, but for many of those readers, *that's exactly what happened.* They shed their faith, if not the moment they put down the book, then not very long after.

I was already an atheist when the book came out, so I didn't need any more convincing, but I was thrilled that Dawkins was accomplishing his goal. He had some help, though. Thanks to other writers speaking out against religion, a backlash to a faith-infused presidency, the internet becoming a powerful force for non-believers, and religious leaders getting caught in various scandals, atheism was finally becoming—dare I say it—*popular.*

But to what end?

Was letting go of God our end goal? Or was it only the first step in a much longer journey?

Those are questions I've been thinking about for more than a decade as a writer and atheist activist. And I'm convinced that those of us who urge people to shed their faith are really promoting a larger goal of critical thinking. Religion is just one of the more difficult hurdles to overcome.

That's why most atheists have no problem pushing for better science education in our schools. It's a method of thinking that relies on evidence and reason. Why wouldn't we support that? It's why most atheists support separation of church and state. It's the best way to ensure freedom of thought for everyone. That's hardly a controversial opinion in atheist circles.

Where it gets more complicated is when we get into social issues in which religion steers the conversation for so many people.

Perhaps there are secular arguments for and against abortion, but the anti-choice movement is undoubtedly fueled by religious rhetoric. Perhaps there are atheists who don't want comprehensive sex education taught to high school students, but the abstinence-only crowd is full of evangelical Christians.

And when it comes to LGBTQ equality, the most vocal opposition to it comes from the Religious Right. From bathroom bills to Kim Davis to conversion therapy to anti-discrimination measures, you will find God at the center of it all. If faith wasn't a factor, how much sooner could we have had marriage equality in the U.S.?

If you're an atheist—or someone who just wants nothing to do with organized religion—then it seems logical that you'd also be an advocate for LGBTQ rights.

But I have known atheists who believe that issue, like other public policy concerns, are *tangential* to their identity. These are the people who say atheism begins and ends with one question: Do you believe in God? If the answer is no, that's it. They might support LGBTQ rights in general, but they don't put much thought into adoption laws or transgender people in the military. They think those are separate subjects, and that advocating for one doesn't necessarily mean you're going to advocate for the other.

I don't think that's true. I think that being an atheist—in this country, at this time, with these issues at stake—means you should be on the front lines of fighting for LGBTQ rights. The same process that led you to become an atheist should make you an activist for civil rights.

At the same time, I'm not always the most articulate person to make this case. I'm straight and cisgender. I've never worked with groups explicitly fighting for LGBTQ rights. I hope I'm a good ally, but there's plenty of nuance on these topics that escapes me.

They don't, however, escape Camille Beredjick. I've had the good fortune of working with Camille for years at FriendlyAtheist.com, where she's covered stories at the intersection of these two worlds. I've always found her articles to be intelligent, interesting, and insightful.

In 2016, long before the presidential election, we began talking about some of the more complicated questions that arise when religion and sexual orientation go head to head. Was religion *always* the enemy when it came to LGBTQ rights? Were there atheists who *opposed* marriage equality (and did they have good reasons for it)? Why were there so many *religious* gay and lesbian people when their holy books seemed to say such horrible things about them?

As I write this, we have a president who relies on evangelical Christians to shape his policies. We're watching the wall of separation between church and state get dismantled on a daily basis. And LGBTQ Americans—and atheists—have a lot to lose in the process.

Queer Disbelief is Camille's response to that. She lays out the issues, shows us why the problems facing LGBTQ people are very similar to the ones facing atheists, and calls on atheists everywhere to join the fight for equality. At the same time, she features the voices of marginalized people and gives credit where it's due to religious groups fighting for equality.

It is rare to see a book that's so thoughtful, so personal, so well-researched, and so inspiring. I was fired up by the end of it.

If this book works as she intends, atheists who open it will be vocal advocates for LGBTQ equality when they put it down.

Why LGBTQ Equality
Is an Atheist Issue

Proposition Hate

THE *New York Times* headline read: "Mormons Tipped Scale in Ban on Gay Marriage."[1]

Ten days earlier—November 4, 2008—California voters had approved Proposition 8, a ballot initiative to ban same-sex marriage in the state. It had been a tiresome campaign, full of anti-gay rhetoric, intense community engagement, and warring editorials about the "real" definition of marriage. The measure was a turning point in California's years-long debate on marriage equality, and it was promoted heavily by conservative religious groups. In particular, the well-connected Church of Jesus Christ of Latter-day Saints—the Mormon Church—spun Prop 8 into a victory at the eleventh hour.

According to leaders of the pro-Prop 8 group "Protect Marriage," Mormons made up the vast majority of door-to-door canvassers for the anti-marriage equality cause.[2] They devised a host of specific talking points against marriage equality, using different arguments based on whether or not the voters they spoke to were religious. On Election Day, they even helped get voters to the polls. But they were careful not to use church buildings as meeting places or a home base, according to *The Times*, "so as to not even give the appearance of politicking at the church." And while LDS members comprised only 2% of California's population, Mormons around the country raised as much as half of the nearly $40 million it took to repeal marriage equality. Other churches were involved in passing Prop 8, too, particularly the Catholic Church. But the urgency of the Mormon Church's involvement, its aggressive fundraising, and its commitment to canvassing were unparalleled.

The 2008 vote was among the first of many chapters in Proposition 8's long story. Protests erupted throughout California immediately upon the measure's passing. Over the course of several years, court after court struck down Prop 8 as unconstitutional, giving same-sex couples hope that their rights to marry would be restored. But it wasn't until a 2013 Supreme Court ruling that same-sex couples could finally marry again in California, and it took another two years for the Court to extend that right to same-sex couples nationwide.

Two years after the vote, and before U.S. District Judge Vaughn Walker overturned Prop 8, the Public Religion Research Institute conducted a survey of Californians about whether they'd vote for it again. Just 22% of Californians told PRRI that Prop 8's passage was a "good thing," 29% believed it was a "bad thing," and 45% believed it had made no difference.[3] When asked whether they would vote in favor of marriage equality tomorrow, 51% said yes.

The survey also documented the role of faith in shaping opinions on LGBTQ (lesbian, gay, bisexual, transgender, and queer/questioning) rights, particularly when religious leaders brought the issue into the pews. PRRI reported "significant Catholic-Protestant differences" in how often various groups heard about homosexuality at church, with Protestants going over the topic more frequently than Catholics. Every major religious group except mainline Protestants heard more negative than positive messages about LGBTQ people at their place of worship. And what happened in the pulpit had an impact at the polls: religious Californians who heard negative messages about LGBTQ people at church were far less likely to support marriage equality.

Looking back, the campaign for Proposition 8 is a prime example of what happens when religious groups unite against LGBTQ people. Prop 8's chief strategist, Frank Schubert, told the *New York Times* that his contingent did not want to frame the debate as "a battle between people of faith and the gays," as that would be a "losing formula." But that's exactly what happened. Despite not wanting to be seen as anti-gay, religious advocates for Prop 8 supported a measure that by its very name—the full initiative title was "Eliminates Rights of Same-Sex Couples to Marry"—sought to demote LGBTQ relationships to second-class status. It took years before that damage could be rectified through the courts.

But the same contempt that enacted Prop 8 still permeates the conversation on LGBTQ rights. Religious extremists argue against same-sex couples having children, fight to legalize employment discrimination, and cite the Bible to dehumanize and degrade LGBTQ people. "Religious freedom" is a buzzword that has come to represent state-sanctioned bigotry. "Religious exemptions" allow right-wing Americans to eschew laws meant to protect everyone equally.

In recent years, religious opposition has been the single greatest force preventing LGBTQ people from equal treatment under the law. That should be jarring to anyone who believes in justice for all, but especially those who understand the sting of faith-based discrimination. Among these groups are atheists (plus agnostics, humanists, non-believers, and others who don't believe in the existence of any gods). Atheists opt out of religious doctrine altogether, but nonetheless face much of the same harsh rhetoric from religious conservatives as LGBTQ people do. The deliberate use of religion to cause harm should infuriate atheists—and spur them to act.

Religious groups—one in particular—forced LGBTQ Californians to wait years for the basic right to marry. It's hard not to wonder: Could organized non-believers have stopped them?

Natural Allyship

The idea that atheists belong in social movements is not new. It stems, in part, from the natural kinship some atheists have with other groups persecuted by the Religious Right.

Some non-believers argue that being an atheist should begin and end with just that: non-belief. They claim that there is nothing inherently political about atheism, and that there is no connection between atheism and progressive social causes like LGBTQ equality, feminism, racial justice, and so on. But remaining silent on issues of inequality—especially when inequality is propelled by religious overreach—is antithetical to the purpose of organizing around atheism.

Over and over, LGBTQ people have been berated, belittled, and bullied based on the faulty premise that God frowns upon them. This erroneous explanation not only targets LGBTQ people but also contradicts ideas many atheists hold dear.

For example: When a pastor preaches that God unleashed Hurricane Sandy as punishment for same-sex marriage, as anti-gay preacher John McTernan did, that's not just an affront to LGBTQ people; it's an affront to science.[4] When a county clerk cites religion as an excuse to deny LGBTQ people equal treatment, as Kentucky's Kim Davis did, that's a slap in the face to the separation of church and state.[5] And when Christian schools that receive state funding fire LGBTQ teachers, as we've seen across the country, it's a clear abuse of power disguised as "religious exemption."

Science, reason, and a government free of religious influence are some of the most crucial tenets of secular humanism. Atheists—even those who believe that philosophy begins and ends with a rejection of God's existence—should be deeply offended when those principles are so egregiously violated.

Atheism itself is still somewhat of a subversive practice. People of faith comprise around three-quarters of the U.S. population; about 24% are unaffiliated or religious "nones," with self-declared atheists making up only 3.4% of the country.[6] As of this writing, there are no openly atheist members of Congress.[7] In some countries, being an atheist, being LGBTQ, or both are cause for persecution or even death. And, of course, there are LGBTQ atheists in the United States and elsewhere who are doubly marginalized for identifying as both. It is in atheists' nature to eschew certain societal norms in favor of ideas that feel more true to them. Joining forces with others targeted by religious groups shouldn't be controversial. In fact, it should be expected.

Some people—though not usually atheists—actually argue *against* taking religion out of politics, citing the civil right to free expression. And sure, the First Amendment has its place in these conversations. A person who pushes homophobia or transphobia under the guise of religion is allowed those opinions privately and even publicly, to an extent. But once religious beliefs are invoked to interfere with the civil rights of others— say, to justify firing a qualified employee, or to provide a legal loophole for segregating LGBTQ customers—the First Amendment exits the equation. Personal beliefs cannot infringe upon the rights of others to pursue life and liberty however they choose. If atheists sit idly by as religious Americans target LGBTQ communities, they are endorsing it.

And yet America's failure to protect LGBTQ citizens is a direct result of the overstepping of religion into politics. It's a flagrant rejection of the Establishment Clause, and a refusal to prioritize objectivity and fairness.[8] Equal rights for LGBTQ people should come naturally to a society that operates on evidence and reason (the kind of society atheists generally advocate for). Atheists should be invested in removing religious influence from the rule of law. And they do their own cause a disservice when they fail to defend LGBTQ people, politically and personally.

As both an atheist and a queer person, I'm doubly baffled by the intensity of religious hatred against my people—*all* my people. I write a lot about LGBTQ issues, and I've received countless anonymous messages (and some not anonymous) outlining all the reasons I'm a hellbound dyke. Sometimes, the message is just a list of Bible verses—as if I'm going to take out my copy of the New Testament and flip through it to learn why my life displeases a higher power whose existence I reject. I'm lucky to have lived mostly in liberal parts of the country (not that religious bigotry doesn't exist in all 50 states) and that I've never faced faith-based discrimination outright. But thousands of others aren't as fortunate.

LGBTQ people are fired, kicked out of their homes, pushed out of local businesses, and refused social and health services because of the "religious consciences" of others. To make matters worse, we don't even know exactly how many LGBTQ people face discrimination every year. As in other situations when victims must choose whether to report what's happened to them, many people refrain out of the fear of retaliation, outing, or worse. (And just because it hasn't happened to me yet, there's no guarantee that it won't in the future.)

LGBTQ people and atheists aren't the only groups hurt by religious fundamentalism. For example, the Religious Right targets women with a similar fervor. Employers fight to deny insurance coverage for birth control on the grounds of religious freedom.[9] Women are fired for being pregnant and unmarried.[10] Puritanical beliefs about women's rights and roles trickle down into other elements of society. The wage gap and sexism in the media aren't necessarily a result of religious misogyny, but they're peddled by a lot of the same people.

And historically—though not long ago at all—people deployed religious arguments to defend segregation and other manifestations of racism. "In the 1960s, we saw institutions object to laws requiring integration in restaurants because of sincerely held beliefs that God wanted the races to be separate," according to the ACLU.[11] Integration was seen as an affront to God.[12] Bob Jones University, a fundamentalist Protestant school in South Carolina, didn't drop its ban on interracial dating until the year 2000.[13]

When you consider how extreme the consequences of bigotry can be, the harassment and disrespect atheists face for their non-belief can seem pretty mild in comparison. Society certainly doesn't embrace atheists, but there are far fewer attacks (physical, legal, and otherwise) on atheist "lifestyles" than on LGBTQ people, women, people of color, or even other religious groups.[14] But plenty of atheists can be and are members of all these groups, facing attacks not for their non-beliefs, but for visible elements of their identity. Virtually every minority group in the world has faced some defamation, discrimination, or mistreatment at the hands of religious extremism, one way or another. It only makes sense that we would rally together in our respective times of need.

Why LGBTQ people in particular? Because when it comes to religious suppression of civil rights, LGBTQ people have too much at stake. In recent years, the Religious Right has focused much of its energy and resources on limiting—or even eliminating—the rights of LGBTQ people. Anti-LGBTQ ideals littered the 2016 Republican Party platform and continue to serve as talking points for many GOP politicians, even though religious beliefs are supposed to be absent from the legislative process. According to the Human Rights Campaign, the largest LGBTQ rights group in the country, only four Republican senators and seven Republican members of the House of Representatives supported marriage equality in the lead-up to the 2016 election. Even Barack Obama, arguably the most progressive president in U.S. history (certainly on this issue), didn't announce his support for marriage equality until the end of his first term, after a handful of states had already enacted same-sex marriage and Proposition 8 had twice been ruled unconstitutional.

LGBTQ issues have never been more visible, and anti-LGBTQ religious extremists have never been more fired up. If equal rights advocates don't fight back aggressively, we can expect sweeping victories for state-approved religious bigotry. That kind of upheaval would deal a significant blow to atheism, too: imagine trying to defend secular education, the scientific method, or the separation of church and state in a country that explicitly favors one belief system over others (let alone over non-belief). We may be a long way off from falling into an extremist religious dystopia, but it's still worth keeping our guard up.

And it's not enough for atheists and LGBTQ people to be allies in name alone. In order for both these groups to be treated with civility and humanity, we must support each other loudly and unapologetically, in our schools and our workplaces, at the dinner table and at the ballot box. In 2015, atheist writer Adam Lee penned an editorial for the *Guardian* with the headline, "If peace on earth is our goal, atheism might be the means to that end."[15] While that sentence might suggest a simplistic answer to a complicated problem, there is little evidence for *more* religious influence leading to social harmony. LGBTQ people have been political targets for decades. As society slowly begins to see us with more empathy than ever before, we deserve the peace we've been denied for so long. Atheists must help us get there.

How I Got Here

I didn't always know I was queer—not everyone realizes it right away—but I've been wondering where I fell on the spectrum of religious belief since I was a kid.

When I was 11 and just starting middle school, some of my new friends were strongly Christian. I didn't have much of a religious leaning; my mother's family is Catholic and my father's family is Jewish, so I grew up celebrating twice as many holidays but lacked grounding in any particular teachings. So when my new friends told me about a Bible study guide they loved, one that was targeted toward "hip" Christian teens, I thought it would be a neat way to join the youth-group-going in-crowd. As far as I was concerned, I was passively agnostic, but I thought having the tools to find faith might make me feel more certain one way or the other. A friend's mom bought me the trendy teen Bible as an early birthday present.

I was ecstatic to receive it. It was brightly colored, used wacky fonts, and had discussion pages at the ends of some sections, making parallels between Scripture and teen issues like school and dating. But there were some red flags right off the bat that made me think this might not be for me. For example, I'd never had strong feelings about premarital sex, but my friends—and this Bible—did. I figured sex would happen when it happened, and between talking with my parents, my lackluster public school sex ed, and *Seventeen* magazine, I had a decent grasp on how not to get pregnant. My Bible's all-or-nothing take on sex and dating made me uneasy, like a stranger giving me serious advice I hadn't asked for. I didn't even bother looking at the discussion notes on gay people; I didn't know yet that they applied to me. (I recently dug that Bible out from my pile of rejected childhood items to find that section. It's not pretty.)

Then I found something that I took more personally. A small section of the sex and dating chapter included a stern footnote about dating non-Christians. "Don't do it," it said. "It's never a good idea."

I asked my parents about it, about whether or not God thought their interfaith marriage—and therefore, my existence—was a bad idea. They said they had talked about it a long time ago and decided that because they both believed in God, the details didn't matter. But it was enough to turn me off of religious exploration for a long time. When I came out as bisexual in high school, I felt even less connected to my friends' stories about church programs and their excitement about applying to Christian colleges. And eventually, I realized I didn't need to explore anymore. The belief just wasn't there.

This isn't to say I disparage or disrespect those who do find comfort in faith. There are thriving communities of LGBTQ people of faith around the world, some of whom belong to progressive houses of worship and others who practice independent spirituality, who find that their faith and their LGBTQ identity strengthen one another. Today, more and more religious groups celebrate diversity, actively support LGBTQ people, and speak out against the institutions that use scripture to oppress and demean. Unfortunately, these groups are in the minority. While there are avenues for LGBTQ people to work with faith groups, the potential for allyship between LGBTQ people and atheists is far more intuitive, and certainly presents fewer institutional boundaries.

When I started writing about LGBTQ issues for Hemant Mehta's blog, "Friendly Atheist"—which is how this book came to be — I was often stumped by the lack of news about the explicit overlaps between LGBTQ people and atheists. Stories about active collaborations between these two groups were sparse. All I seemed to read (and write) were stories of outrageous homophobic and transphobic behavior by conservative churches and evangelical politicians, all in the name of God. What I didn't immediately realize, though, is that religious groups oppressing LGBTQ people is an atheist issue. Any abuse of religious freedom, particularly at the expense of a marginalized group, is an atheist issue. That's how I reframed my work for the blog, and that's the lens through which I wrote this book.

These chapters are an examination of the ways atheists and LGBTQ people are natural allies; the ways these groups can learn from and support one another; the reasons atheists have a responsibility to support human rights issues like LGBTQ equality; and most importantly, why it's crucial that we do so without delay or hesitation.

Notes on Language
As with any culture or community, the language of the LGBTQ movement is constantly changing. Being intentional and

thoughtful in our word choices plays a huge role in promoting acceptance outside the movement and within it. For the purposes of this book, it's important to note a few distinctions and linguistic choices and why we've made them.

The acronym *LGBTQ*—for lesbian, gay, bisexual, transgender, and queer or questioning—will be used to refer to the greater community of people who don't identify as straight and/or cisgender. Many people describe their sexual orientation or gender identity with a word not included in this shorthand, but aside from adding letter after letter to an infinite acronym, the community has not come to consensus about how to linguistically include every identity in one word.

Sometimes, the word "queer" is used as an umbrella term for anyone whose sexual orientation or gender identity falls outside the mainstream; however, I will generally not use it in that way in this book, with a few exceptions. The word "queer" has a deep history as a biting slur targeting LGBTQ people, especially gay men.[16] It was used as a symbol of protest in 1990, when a group called Queer Nation formed calling for an end to homophobia.[17] In recent years, "queer" has been reclaimed by some LGBTQ people as their own identity, as a more radical descriptor for gender and sexual identities that challenge norms. However, for others, the word still has sharp connotations as pejorative or even threatening, and in many regions and contexts, it's still used that way.

Throughout this book, I've avoided using the word "queer" unless referring specifically to a person who identifies with the term, or to the broader *issues* of gender, sexuality, and equal rights. The goal is not to impose the label of "queer" on people who do not care to use it, but to recognize its usefulness in describing identities that fall outside the mainstream. "Queer theory," for example, is an academic study encompassing gender, sexuality, and other identities and power systems that shape how we interact with each other and the world. The title of this book is a reference both to the overlap in LGBTQ and atheist ideals, and to the ways that atheism is inherently queer, as in different or unusual. (As I'll say throughout the book, an identity or belief being uncommon doesn't make it bad.)

Some of the people I've interviewed use the singular pronoun *they* to describe themselves, rather than *he* or *she*. This is another way to convey an identity that isn't strictly male or female, or to refer to a person without invoking gender at all. Use of the singular "they" dates back at least to Shakespearean English, and it is used increasingly across the United States, from newspapers to classrooms.[18] To avoid confusion, I'll indicate when an interviewee uses "they" as needed. It's not a typo!

The word *transgender* refers to people who identify as a gender other than the one they were assigned at birth. Conversely, the word *cisgender* refers to people for whom this is not the case—those who identify with the gender they were assigned. Explicit inclusion of transgender people is one of the reasons why it's critical to use more inclusive terms like LGBTQ rather than umbrella terms like "gay" when referring to the movement for equal rights. In order to adequately address discrimination based on gender identity and expression, it's crucial to include and center transgender people in the cause. The language of the movement should reflect that.

To that end, it should be noted that the "LGBTQ community"—like the atheist community, or communities of faith—is not a monolith. While LGBTQ people may share some common goals, other factors like race, class, nationality, socioeconomic status, etc. influence how LGBTQ people experience the world and the ways in which they face oppression, marginalization, and empowerment. For example, the campaign for marriage equality was a huge victory to LGBTQ people for whom marriage is desirable and accessible. But the legalization of same-sex marriage contributed little, if at all, to the well-being of LGBTQ homeless youth, of whom there are an estimated 320,000 to 400,000,[19] or to the safety of transgender women of color, who face devastatingly high rates of assault and murder.[20]

Finally, there is no single agreed-upon glossary of LGBTQ terminology, and likewise, an infinite array of opinions and experiences within LGBTQ and (non-)religious communities. While I chose my language and statements thoughtfully and with the best of intentions, I'm limited to writing about my own experiences and those of the sources I consulted. (If readers disagree with anything I've said or words I've used, I hope you'll reach out.) This book was written with the ambition to talk about our communities with kindness and respect; ideally, it will be read in the same way.

Common Ground

Evil Little Things

JESSICA Ahlquist was a teenager when she became the country's most-talked-about atheist. Ahlquist was a high school student in Cranston, Rhode Island, a deeply Roman Catholic city. Baptized in the Catholic Church, she had stopped believing in God when she was 10. And in 2012, at age 16, she served as a plaintiff in the ACLU's lawsuit to have an eight-foot-tall prayer mural removed from her school's auditorium.[21]

The prayer had hung for nearly 50 years, a gift from a graduating senior class. It began with the words "Our Heavenly Father," and asked for God's grace in modeling good morals like kindness and honesty. Ahlquist said the mural made her feel like she didn't belong at Cranston High School West, a public school in a religious community, but a public school nonetheless. A federal judge ruled in her favor, and the school was ordered to take down the prayer.

This victory for the Constitution came at a personal cost to Ahlquist when her town largely turned against her. She faced harassment and even death threats (because nothing says "good Christian" like threatening to kill someone who disagrees with you). She had a police escort at school. State Representative Peter G. Palumbo—an elected official and grown man—called her an "evil little thing" during a radio interview. All this because she had the audacity to stand up for separation of church and state at her school, and because the court took her side.

Ahlquist also received a significant showing of support from atheist and humanist groups, including scholarships, awards, invitations to speak at events, and other forms of recognition.[22] She's been out of the public eye recently, but her bravery inspired others to speak out about inappropriate religious symbols in their schools.[23]

Now, rewind to about two years before Ahlquist's fight. In another part of the country, in Fayetteville, Arkansas, another student pushed back against a school tradition that didn't make sense to him. This time it was Will Phillips, who was just 10 years old when he called out an injustice he noticed in the world. In 2009, Phillips decided to stop saying the Pledge of Allegiance at school to protest the way LGBTQ people were treated in the United States.[24]

"I've grown up with a lot of people and I'm good friends with a lot of people who are gay," he said in an appearance on CNN sitting next to his dad, Jay Phillips. "I think they should have the rights all people should, and I'm not going to swear that they do. . . . I really don't feel that there's currently liberty and justice for all."

Phillips continued his work as an LGBTQ activist for the next several years. His protest ended in 2013, when the Supreme Court overturned the Defense of Marriage Act.[25] That year, he gave a speech and led a modified version of the Pledge at the Northwest Arkansas Pride Parade.[26] He gave the crowd the chance to repeat after him, with a caveat.

"I'm not one for pressuring people to say the Pledge against their wishes, like *some* people, but if you'd like to, please repeat after me," he said to laughs and applause. He skipped the phrase "under God." *One nation, indivisible, with liberty and justice for all.* (That's how the Pledge was originally written in 1892. "Under God" wasn't added until 1954, a move by President Eisenhower to respond to the threat of communism.)[27]

It makes sense that atheists and LGBTQ people—and their kindhearted young allies—would feel unsettled about enshrined rituals that deliberately exclude them. Both groups espouse a "lifestyle" that differs from what's recommended by most mainstream religions; therefore, both are subject to religious persecution in some form or another. Add to that the huge historical influence of Christianity in the United States, and the societal expectation to pledge liberty to a country that treats some citizens as second-class— no wonder there's a disconnect. However, this persecution takes many different forms, and the two groups definitely don't experience it with equal frequency or intensity.

In his book *Born Atheist,* author Tim Covell dedicates a chapter to the relationship between LGBTQ people and the church, particularly the various sources of religious bigotry against LGBTQ people and their relationships. "Without religion, there is no reason other than prejudice to deny gays equal rights, including the right to marry," Covell writes. "Gay people are born that way, and it is grossly unfair to apply ancient rules to deny them equality in the modern world. ... As in so many other instances, religious scriptures, written by men and fixed in time, have been unable to adapt to a changing world."

Covell's book was originally published in 2010, so some of his points, such as the then-refusal to legalize marriage equality, are no longer relevant. But the idea that anchors his argument is still pertinent; religious extremists cite expired, vague stories to undermine LGBTQ people, and the law often rules in their favor. Prejudice may be less socially acceptable than it was 10, 20, or 50 years ago, but religious freedom is still considered a valid reason to discriminate in too many cases. And if weak interpretations of scripture count as justification for bad behavior, then we're in even more trouble.

Covell also writes that it can be hypocritical to form your opinion about homosexuality based on the Bible. Christians don't generally stone disobedient children or adulterers, he says, even though that's the punishment the Old Testament designates for those transgressions. Likewise, most Christians in the United States don't usually call for the death of LGBTQ people (though in countries like Uganda, some do), even though that's what a literal reading of Leviticus might suggest. "If gays are okay, the scriptures are wrong," Covell writes. "If the scriptures are right, then gays should be killed."

Rather than call for the death of LGBTQ people, it's more common for anti-equality advocates to condemn gay relationships and cite the Bible as justification. But even this gives holy texts too much credit. The First Amendment of the Bill of Rights—"Congress shall make no law respecting an establishment of religion"—has long been interpreted to mean it's out of bounds for religious beliefs, or lack thereof, to govern society. Whether or not Christians follow the entire Bible in a literal sense is irrelevant; Scripture should be entirely absent from law anyway. If there aren't good secular reasons for public policies, we shouldn't pass them.

Are there any non-religious reasons one can cite to oppose equality? Absolutely—but those are harder for politicians to justify. Put simply, it's prejudice.

In 2009, four researchers found that sensitivity to the feeling of disgust is associated with "intuitive disapproval of gay people."[28] There's a strong link between morality and disgust, they wrote. Disgust responses are emotional, quick, and intuitive. They don't require intentional, logical reasoning or consideration of values and principles. And sex is one category to which our "ick factor" may be highly attuned.

"Because gay people almost by definition engage in 'unusual' sexual behavior," the researchers wrote, "one would expect more negative reactions to this outgroup on the part of those who are particularly disgust sensitive." Or, for our purposes: gay people are icky.

It's pretty easy to identify someone who's grossed out by same-sex attraction but doesn't want to say it. Usually, it's the same type of person who talks about gay sex *way more* than any average gay person does (looking at you, Pat Robertson). It's someone who looks for biological arguments against homosexuality, like the inability of two men or two women to have a baby. Of course, these pairings aren't the only couples incapable of procreation; infertile couples and elderly couples are also biologically prevented from having a kid, but you don't see COMMENTS IN ALL CAPS demanding an end to their marriages.

As it turns out, disgust reflex isn't protected under the Constitution. Religious freedom is. Which is why the latter is the language we're used to hearing when beliefs and rights conflict. In cases where business owners or politicians refuse to serve LGBTQ people because it violates their religious beliefs —which is illegal anyway—what they might be saying is that they think we're disgusting.

There's also a contingent of activists, many of them LGBTQ themselves, who protest causes like marriage equality and LGBTQ inclusion in the military on the grounds of anti-assimilationist principles and opposition to those institutions themselves. The issue for them isn't LGBTQ people getting married;

it's the government sanctioning marriage at all. Similarly, they don't fight for LGBTQ inclusion in the military because they oppose the military as an institution. In many ways, that's a valid argument. The politics of marriage and the military are complex, and both these fixtures of society have their flaws. While they are important, heralding them as indicators of "true" equality is entirely wrong. (Case in point: Marriage equality and military service for lesbian, gay, and bisexual people are both legal, but while neither of those institutions has "suffered," LGBTQ people are obviously still not equal.)

But beyond marriage and the military, two powerful societal institutions, LGBTQ people still lack some basic protections we need before we can pursue a life of our own choosing: comprehensive and accessible health care, a safe and harassment-free education, and housing guaranteed free from discrimination are just a few.

And then there's the ongoing debate about the word *homophobia* itself: Is it really a phobia, or are you just a bigot? Ignorance and disdain are two different beasts, yet they commonly overlap to spawn hate and stigma. Here, too, atheists can relate. To someone who's never met anybody outside of their religious community, the mere idea of a person who doesn't believe in God can be terrifying and confusing—and may even seem impossible. In cases like these, it's easy for misunderstanding of atheism to turn into distrust and disapproval.

In the privacy of your own home and your own mind, you're allowed whatever beliefs you like, however toxic and unkind they may be. It's when those beliefs permeate into other people's lives—which they inevitably will—that they become more urgently problematic. Even though homophobia and transphobia can stem from multiple sources, anti-LGBTQ advocates have had the most success when tying their prejudiced ideals to religious freedom. But that doesn't make them legal, and it doesn't make them right.

The social bookmarking site Reddit is primarily young, white, and male.[29] So are most atheists, according to the Pew Research

Center.[30] It makes sense, then, that one of the site's larger "subreddits," or forums on a specific topic, is r/atheism, with more than two million subscribers. It's a hotbed for conversations about atheism in the modern world—and sometimes, atheists disagree about what that looks like.

In 2016, the moderators of r/atheism started a conversation referring to a recent "uptick in vocal opponents to posts about LGBT issues on r/atheism." The moderator account posed this question to the forum: "How relevant are LGBT topics to r/atheism?" Obviously, this is a hyper-specific question, about one issue on one forum on one website. But the conversation that ensued highlighted the main reasons atheists and LGBTQ people click: "The majority of anti-LGBT sentiment stems from something religious, and thus it is fair game for inclusion here." One user stated that, in particular, conversations about LGBTQ people's "freedom from oppression" should be welcomed on r/atheism; after all, overcoming the impositions of religion in society are a common thread for both groups.[31]

It's true that LGBTQ people and atheists both face marginalization, and that institutional religion is a major cause for their hardship. However, the two groups' experiences are far from identical, and it's irresponsible to suggest they are.

In 2013, queer atheist writer Chris Stedman wrote a column for *Religion News Service* titled "Atheism is not the 'new gay marriage' (or the new anything else)."[32] He argued that suggesting too close a parallel between atheist and LGBTQ communities was "shallow at best and erasure at worst." Instead, he called for a cross-community approach to social justice, recognizing that our struggles can be connected even if they're not intertwined.

Politically and personally, atheists and LGBTQ people overlap. LGBTQ people are more likely to be atheists than the general population ; atheists are more likely to support LGBTQ rights. In some cases, discovering that you're LGBTQ is the spark that causes you to leave the faith in which you were raised. Atheists should support LGBTQ people even in fights that don't affect them personally, but in order to get there, it's worth examining the ways in which those issues really do impact atheists, too.

On the Books

Since 2015 or so, "religious freedom" bills—or, as some call them, "license to discriminate" bills—have swept state legislatures with unprecedented force. Part of that momentum was because of the Supreme Court's decision to legalize marriage equality, though the political motivation behind the laws isn't new.[35]

Back in 1993, Congress passed the U.S. Religious Freedom Restoration Act (RFRA) to "ensure that interests in religious freedom are protected."[36] It had 170 bipartisan cosponsors and was even introduced by a Democrat, New York's Chuck Schumer, who was then a member of the House of Representatives. In 1997, the Supreme Court ruled that RFRA applied only to the federal government, resulting in many states creating RFRAs of their own.

"The law passed with the backing of a broad-based coalition," CNN's Ray Sanchez wrote of RFRA, "but it wasn't set against the more recent backdrop of gay rights or the wave of marriage equality laws and court rulings that culminated in the *Obergefell* decision."

Since then, religious freedom laws have seemed more targeted and less transparent. With some tweaks in wording, the gist of each bill is the same: the government cannot punish businesses and religious groups who deny services based on "sincerely held" religious beliefs or convictions. About 30 states either enacted or considered religious freedom laws since the RFRA law of 1993, according to CNN.

Anti-LGBTQ activists who support these bills often use same-sex weddings as an easy illustration of the supposed problem. For example, they claim a baker shouldn't be forced to make a wedding cake for a same-sex couple if the baker's religion disapproves of same-sex marriage. Nondiscrimination laws involving public accommodations should prevent this kind of targeted bigotry. Unfortunately, those laws don't protect LGBTQ people everywhere. In fact, there's no federal law protecting against discrimination on the basis of sexual orientation or gender identity, and fewer than half of states have enacted their own policies doing so.[37]

This, in itself, is terrifying. In places like Georgia and Mississippi, lawmakers want business owners to be able to shut out customers because of their "sincerely held" convictions. In one gross violation of privacy, a baker in Ohio accepted an order from a customer, found the customer on Facebook, figured out that the customer had ordered a birthday cake for her same-sex partner, and canceled the order.[38] (This happened in the city of Toledo, which has LGBTQ protections, but elsewhere in Ohio, it could have been totally legal.) As of this writing, the customer has not taken legal action against the bakery (or hasn't announced it publicly if she did), but the baker certainly would have lost.

LGBTQ people also worry the law could trickle down to places like hospitals and doctor's offices, and that they could be refused necessary medical treatment. In Michigan in 2015, a pediatrician refused to care for a 6-day-old baby with two moms.[39] "After much prayer following your prenatal, I felt that I would not be able to develop the personal patient-doctor relationship that I normally do with my patients," their doctor told the couple. "Please know that I believe that God gives us free choice and I would never judge anyone based on what they do with that free choice." The doctor's decision violated the American Medical Association's code of ethics, but not Michigan state law. And because the pediatrician's actions were technically legal, the couple didn't sue (again, at least not publicly) and presumably found another doctor.

And LGBTQ people are just one population that could be targeted. Some state-level RFRAs are specifically applicable to convictions on marriage—that is, they exist to protect people opposed to marriage equality—such as the "Marriage and Conscience Act" proposed in Louisiana in 2015.[40] Others are more vague. Depending on your interpretation of an RFRA, unwed mothers, pregnant teenagers, interracial couples, and even people who appeared to belong to another religious group could qualify to be booted from a Christian-owned mom-and-pop soda shop. (Obviously, there's no visible marker that conveys to the world you're an atheist the way there is for some religions. But if you were wearing your "I'm An Atheist" T-shirt that day, you might also be out of luck.) RFRA laws may start at anti-LGBTQ discrimination, but there's no telling where they end.

The Supreme Court has sent mixed messages on "religious freedom" recently. The marriage equality decision was an obvious victory. However, the Court's ruling in *Burwell v. Hobby Lobby Stores, Inc.* scored a point for religious discrimination. The Court ruled that based on religious beliefs, a business could abstain from covering employees' birth control prescriptions under their health care plan. In her dissent, Justice Ruth Bader Ginsburg pointed out that religious business owners could use the same logic to deny access to other necessary medical care, like blood transfusions, antidepressants, or vaccinations.[41]

And as recently as June of 2017, the Court announced that it would hear the case of Masterpiece Cakeshop, a Colorado bakery that lost a discrimination case for refusing to bake a cake for a same-sex wedding.[42] The outcome may set the stage for these disputes in the future.

Now that marriage is signed, sealed, and delivered—knock on wood—another battle for the anti-LGBTQ cause concerns the rights of transgender people to live fully as the gender with which they identify. It's a little harder, but not impossible, to make a religious case against trans rights. There's no Bible verse suggesting a trans person should be stoned to death in the way some verses about gay people have been interpreted. But throngs of people claim that undergoing a gender transition is an act against God, a betrayal of the way one was created.

Laws that oppress transgender people are less likely to invoke religious freedom. Instead, they claim that denying trans people's rights is necessary for the purposes of safety and privacy (here comes that disgust reflex again). This talking point especially comes into play in the case of "bathroom bills," so nicknamed because they dictate which public bathrooms trans people can legally use. Political bigotry seems to particularly target transgender women, whom some conservatives call "confused" or "men in dresses." Virtually all of the science on trans people proves these accusations wrong.

One of the most visible battles for trans rights is the case of Gavin Grimm, a transgender teenager whose school forced him to use the women's bathroom. Grimm's case was supposed to be heard by the Supreme Court in the spring of 2017, but as of this writing, the Court sent the case back to the 4th Circuit Court of Appeals. (That happened after the Trump administration revoked President Obama's guidance extending protections to transgender students, a move that presents its own set of fears.)[43] If a decision comes out in favor of trans students, we can almost certainly expect that social conservatives will find a religious argument in retaliation.

Finally, our great nation has a nasty habit of leaving ancient laws on the books, even when they've been deemed unconstitutional, and even when there's virtually no way to enforce them. LGBTQ people and atheists are two groups that often bear the brunt of these laws.

When the United States of America was founded, the country inherited sodomy laws—laws banning consensual sex between men, as well as other acts that inhibited procreation, like masturbation and abortion—from Britain. Its justification was tied to traditional Judeo-Christian morals, which maintained that sex was reserved for procreation between married couples.[44] The majority of these laws were struck down from the 1970s through the 1990s, while others were rewritten to apply only to gay people.[45] The Supreme Court only struck down sodomy laws across the country in *Lawrence v. Texas* in 2003—yes, that late. In 2014, a dozen states still had not taken their sodomy laws off the books;[46] such laws are unconstitutional and unenforceable, thanks to the Lawrence decision, yet they remain as symbols of past norms.[47]

Similarly baffling laws exist barring atheists from holding public office in seven states.[48] Just like old-timey sodomy laws, these bans are virtually unenforceable under modern nondiscrimination laws, perhaps even more so than laws targeting LGBTQ people. Discrimination on the basis of one's religion (or lack thereof) is prohibited by the Civil Rights Act, but there are no federal laws banning discrimination on the basis of sexual orientation or gender identity. Way back in 1961, the Supreme Court ruled in favor of Roy Torcaso, an atheist who refused to say he believed in God in order to become a notary public in Maryland. Decades later, however, Maryland is one of the states where it's still technically illegal to hold public office as an atheist.

In both these cases, the true harm of these laws may not be their legal consequences, but their social implications. Even if they don't lead to prosecution, our laws indicate that there is something wrong—illegal, even—about adults having consensual sex. Even if atheists are sworn into office in those states, the rules they swear to uphold deem them unworthy leaders.

Discriminatory laws do more than burden people with unfair penalties and punishments. They instill fear of the "other" and communicate that some people are more deserving of protection than others. And their long history of targeting both LGBTQ people and atheists is far from over.

Social Differences

I'll be honest with you: There have been days when I wished I believed in God. It's not an incessant, gnawing feeling, but every once in a while I wonder what it would be like to feel that *someone* was out there, watching over me; to know that my future wife and I will meet again on some eternal plane; to believe I was never alone.

But I don't believe that. I can't make myself believe it, as much as I tried to when I was 11 and all the cool kids were doing it. And for the most part, I'm comfortable with that.

There's disagreement about the role of choice in atheism, and religion more broadly. None of us thinks about the possibility of a god until someone tells us about it. Your first conscious thoughts as a baby are less about the creation of the universe and more about when you're getting your next meal. But does that mean babies are atheists until further notice? Are dogs atheists because they can't bark out that they believe?

Arguably not. In fact, few people actually self-declare as atheists. About 3% of Americans identify as atheist and another 3% identify as agnostic, according to PRRI data, as compared with about 14% who are simply "secular."[49] Even if you can't choose your (non)beliefs, you can choose how you convey them to the world, and some people prefer to be non-affiliated rather than identify with the label of *atheist.*

That said, realizing you're an atheist is dependent upon knowing that other people believe in God. But a girl who has a crush on another girl in elementary school doesn't necessarily know that she's in the minority.

Being LGBTQ is decidedly not a choice. We haven't figured out exactly what "causes" it, but infinite anecdotes and at least some research confirm that there's no defining moment when you choose your sexual orientation or gender identity.[50] Thanks to lifetimes of homophobia and transphobia ingrained in society, there's no doubt that some LGBTQ people wish they were different, or at least felt that way at some point in their lives. I remember sobbing in the shower as a teenager, wishing my crush on a girl was just a fluke, knowing I could never tell anyone about this awful defect I'd discovered in myself. I never felt that kind of devastation about realizing I was an atheist, but that doesn't mean there weren't moments of discomfort in the process.

In his book *Far From the Tree*, author Andrew Solomon calls being gay a "horizontal identity," as most gay kids are born to straight parents and learn about gay identity and community from outside sources. Solomon himself is gay and writes about how being different from your family affects you both.

"Many parents experience their child's horizontal identity as an affront," he says. "A child's marked difference from the rest of the family demands knowledge, competence, and actions that a typical mother and father are unqualified to supply, at least initially."[51]

Indeed, when you realize something about yourself that wasn't passed down from your parents, like being an atheist or LGBTQ, a coming-out conversation is usually not far off. Coming out as LGBTQ can be devastating or uplifting, depending on how your audience responds.

As public opinions of LGBTQ people improve, you'd think young people coming out could expect a marginally better reaction from their families than they did 10 or 20 years ago. Sadly, that's not the case for everyone. As many as 40% of homeless youth identify as LGBTQ, and the most common reason they become homeless is because their families rejected them. According to the True Colors Fund, a non-profit working to end LGBTQ youth homelessness, half of all LGBTQ teenagers get a negative reaction from their parents when they come out, and over a quarter are thrown out of their homes.[52]

There's a link front and center on Reddit's r/atheism home-page that says, "Thinking of coming out to your parents? Read this first." The phrase "coming out" has been associated with the gay community (and later, the rest of the acronym) since the 1960s, and if you're someone who's never had to "come out" to anyone as anything, seeing it used in this context might give you pause. Unfortunately, coming out as an atheist can have hard consequences for people from religious backgrounds, just like coming out as LGBTQ is dangerous in some families.

The Reddit advice page starts with: "Should I come out to my parents as being an atheist? The short answer is no." That's followed by this lengthier explanation:

> The slightly longer answer is that if you are not in a position where that is likely to end well for you, you should probably wait until you're more self-sufficient. However, you know your own parents better than we do. You could try breaking the ice on the subject of atheism to get a feel for their reaction to it in general, if you're not sure. Always keep in mind that for many people religion is a highly emotive subject, and for many parents who have been raised to believe in the "moral superiority" of religious belief, a child who comes out as an atheist can be interpreted as a betrayal of them or as a failure of their own. . . . A common proverb here is "The best place to come out to your parents is at a home you own, over a dinner that you paid for yourself."

There are a lot of similarities to be found between coming out as an atheist and coming out as LGBTQ. In both cases, your family might think there's something wrong with you, or that you've temporarily "lost your way" from the path they set for you. Both announcements might lead to "(more) frequent church visits, and maybe a talk with the priest/pastor/counsel-or," as r/atheism says of coming out as an atheist. Depending on your background, either could elicit a response along the lines of "That's not how we raised you." And in the most extreme sit-uations, either could lead to an outright rejection by your loved ones, getting thrown out of the house, or even being assaulted or abused by an unaccepting family member. These responses range from heartbreaking to life-threatening, and their effects stick. Nobody wants to be told they're not the kind of kid their family wanted.

In one study, a group of researchers from the University of Minnesota found that atheists were second only to Muslims as the most disliked and distrusted "cultural outsider" group in the country. Nearly 42% of respondents said that atheists "do not at all agree with my vision on American society." "Homosexuals" and conservative Christians were the next two most commonly chosen groups.[53]

"There are no mainstream, cultural expressions or depictions, on television for example, to present atheism to the general public," sociologist Penny Edgell said in a university statement. "It's only in the last decade that a secular coalition of American atheist and non-religion organizations have gotten together. I expect that in the near future we'll see more effort on their part to change perceptions and lobby to change policy."[54]

Her point about cultural expressions of atheism is not necessarily true. There are plenty of big-name atheists in pop culture—Bill Maher, Ricky Gervais, Sarah Silverman, Penn Jillette, and plenty of others have spoken publicly about being atheists—but their atheism may not be as central to their public image as, say, Ellen DeGeneres being a famous lesbian role model. And with fewer high-profile conversations about what it means to be an atheist, it makes sense that misunderstanding runs high.

The Minnesota researchers wrote that "anti-atheist sentiment is strong, persistent, and driven in part by moral concerns about atheists and in part by agreement with cultural values that affirm religiosity as a constitutive moral grounding of citizenship and national identity." It's the old debate about whether there can be ethics without religion, and society seems to have made up its mind—with one exception.

"In other words, Americans have moral objections to atheists, yes — but they also believe that having some sort of doctrine makes you a moral person," wrote *Mic*'s James Dennin.[55] "Unless, it would seem, that religion is Islam."

As for LGBTQ people, support is steadily rising, but we're not in the clear yet. Some 63% of Americans say homosexuality should be accepted by society, and a little over half support same-sex marriage.[56]

With such negative attitudes come negative stereotypes, all of which you've heard. Gay men are stereotyped as effeminate and flamboyant, lesbians as angry and mannish, bisexuals as greedy and oversexualized, and transgender people as confused and disturbed. (Oh, and we're all "deviant.") It should go without saying that stereotyping is harmful; it unfairly assumes that we're all the same, and it assigns negative connotations to some qualities that are otherwise pretty neutral.

For example, there's nothing wrong with being unsure about your identity and taking time to figure it out. There's also nothing wrong with being butch or effeminate or liking sex. What is wrong is assuming all LGBTQ experiences are identical, or that anyone should be treated differently or unfairly because of them. Some gay men are flamboyant and some aren't, and it's none of your business either way.

On the flip side, your typical atheists are often depicted as cold and callous, immoral and arrogant in the absence of religious principles to guide them. (And don't forget about our War on Christmas!) In reality, atheists come in all personality types and live by a wide spectrum of morals, just like many religious people. Some of us even put up Christmas trees.

But layer after layer of unfair portrayals, from pop culture and media coverage to social expectations, take their toll. Research has indicated suicide attempt rates are higher among LGBTQ people than straight and cisgender people,[57] and among non-believers than people of faith.[58] Suicide is a complex subject, and there's never an easy explanation for why it happens. What we do know is that the vast majority of people who die by suicide have a mental illness, and that millions of people face hurdles to getting mental health care, from the costs of care to the stigma around mental illness itself.

For LGBTQ people, mental illness can be exacerbated by rejection from family and friends, pervasive discrimination, and bias in society, or experiences like bullying in school. Some religious extremists would wrongfully claim that homosexuality or being trans constitute mental illnesses themselves, therefore simply *being* LGBTQ is what drives one to suicide. That's just not true; the implication that there's something wrong with being LGBTQ, in fact, is exactly the kind of ideology that hurts LGBTQ people so gravely.

When it comes to suicide rates among atheists, some Christians have tried to explain the trend by claiming the absence of religious opposition to suicide makes non-religious people more likely to die that way. That's also not true. Suicide is a decision made out of extreme suffering, not moral failing, and attributing it to the lack of a deity is deeply harmful.

Lauren Nelson wrote this for Friendly Atheist in 2016, after Christian talk show hosts suggested atheists have no reason to value life without God:

> In many faiths, suicide is cast as sinful, a barrier to Heaven or rewards after death. Such a perspective not only compounds the intense emotions of the suicidal but enhances the grief experienced by those left behind. And it's bullshit.
>
> Those who end their life do not do so out of cowardice or weakness. They do so because they are in extreme pain and dealing with tremendous struggle. Sometimes those struggles are known to loved ones, sometimes they are not. And while the causes of most suicide attempts may be treatable, resources for treatment are frequently scant. Those who have lost loved ones to suicide are entitled to their own emotions on the subject, but social condemnation of those who lost their lives to suicide is wholly inappropriate. It's callous, ignorant, and only further contributes to the stigma surrounding mental illness. Who on earth wants to get help for suicidal ideation when it's painted as a fault?"[59]

Many of the same religious groups that shun suicide also stigmatize mental illness. A 2014 study by the conservative Christian group Lifeway Research found that nearly half of evangelicals said "mental illness can be overcome by 'Bible study and prayer alone.'"[60] That pretty much proves Nelson's point.

"The key difference between most atheists and the religious has nothing to do with whether or not we see the loss of life as tragic," she wrote, "but that we don't feel the need to use shame as a preventative measure or reaction to it."

LGBTQ communities have responded to high suicide rates in robust ways. Groups like the Trevor Project and the Trans Lifeline run crisis hotlines specifically for LGBTQ youth and transgender people, respectively, and organizations are investing more resources into researching, understanding, and supporting LGBTQ mental health. There's room for growth in both our communities, but also a great deal of misunderstanding about how and why some of us hurt so much.

Perhaps one of the most fascinating social overlaps between atheists and LGBTQ people is the unbridled fear we've ignited in the Boy Scouts of America. To this day, open atheists are not allowed to participate in the BSA as either youth members or adult leaders. The BSA only recently lifted its national ban on gay, bisexual, or transgender scouts[61] and adult leaders, but individual troops can still discriminate against LGBTQ adult leaders depending on their charters (some troops are chartered to churches, for example).[62] Technically discrimination is still permitted; it's just that LGBTQ adults who aren't welcomed in a conservative troop must find a more liberal one.

In 2014, a blog about the Boy Scouts run by Eagle Scout Bryan Wendell posed a question to R. Chip Turner, Chairman of the BSA's Religious Relationships Task Force.[63] The question, submitted by a reader, was about "handling advancement when a Scout says he doesn't believe in God." Here was Turner's answer:

> The shortest answer is that we should help Scouts and their families come to realize that a belief in God is integral to Scouting and is a key element in character building. This does not reflect a change in BSA policy nor does it place Scouters in the role of religious leaders.

> By signing the membership application, each leader has already acknowledged the Declaration of Religious Principle which affirms a belief in God, calls for an appreciation for the faith of others, and acknowledges the importance of faith in citizenship development.

The first sentence of that declaration says that "no [Boy Scout] can grow into the best kind of citizen without recognizing an obligation to God."[64] Once again, there's a pattern of distrust and disgust at play here. Belief in God is required to be the "best kind" of person. LGBTQ adults may not be suitable to interact with children. The BSA's religious roots may have made sense for the organization at one point, but their policies are outdated and alienating to a growing number of boys and men who just want to go camping, make friends, and be Scouts. In effect, the BSA's restrictions are preventing many boys from advancing the BSA's mission.

Whatever the reasoning, the consequences are clear: LGBTQ people and atheists are told they don't belong because of a characteristic they can't control.

Persecution Abroad

When Donald Trump accepted the nomination for president at the 2016 Republican National Convention, he tried to convince left-leaning viewers that he was an ally to LGBTQ people. Speaking about the shooting at the Pulse nightclub in Orlando, he told the crowd, "As your president, I will do everything in my power to protect our LGBTQ citizens from the violence and oppression of a hateful foreign ideology."

Of course, he was referring to the terror group ISIS and "radical Islamic terrorism." It's true that homophobia and transphobia run rampant in some foreign countries. ISIS has circulated videos of alleged gay people being beheaded and thrown off buildings in the name of Islam.[65] Homosexuality is punishable by death in some 10 countries and illegal in more than 70. But in some cases, American conservatism—specifically the religious kind—has some influence in what happens abroad.

For example, there's the case of Scott Lively. The conservative pastor from Massachusetts has made several trips to rampantly anti-LGBTQ nations like Uganda and Russia. Video footage shows him in Kampala in 2009, speaking to members of the Ugandan parliament and claiming that "homosexuals prey on children."[66] At the end of that year, Ugandan officials introduced the Anti-Homosexuality Act calling for the death penalty for LGBTQ people.

Since then, Lively has been on trial. He was sued by Sexual Minorities Uganda (or SMUG), the country's leading LGBTQ rights group, for international crimes against humanity. SMUG alleges that Lively essentially authored the anti-gay bill. Lively denies it.

The bill never made it into law, but homosexuality is still illegal in Uganda, and anti-LGBTQ violence is omnipresent. In 2011, while the Anti-Homosexuality Act was still being considered, a prominent Ugandan LGBTQ activist named David Kato was beaten to death in his neighborhood.[67] Kato had been targeted in a Ugandan newspaper that published the names and photos of LGBTQ people; above Kato's photo, on the front page of the paper, read the words "Hang Them."

SMUG released a statement mourning Kato and condemning his murder, calling on religious leaders to stop persecuting LGBTQ people. Activist Val Kalende wrote that "David's death is a result of the hatred planted in Uganda by U.S. Evangelicals in 2009. The Ugandan Government and the so-called U.S. Evangelicals must take responsibility for David's blood."[68]

Elsewhere in the world, Russia passed a law banning "homosexual propaganda," or any public mention of LGBTQ people or causes. The law is aimed at "protecting children" from the influences of LGBTQ people. In a 2015 letter to his "pro-family" supporters, published on his personal blog in response to the lawsuit, Lively wrote:

> The beauty of the Russian law is it cuts right to the heart of the real problem of LGBT advocacy: the recruitment of children. What I mean by recruitment of children is not primarily the sexual exploitation of young people by adult homosexuals, though that represents a dark current within the larger "gay" culture, especially among the men. What I mean is the normalization of homosexual conduct and culture to children and youths, leading them to engage in homosexual experimentation among themselves and subsequently self-identify as "gay." An entire generation of American, British and Canadian children has been enslaved to this corrupt culture and ideology through the very propaganda that Russia has now banned. . . .

> I have been falsely accused of masterminding the Ugandan Anti-Homosexuality Bill which initially included the death penalty for repeat homosexual offenders, though I had strongly encouraged the Ugandan Parliament to em-

phasize rehabilitation and prevention, not punishment in my address to its members in 2009. However, I am proud to say that I believe I played a small part in the adoption of the Russian law by advocating for such a policy in a 50-city speaking tour of Russia and the former Soviet Union in 2006 and 2007, ending in St. Petersburg where I published my Letter to the Russian People outlining my public policy recommendations. St. Petersburg became the first city to pass the law a couple of years later.[69]

Even if Lively claims he isn't responsible for the call to literally kill LGBTQ people in one country, he's "proud" to have helped ban gay people from openly existing in another. That's not much better.

There are examples of atheists abroad facing similar terrors. In 2016, a graduate student and secular writer named Nazimuddin Samad was found murdered in Bangladesh.[70] Al Qaeda in the Indian Subcontinent (AQIS) claimed responsibility for Samad's murder, accusing him of being an "enemy of Allah" and of insulting Islam. Samad was the sixth atheist writer in 14 months to be murdered in Bangladesh; earlier, a jihadi group had published a "hit list" of more than 80 atheists in the country.

Sex between men (or "buggery") is banned in Trinidad and Tobago, punishable by up to 25 years in prison.[71] Cherrie Ann Joseph, an atheist who lives there, told me she has observed Western Christian influence in political attitudes toward LGBTQ people.

"We can be a pretty intolerant and at the same time indifferent society," she said. "Coming out as LGBTQ or atheist is challenging, but most people just live and let live. A number of fundamentalist Christian groups are increasingly intolerant (sadly influenced by the American Christian right and the prosperity doctrine), but they are largely ignored beyond their own communities in day-to-day interactions. Unfortunately, their influence extends to the legislature, so we don't yet have equal rights for LGBTQ people."

And violence against LGBTQ people doesn't stop at the U.S. border, while violence against atheists is almost non-existent in the States. In 2015, the FBI documented more than 1,300 hate crimes against LGBTQ people, about 20% of all the hate crimes reported that year.[72] But hate crimes against atheists? The FBI reported just two. And in fact, both of these numbers pale in comparison to race, ethnicity, or ancestry-based hate crimes, of which there were more than 4,000 that year.

Chris Stedman wrote about the faulty comparison back in 2013. "Personally speaking," he writes, "I rarely fear for my safety as an atheist in the U.S., but I frequently do as a queer person. I have been physically assaulted for being queer, and many of my Muslim and Jewish friends have also been the victims of hate crimes. ... So when an atheist like Bill Maher or Richard Dawkins—powerful, influential, financially comfortable, heterosexual white men—implicitly or explicitly attempts to parallel his experience of life to those of people in other marginalized communities, it's difficult not to cringe."

The ideal number of hate crimes against any group is zero. But as a point of comparison, atheists simply do not face the same imminent physical danger that LGBTQ people do—not in the United States, that is.

 voices **John Webster**

One of the most critical questions I've asked myself and others in researching this book is not just about *whether* atheists should join the fight for LGBTQ rights, but *why.* Given the overlap in experiences and history, it's easy to say that a friendly working relationship makes sense. It may not be productive to think of institutionalized religion as a "shared enemy" between these two groups, but it is true that both are likely to have been harmed in the name of religion. For some, that common ground is enough to support one another's causes.

But there's also disagreement in the atheist community about whether being an atheist comes with any intrinsic values, aside from non-belief in any gods. Atheists believe in freedom from religion, but what about freedom from discrimination? Freedom from hate speech? Freedom to marry, have children, or change one's gender marker? It's easy to answer the general questions, but it gets more difficult as the scenarios grow more specific. And while atheists tend to skew liberal, there are plenty of socially conservative atheists as well.

I asked around and dozens of people offered their takes, from opinionated friends and friends-of-friends to strangers on the internet (sorry, Mom). Throughout this book, I'll feature some of the most interesting conversations I had with people across different faiths, genders, and sexual orientations. Some of these conversations highlight important personal experiences with and without religion that can inform our work as activists. Others ask and answer questions that make us reflect on who we are and our responsibility to support one another. In some cases, I've changed a source's name at their request for privacy (those names are marked with an asterisk), or edited and condensed interviews for clarity.

The very first person I heard from in my call for perspectives was John Webster, a gay atheist and former Jehovah's Witness, whose powerful story landed in my inbox as soon as I started researching. Webster left the Jehovah's Witnesses recently, a process he described as "slow and painful and wrought with guilt and anxiety," after a decade of trying to convince himself that progressive change could happen within the church. He shared his thoughts with me in response to a question posed online about whether he, as an atheist, would take up the causes of other social movements. Unapologetically, he said no. Webster said:

> I got thinking about this and talked it over with several like-minded friends. Our common background is being gay and formerly zealous Jehovah's Witnesses. I was actually uncomfortable with the notion of not being willing to stand up and take part in activism and that was our discussion. I was about to add here "for a cause I believe in," but that's the issue.
>
> Forgive my reticence, but I left the Jehovah's Witnesses pretty much one year ago now, and this has been a turbulent (though super-positive) 12 months of growth and re-assessment of pretty much anything I ever took for "truth." Seeing things from outside the "organization" has been sobering, to say the least. I would liken it to a painful divorce from a partner you once truly loved and respected, whom you now see as a vile cheat and vindictive bully.
>
> I poured 30 years into that "relationship" and believed pretty much up to the end that I was doing the most noble thing I could with my life, remaining chaste and faithfully following the "headship" of the so-called "faithful and discreet slave." I did so willingly and with purpose, self-righteously turning my back on my Catholic upbringing,

convinced it was my calling to help blinded unbelievers to attain a "relationship with God."

Yikes.

I now see all religions as pretty much the same, each convinced that they are "the truth" to the pious self-righteous dismissal of anything "other."

Point is, I was very disillusioned by the whole experience.

I "believed" in my heart of hearts that I was doing the right thing, fighting for the only right cause ... "the vindication of Jehovah's Sovereignty!" It even just SOUNDS noble, doesn't it?

Would I be willing to support and/or work for LGBT activist groups? Well, in principle I'm there for you. But forgive me for being a bit gun-shy at this juncture to throw my energies (a bit sapped at this point) to "the next cause." I would say that it's in my DNA to rally behind and support the weak and disenfranchised of the world, but I've kinda been burned by causes. I would need to know that I was involved in something of meaningful value and not tainted by corruption and endorsed by people for whom I have respect.

Webster is certainly not the only person who feels like he's been burned before when it comes to organizing around common beliefs. Organizing for a cause, though historically a powerful form of protest or political action, can be disastrous. There's never been a social movement without its share of problems—an unclear objective; fragmented leadership; underlying inequality in how people of different races, genders, or socioeconomic classes are able to participate—and neither the LGBTQ rights movement nor the atheist movement is an exception. This could be part of the reason why some atheists don't see the purpose of "organizing" as a broader atheist community at all: it sure sounds a lot like a church group, minus the communion wafers.

But there are other factors to consider, too. Joining forces with people who share your worldview can be a form of solace, almost therapeutic. This is especially the case when you've grown up thinking you were the only person who felt the way you did, an experience many LGBTQ people and atheists can relate to. When I reached out to Webster to ask permission to reprint his story, he replied, "I've never been happier, and would be pleased to have a part in helping similarly troubled current Jehovah's Witnesses find the courage and argumentation (because that's what you need) to move on with their lives, should that be their wish."

Seeing Eye to Eye

What can we take away from all of this? Even if LGBTQ people and atheists don't experience the world in the exact same way, we have comparable goals—as movements and as people—and face some of the same challenges. We want to go to work knowing we won't get fired for our beliefs. We want to feel safe walking down the street. We want to build families and friendships and relationships however we damn well please. And too often, we're pushed down by people whose beliefs don't match ours, people who think we're broken and sick, and people who just don't get us. On good days, it's annoying; on bad days, it's dangerous.

Allyship between our two groups might not be part of the contract you sign when you become a card-carrying atheist. And when you look from a distance at victories like the Supreme Court's decision on marriage equality, that kind of work might not seem necessary. But in reality, LGBTQ people are still suffering, be it at the hands of legislated religion, outdated school curriculum, or stubborn family members. Atheists have been there, too. Ensuring full and unconditional equality for LGBTQ people is not just a political concern, but a matter of human rights. And as a group with skin in the game, atheists should be among the first to join the fight.

Believing in Something

Being Good Without God

IN SAN Antonio, Texas, nearly 15% of the population lives in poverty—more than 350,000 people.[73] And in early 2017, the city's mayor showed she was woefully ill-equipped to talk about it.

At a mayoral candidate forum a few weeks before the election, the director of the city's Christian Resource Center asked incumbent Mayor Ivy Taylor what she believed was the systemic cause of generational poverty. The mayor's answer was outlandish.

"I'll go ahead and put it out there," she told the SACRC director. "To me, it's broken people... people not being in a relationship with their Creator, and therefore not being in a good relationship with their families and their communities... and not being productive members of society. I think that's the ultimate answer."[74]

Taylor is a registered Democrat and a Baptist who describes herself as "fiscally conservative and socially conservative." As a city councilwoman, she voted against an LGBTQ nondiscrimination ordinance.[75] When the ordinance was enacted anyway, she called the issue a "waste of time."[76] So it's no surprise that she faced a significant backlash when video of her comments at the forum circulated online.

She released a statement on Facebook claiming the video had been intentionally edited to harm her (it wasn't) and that her faith in God had led her to public service to begin with:

> I have devoted my life to breaking the chains of generational poverty—as an urban planner, the District 2 Councilwoman, and now Mayor. I've done so because of my faith in God and my belief in Jesus's ministry on Earth. I believe we are all called on to help lift our brothers and sisters out of poverty. I also believe in Original Sin, and that was the context for my comment in the YouTube video clip. We're all "broken," from the richest among us to the poorest, until we forge a

relationship with our Maker. I could have expressed myself more clearly in explaining my belief at the forum.

Taylor's comments were unfair and uncalled for on a number of levels. There are complex, overlapping systemic causes of generational poverty, and the absence of religion isn't one of them. Research also suggests Taylor is flat-out wrong; atheists and agnostics have some of the highest average incomes in the country, according to Pew data,[77] and a Gallup poll found that the world's poorest countries are also the most religious.[78] Finally, it's absurd to suggest that people living in poverty are "broken," or that they are lesser members of society, or that finding God is the answer to persistent economic disadvantage. That kind of thinking is cruel coming from anyone, let alone a public servant. (This story does have a happy ending, though, if you could call it that—Taylor lost her bid for reelection as mayor in June. She thanked God profusely in her concession speech.[79])

Atheists aren't "broken," either. The absence of belief isn't the same as the absence of empathy, morality, community, or any of the other things people often get from their faith. In fact, for plenty of atheists, not believing in a god makes us *more* strongly connected to ideas of justice and morality. We're not accountable to a higher power, but to ourselves and our surroundings. We live by certain principles not because we fear retribution in the afterlife, but because we know them to be true and good. In her misguided comments, Taylor invoked a common stereotype against atheists: that we're cold and cruel, with no values or consideration for our fellow person. That's simply not true.

While atheists may not believe in a god, there's a lot that we *do* believe in—including, for many of us, justice and equality for LGBTQ people. Whether your support for equal rights comes from the shared struggle of religious discrimination or whether you recognize it as simply the right thing to do, atheism and pro-LGBTQ ideals often go hand in hand.

Who We Are

By nature, atheism is not a belief system, but the absence of one. And just as there is no monolithic LGBTQ "community," there's no singular atheist community, either. Atheism isn't traditionally passed down through families, and you're unlikely to find an "atheist neighborhood" in your city the way you might find one that's heavily Jewish or Muslim, for example.

Here's how the organization American Atheists defines the diversity of atheists:

> The only common thread that ties all atheists together is a lack of belief in gods. Some of the best debates we have ever had have been with fellow atheists. This is because atheists do not have a common belief system, sacred scripture or atheist Pope. This means atheists often disagree on many issues and ideas. Atheists come in a variety of shapes, colors, beliefs, convictions, and backgrounds. We are as unique as our fingerprints. Atheists exist across the political spectrum. We are members of every race. We are members of the LGBTQ* community. There are atheists in urban, suburban, and rural communities and in every state of the nation.[80]

The Pew Research Center has also reported some general data on where atheists in the United States stand on different issues, although it can be difficult to track. For example, some self-described atheists Pew interviewed said they believed in a god or universal spirit, while some respondents who did identify with a religious group also said they didn't believe in any gods.[81] Data-wise, the definition of "atheist" itself is murky.

For one, there are more self-identified atheists and religious "nones" in the country than ever before. Fifty-six percent of those atheists call themselves political liberals, and only 10% consider themselves conservative. Ninety-two percent of atheists support marriage equality and 87% support abortion rights. Two-thirds of atheists said they seldom or never discuss their thoughts on religion with religious people, and about a third of atheists "look primarily to science for guidance on questions of right and wrong."

But despite not being an organized religion, atheist groups have formed. Organizations like American Atheists as well as the Freedom From Religion Foundation, the Secular Student Alliance, the American Humanist Association, and dozens of others serve to gather atheists with common goals, advocate for the separation of church and state, and provide news, resources, and even scholarships for atheists. Many of these organizations consider LGBTQ equality to be an important part of their mission.

For example, the American Humanist Association lists LGBTQ rights as a key issue on their website. Discrimination on the basis of sexual orientation and gender identity violates a person's right to free expression, the site says, and yet LGBTQ people often face discrimination because of religious ideology disguised as "family values."

Sincere Kirabo, social justice coordinator for the AHA, says there's a direct connection between humanism and LGBTQ rights. "The American Humanist Association supports the LGBTQ liberation movement because we recognize the direct connection between humanist values and acting in solidarity with marginalized groups seeking increased sociopolitical power and freedom currently not being distributed in an equal or just manner," he told me.

He added: "Humanism refers to a determination to lead an ethical life based on human-derived reason and social responsibility without relying on imagined supernatural influence to guide or inspire action. Based on this, humanist philosophy is little more than feel-good rhetoric if its ideas aren't implemented to engage in social change actions that improve unjust conditions within society that negatively impact quality of life."

I also talked to Nick Fish, national program director at American Atheists, who said there's a "very natural allyship" between LGBTQ people and atheists.

"I think that it's obvious to all of us here that this is something that we need to do," Fish said. "Not only because it's the right thing to do, but also because it gives us a lot more power and a lot more activated, excited, and seasoned activists who are willing to fight for these issues."

Fish said that American Atheists engages with the LGBTQ movement in a number of ways. They work with LGBTQ organizations "whenever possible" to collaborate on lobbying efforts, letters of support, and community events. From a policy standpoint, the group has been monitoring and fighting religious freedom restoration laws across the country that aim to legalize faith-based discrimination. (LGBTQ discrimination is "very easily the clearest example" in the last two decades of using the state to enforce religious dogma, Fish said.) They attend Creating Change, the National LGBTQ Task Force's annual conference of thousands of activists, to both make sure atheists are represented and to lend their support to LGBTQ causes.

Because nearly half of LGBTQ people have no religious affiliation, Fish said, it would do both groups a disservice to ignore the overlaps in membership. The atheist movement will be stronger when dedicated LGBTQ activists participate, and vice versa.

"If you're doing LGBT activism and you're not thinking about the half of the people who are nonreligious when you're doing it, you're necessarily excluding this huge segment of people, alienating them, and losing them as potential activists," Fish said.

I asked Fish whether atheists should fight for LGBTQ equality because of their atheism or simply because it's the right thing to do. He said that it's about elements of both.

"It's something that most Americans are on our side on, so we think it's something that's right for the fight, and a good way for us to show that church/state separation matters because it's impacting actual people," he said. "If we can be a part of that... we're not co-opting, we're coordinating. We're not taking over, we're supplementing."

voices   **Philip***

Philip is a gay man who grew up in California with Southern Baptist missionary parents. He says there are a lot of ways to describe his beliefs and identity—ex-Christian, atheist, agnostic, apatheistic, dystheistic, humanist, rationalist, "big old nerd"—but that he feels a definite connection between being an atheist and being gay. We talked about his experiences growing up in a religious household and what it means to be a "gaytheist."

Can you tell me about your experience with religion?

I was raised by Southern Baptist missionaries, rebelled against that very strongly and politically oppose Christianity strongly. I don't believe in the existence of any gods, I don't trust humanity to know or not know for certain things like that exist, I honestly don't think the existence or nonexistence of gods should be relevant or interesting to humans, and that most of the characterizations of gods people believe in are pretty damn unethical and undeserving of worship.

Religiosity and spirituality make me gag, but I try to be friendly and kind to believers in the hope that maybe they'll do the same in turn to unbelievers. I try my damnedest to keep my "militant atheism" the act-only-in-self-defense kind. I feel like atheists and gay people are natural allies because we have the similar experiences of prejudice from religious people and we have benefitted from the same kinds of protections. In one respect, I feel like being gay is often a free ticket to the wonderful world of skepticism and disbelief.

You mentioned being raised Southern Baptist and rebelling against it—can you tell me anything about that process? Did it have anything to do with being gay?

I think I would have seen the plot holes in Christianity with or without being gay, but it certainly helped. I didn't come out until I was a legal adult because my family would have sent me to "reparative therapy" treatment. They still tried to convince me to go to an Exodus International conference, and forced me to attend their church. We were on very bad terms for a while and they tried to control me financially. When they realized I could (and would) disappear from their lives if they continued that approach, we developed an unspoken ceasefire. They haven't really come around, but they're more used to it now.

Is there any relationship between your atheist identity and your gay identity?

There's absolutely a connection between my gay and atheist identities. "Gaytheist" is a portmanteau a lot of people have independently suggested because there's such an overlap in the two communities.

"Gaytheist" is a great word. Can you give me an example of what that looks like to you?

I was involved with an LGBT student club for a number of years and took an active leadership role, and one of the problems I noticed in the first few years were some culture gaps around religion. The majority of the club members were gaytheists (even if they didn't think in those terms) and pretty hostile to religion in general. Prop 8 passed in California during my college years, and that was a big trauma in the queer campus community, so most of the club wasn't particularly charitable in that direction.

Occasionally, students who came from a strong faith background would be rubbed the wrong way by anti-religious statements made by individual club members – either because of insensitivity or personal resentment – and some queer believers felt like a minority within a minority. Club officers were better-behaved about it to begin with, but at my insistence we took initiative to make it clear that exclusionary comments weren't tolerable and to clarify that the club's purpose was to support all LGBT students, and the club couldn't serve that purpose if people weren't able to talk about religion in a respectful way.

I think that the out LGBT community has (on average) moved far enough away from religious culture that we're not as good at relating to the struggles LGBT believers have. Conversely, I think straight people from religious backgrounds have grossly inadequate sympathy for gaytheist resentment of religion; it's pretty damn galling to be told to respect and be courteous to people who literally want to destroy what makes you who you are. It's to be expected that some gaytheists are going to be prickly.

Do you think atheists have an obligation to support LGBTQ people, as a fellow group marginalized by religious extremists? Why/why not?

I guess I'd agree that atheists are obligated to support queer folks to be ideologically consistent, but I would be legitimately surprised to find an intentionally homophobic atheist group out there. I think that, even while the atheist movement is dominated by straight men, most agree that sexual prejudice and sex-negativity are some of the worst things existing religions give us.

I'm a Believer

In 2017, a PRRI report on religious trends found that LGBTQ people are less religious and more likely to be atheists than the general population. More specifically, 46% of LGBTQ people had "no religious affiliation," compared with only 24% of the general U.S. population at the time.[82]

It's not outrageous to think that widespread homophobia in many faith institutions could influence the religious leanings of LGBTQ people themselves. Majorities of LGBTQ people said they viewed Evangelical, Catholic, and Mormon churches and the Muslim faith as "unfriendly" toward LGBTQ people. Just under half said the same about the Jewish faith and non-Evangelical Protestant churches. Most organized religion in the United States falls under one of these groups, and there are plenty of reasons why some might want to stay away.

However, the next most common faith held by LGBTQ people after "no affiliation" in this study is Christian—41%, just a little lower than the number who don't identify with any religion. (In general, about 70% of Americans consider themselves Christian.) That high of a percentage may sound oxymoronic when you consider the swaths of people who use Christianity to undermine LGBTQ identity and relationships. But religion isn't a singular experience, especially for LGBTQ people of faith.

Bryan, a transgender man from the Midwest, grew up going to Catholic Mass with his family every Sunday. When he moved away to college in Illinois—before he had come out as trans—he started off going to church every week like he was raised, but the routine faded by the winter. He went through a period of depression, and after going to a college drag show he started to question his gender identity. Around the same time, he started going back to church more regularly.

"I started to take comfort in going to Mass, but at the same time my mental state was rapidly deteriorating because of questions about my gender," he told me. "One day it became too much and I couldn't get out of bed unless it was as a man. So I did. I was Bryan from that point on. I came out to everyone I knew in that one day." He was 20 at the time.

Bryan said his friends and the Catholic community at school accepted him right away. Another member of the Catholic student group had come out as a transgender man a few years before, so the program staff were educated and armed with resources. Bryan became increasingly involved with the campus Catholic center, went to daily Mass as often as he could, and became a Sunday school teacher. One day in his senior year, he had an out-of-body experience at Mass and felt called to become a priest. He's an engineer now and still exploring how he can pursue that calling—he says he's reached out to some priest friends and their networks for guidance—but he knows it's unlikely. While the Catholic Church has no official doctrine regarding being transgender, the catechism states that "homosexual acts are intrinsically disordered"[83] and that anyone who is gay or lesbian is called to a life of chastity. It doesn't seem difficult to extrapolate from there.

Still, he says, being Catholic is a part of who he is. I asked him why he feels called to Catholicism even though other denominations of Christianity would be more likely to ordain him.

"There are a whole bunch of reasons I feel called to stay Catholic. I would be lying if I said being born Catholic wasn't one of them," he said. "I also love the history of the Church. I like that it has been around for so long and that there is a long line of saints that I can look back to for guidance. I love that I can go to Mass every day if I want to. And I love that Mass will look pretty much the same anywhere I go. It is a beautiful representation of a global community.

"[And] I love confession. That I can go in and lay bare all of the shit I have gotten myself into and come out feeling clean and ready to do better. I would love to be the person to be able to assist other people in unloading themselves like that."

Most of the people he's met through his faith have been kind and accepting of his gender identity, Bryan said. One exception: when a Catholic missionary asked if he had considered becoming a nun and recommended a group for celibate gay and lesbian (but not transgender) Catholics. Even then, he talked about that incident with his priest, who supported him completely.

"I don't know that I can imagine not having religion in my life," Bryan said. "The period where I didn't was the darkest time in my life. I am sure part of that was because I was still in the closet, but those two things are very tied together in my story."

Bryan said he understands how a partnership between LGBTQ people and atheists makes sense, even though it's outside of his experience. He also doesn't fault LGBTQ people who feel wronged by religion, he said.

"There are a lot of not-great people out there saying a lot of hurtful things in the name of God," he said. "I think the thing I try to remember is that religion may be a divinely inspired human institution, but it is human nonetheless. We make mistakes. The God I believe in doesn't hate people for being gay or trans."

Like many of the LGBTQ people of faith I spoke with, Bryan does see a relationship between those two identities, including how he communicates them to the world.

"I can't know for sure that God is real or that, if He is, He doesn't hate me for being trans. All I have is the joy I feel at Mass or those brief moments of connection when I feel His presence. The funny thing is, it is the same with being trans. There is no proof. Genetically, I am female. There is nothing to prove I am a man. All I have is the feeling deep down that being a man brings me peace."

Another telling statistic from the Pew survey found that of religious LGBTQ adults, about a third reported "a conflict between their religious beliefs and their sexual orientation or gender identity." Just under a third of all LGBTQ people said they "have been made to feel unwelcome in a place of worship."

Charlie, a progressive Christian from Washington State, is bisexual and married to a woman. He wasn't raised religious, but he and his wife joined an Anglican church just before they were married and are now taking time to worship privately.

"I don't think I'd be welcome at churches, men's groups, or church culture because I am bisexual," he said. "At times, I've thought my life would be easier if I weren't attracted to other men. My marriage might be simpler, my relationship to other Christians would be simpler, I wouldn't have to come out to anyone and I can go quietly about my life. But even if I pretend I'm straight, boys won't be less cute, and then we're back to square one."

Like many progressive people of faith, he said his beliefs differ from those of fundamentalists who "get all the airtime"

on what it means to be a Christian. "The loud people scream-
ing, your Falwells and your Dobsons and your Bachmanns,
aren't the only voices out there," he said. "There isn't a single
exclusive Christian answer for anything."

The same goes for the Bible. It's well-known that religious
conservatives often grasp at a couple of verses to justify their
sweeping homophobia and transphobia. Charlie said he sees
the Bible as a product of a specific historical and narrative context. Of course it doesn't make sense as a verbatim guidebook
for 21st-century society.

"Unfortunately, I did at one point understand portions of
scripture to be against queer and trans people," he said. "But,
after I got my head out of my ass, I realized that those are cultural presumptions assigned to the Bible by hateful people like
[Jerry] Falwell and Pat Robertson, and that is what permeates
the culture."

Bryan and Charlie are both in their 20s, making them statistical outliers. In 2014, the Pew Research Center reported that
young LGBTQ people are less likely than older ones to be religious.[84] Pew also found "no significant differences in religious
affiliation levels" between white LGBTQ people and LGBTQ
people of color, or those with a college degree and those without. Geographic location in the United States does play a role,
though; 57% of LGBTQ Southerners reported being religious,
compared with 41% in the Northeast. Those in the West and
Midwest fell somewhere in the middle.

Finally, LGBTQ people are more likely to be Democrats
regardless of their religious beliefs—76% who are religious and
83% who aren't said they identify as Democrats. Nationwide,
Americans are becoming less religious, but the most dense
pockets of religion remain clustered in reliably red states.[85]

And religious conservatives' stronghold on homophobia and
transphobia isn't letting up. In 2016, David Gushee wrote for
Religion News Service that on the question of LGBTQ equality,
"middle ground is disappearing."[86] Gushee wrote that "you
are either for full and unequivocal social and legal equality for
LGBT people, or you are against it." Clear political divisions
already show who's on which side.

Gushee wrote that most of the federal government, the education sector, corporations, medical associations, the media, the non-profit world, the sports world, and the secular and progressive-religious circles are committed to being pro-LGBTQ (granted, Barack Obama was president at the time he wrote it). The stalwart opponents are conservative religious groups, the parts of the country where those groups have the most sway, and a few of their leaders in government and elsewhere in the public eye.

"These institutions and their leaders are interpreting pressure to reconsider as pressure to succumb to error, or even heresy," Gushee wrote. "They are interpreting social changes toward nondiscrimination as mere embrace of sexual libertinism. They are attempting to tighten doctrinal statements in order to tamp down dissent or drive out dissenters. They are organizing legal defense efforts under the guise of religious liberty, and interpreting their plight as religious persecution. They are confident that they have the moral high ground, and from their remaining, shrinking spaces of power they still try to punish those who stray from orthodoxy as they understand it."

Maybe that's how the rightmost right-wingers are approaching the fight for (or rather against) LGBTQ rights, but as research has pointed out, their numbers are dwindling. LGBTQ people of faith like Bryan, Charlie, and many others are setting the stage for new ways of experiencing religion, focusing on takeaways like community and compassion rather than tradition and fear. If we're to believe the trends, that approach to religion—or simply having no religion at all—might soon be leading the pack.

 voices   **Brandon Beck**

Brandon Beck has made a name for himself in LGBTQ spaces as an openly transgender teacher and activist from Texas. His story flips the traditional leaving-the-church narrative you might expect from an LGBTQ person on its head: Beck identified first as an atheist, but later became a Christian after coming out as a pansexual trans man. He spoke with me about his experiences of finding faith at the intersection of his identities.

How did changes in your beliefs align with coming into your identity as pansexual and transgender?

I was a very "devout" atheist until my mid-twenties. At that time, I was also an alcoholic and drug addict. I was self-medicating to not have to face the realities of being a trans man in a world that never talked positively about trans people. You see, I am the same age Brandon Teena would have been had he not been murdered.*

I had finished college, but as many Gen X-ers did, I faced a strong sense of ennui, and had returned to live with my parents, doing odd jobs and going to graduate school. One of my odd jobs was playing bassoon in a local orchestra. The conductor happened to also be a minister. He befriended me and took me into his family, in a way. He and his wife and two children helped me feel good about myself. The better I felt about myself, the less I wanted to drink and do drugs. But the less I drank and did drugs, the more I was faced with the reality that I had some serious gender identity issues to face.

I saw so much contentment and faith in this family I had met that I asked them to teach me. So I read the Bible and attended church with them and came to believe in Christ's allegories and in the communion and fellowship of church. But I very soon realized that the church they were taking me to didn't believe in me. I slept with men and women. I was divorced. I wanted to understand why I felt like a man. There was no place in their church for this, even though the Bible they showed me led me to believe that I was perfect the way God created me, and that the first thing God taught us was to love each other. So I left that church, transitioned, and found a new church home where love is love.

Do you see any relationship between your faith identity and your LGBTQ identities?

I really see a strong relationship between being trans and Christian. It was through my faith that I was made whole and through my wholeness that I was able to love myself enough to be able to transition. I out myself as trans and Christian because people tend to view those as disparate. To me they are integrated. I believe that my God knew I am trans and that He decided how I would transition and that He helps me tell my story of faith and transness.

---

* Brandon Teena was a transgender man murdered in Nebraska in 1993, at the age of 21. His story was the subject of the award-winning film *Boys Don't Cry*, and his death inspired increased advocacy for hate crimes legislation in the United States.

Have you ever faced any kind of pushback from religious communities for being LGBTQ, or, on the flip side, from queer communities for being a person of faith?

My extended family is Catholic and use their religion to judge me harshly. They have all but discontinued communicating with me and no longer invite me to family gatherings. On the other hand, my mom's Baptist cousins love me and support me, [as they show by] praying for my "salvation." They find it hard to believe that I'm really both Christian and trans. The family that took me under their wing all those years ago hates that their church was an unsafe place for me and that their doctrine was against who I am. They are still my friends even though their lead pastor and many of their congregants are not.

In the queer community, I am much more often judged for being a Christian than I am for being queer in the Christian community. I mentor many young trans people, and they adamantly oppose my Christianity. They speak as vehemently against Christianity as they do against cis-het [cisgender and heterosexual] narratives. Part of my mentoring is to teach them to love in order to be loved, to seek understanding in order to be understood. I often don't come out as Christian to them until I've heard them make these anti-Christian remarks. Then, they're at a point where they respect me, even possibly admire me, and I tell them, "You know, not ALL Christians are the same. I mean, I'm a Christian." And their minds are blown and they rethink their statements.

How do you respond when religion is used to oppress LGBTQ people?

When religion is used to oppress LGBTQ people, I am hurt. I try to find ways to counter these attacks with words, written or spoken, or with demonstrations of my own dual nature of being queer and Christian.

Losing Your Religion

In 2017, the largest "religious group" in the United States was comprised of people with no religion at all. Twenty-four percent of Americans claimed "no formal religious identity," according to a survey released by the Public Religion Research Institute, a higher number than any single Christian denomination.[87] The number of unaffiliated Americans grew slowly between the 1970s and the 1990s, hovering around the single-digits, but has accelerated quickly in the 2000s.[88]

The majority of these unaffiliated people "formerly identified with a particular religion," PRRI had previously reported.[89] That points to a mass migration of people away from the religions they grew up with. One big reason for that shift is how religious institutions treat LGBTQ people.

According to PRRI, nearly a third of people who left their childhood religion cited "negative religious teachings about or treatment of gay and lesbian people" as one of their reasons for doing so. (That's a big number to stand up for a relatively small group.) Former Catholics, young adults, and women were more likely than members of other religions, older people, and men to hold this view.

This is a helpful measure because it gives a glimpse of how people have started to care more about LGBTQ issues over time. As LGBTQ issues have become more widely talked-about in the political realm, churches have started to make decisions about where they stand on these issues, and how public to be about those stances. For example, it's easier than ever to look up whether your childhood place of worship supports LGBTQ people. Maybe it's aligned with a larger denomination that opposes LGBTQ rights, maybe it loudly and proudly performs same-sex wedding ceremonies, or maybe it's silent on the issue. If you were teetering on whether or not to stick with religion, it's easy to find that last straw that either pushes you out the door or compels you to stay—if LGBTQ inclusion is important to you, that is.

In 2015, the Mormon Church took its institutionalized homophobia to a new level. Mormon officials introduced a rule announcing that married same-sex couples were apostates of the church. As such, the children of same-sex couples could not join the church or be baptized until they turned 18 and denounced same-sex relationships, including their own parents' union. The new section of the church's handbook declared that "a natural or adopted child of a parent living in a same-gender relationship, whether the couple is married or cohabiting, may not receive a name and a blessing."

For hundreds of Mormons, gay and straight, that was the last straw. More than a thousand people waited in line in Salt

Lake City about a week after the announcement to formally resign from the church. In doing so, they removed their names from a Rolodex of people who stood by the church's homophobic decision, even if they didn't personally agree with it themselves.[90] One woman told *The New York Times* that she had stopped attending services two years earlier, but this was the end of the line.

"I hoped that I could live harmoniously with the church even though I wasn't a believer anymore," she told *The Times.* "But the stance and the retrenchment and the harm that is being done to people in this community is beyond what I can live with."

It's also no coincidence that more young people than ever identify as LGBTQ. Most people who abandon faith after being raised in religious households do so before the age of 18. And fewer than half of Americans from age 13-20 identify as "exclusively heterosexual," according to a 2016 study by the J. Walter Thompson Innovation Group, a "trend forecasting agency."[91] Generation Z, as it's called, embraces gender and sexual diversity more than any other generation on record. As their attitudes rush forward, traditionally conservative religions are hovering behind.

This is an especially interesting conversation when you consider the relationship between religious identity and perceived morality. Only 21% of non-religious Americans say you need to believe in God to have good morals, according to PRRI. In contrast, a few groups strongly believe that you need faith to have morals: black Protestants (78%), white evangelical Protestants (59%), and Catholics (59%). From debate teams to high school philosophy classes, the question of whether there can be morality without religion is a classic. But what about morality *with* religion—that is, certain religions that call for violence and hatred under the guise of "family values"? What does "morality" look like if it doesn't encourage compassion and acceptance?

Morality guides our sense of right and wrong, good and bad. It would seem, then, that treating everyone with dignity, respecting bodily autonomy, and trusting people to live in the way that brings them the most peace and happiness are the moral things to do. Yet when it comes to LGBTQ people—and many others—some religious conservatives operate under a different understanding of the issue. In these cases, the concept of "morality" is derived from a narrow interpretation of the Bible, strict adherence to ancient gender roles, and a perpetual fear of those who are different. Sometimes, a conservative Christian might decide that scorning an LGBTQ person—rather than the seemingly obvious decision to just be nice—is the moral thing to do.

You've heard the story before: Parents send their gay kid to Bible study or even conversion therapy supposedly out of love, because they genuinely believe that's what is best for their child. Or, more broadly, there are the proselytizing Christians who believe loving their neighbors means telling them they are going to hell. Actor and evangelist Kirk Cameron is a prime example of this.[92] He's made a series of awful remarks about LGBTQ people over the course of his new career as a fundamentalist Christian speaker. After the fact, when the media starts blasting him for statements that are both false and horrifying, he'll make the excuse that he's speaking out of love and shouldn't be targeted for expressing *his* view of truth and morality.

"The truth is always love speech, it's not hate speech," he told a group of Liberty University students in 2012. "The truth communicated with compassion, with a desire to see people in a right relationship with God, helped and healed and whole, is the most genuine form of love speech you can give anyone." Sounds well-intended (if a little creepy), right? Less so once you realize he was defending comments he'd made to TV host Piers Morgan, calling homosexuality "ultimately destructive to so many foundations of civilization."[93] Nothing about that is loving. (Or accurate, for that matter.)

"Morality" (and apparently "love") is relative, and in some cases, it's certainly not always synonymous with kindness and decency. But if you consider whose idea of morality is the least hurtful, many non-religious people could easily out-moral groups who claim to be the bastion of good values. And because atheists aren't guided by holy books that could be interpreted as anti-LGBTQ, it's fair to say that we are more likely to embrace ideas of morality and love that *don't* require telling decent people they're destructive to society.

Sometime between the ages of two and now, you probably heard that the "Golden Rule" is to treat others the way you'd want to be treated. At my first job working in the LGBTQ rights movement, I learned about the "Platinum Rule," which says to treat others the way *they* want to be treated. That means referring to a transgender person by the name and pronouns they use, regardless of your views on transgender identity. It means fulfilling the obligations of your job as a city clerk to marry same-sex couples, even if you don't support their unions. It means treating LGBTQ people with kindness, even if you hold hate in your heart.

There's also the subset of "But I Have Gay Friends" religious conservatives: those who claim they're O.K. with gay people existing, but who don't want to give them any rights that might conflict with their own faith. You often hear this excuse from socially conservative politicians, who might proclaim their tolerance in the same breath as they announce sweeping anti-LGBTQ legislation. Senator Ted Cruz held a fundraising event at a gay couple's home, but he also attacked LGBTQ rights throughout his presidential run. Pastor Rick Warren has both compared marriage equality to incest and pedophilia and bragged about having a "wonderful conversation" with lesbian singer Melissa Etheridge. Donald Trump proclaimed himself a "real friend" of the LGBTQ community while campaigning, then called for a ban on transgender people in the military after he was elected. The list goes on.[94]

And then there are those who never act on their homophobia and transphobia, or only do so in their intimate social circles. These kinds of attitudes are less imminently dangerous, but they shouldn't be let off the hook.

No matter your beliefs (or non-beliefs), it's still not "moral" to hate LGBTQ people quietly, condemning their existence internally while being considerate and respectful to their faces. That's sort of like when Christians say that it's O.K. to *be* gay, as long as you don't *act* on that gayness. The reason that argument fails is because you're not any less gay if you abstain from gay sex. Telling someone that they can desire a consensual sexual relationship but can't actually have it does not count as acceptance. (That applies to Pope Francis, who once said about the possibility of gay members of clergy, "Who am I to judge?", but still presumably accepts Catholic doctrine on matters of homosexuality.)

Likewise, you're not any less homophobic just because you don't say homophobic things. If the feelings are there, they're there, and eventually, they are going to spill out. It might be a microaggression to a person on the street who looks a certain way, or a tongue-in-cheek comment in front of someone you didn't know was gay—maybe a friend, maybe a cousin, maybe your own kid. And if others hear those slip-ups, you're sending them the message that you're OK with bullying people who are different. Subtle bigotry is still bigotry. It may not break the law, but that doesn't mean it doesn't do harm.

Obviously, everyone has the right to their beliefs and expression, privately and publicly. I'm not advocating for the Thought Police to take you away in the night if you grimace at a gay couple in public. Rather, this is an invitation for us to check our implicit biases and beliefs about how the world should work. It's too easy for us to look at an extreme example of racism, sexism, homophobia, or the like and separate ourselves from it, thinking, "I'd never do that, so I can't be racist/sexist/homophobic." That's just not true. You may feel Westboro Baptist Church is grotesque in how its members talk about homosexuality, but you're hardly better if you think gay couples are inherently inferior parents. Bigotry comes in shades, and a person doesn't have to be violent to be part of the problem.

All of this suggests that one person's morality might not be moral to someone else, and that religion and compassion aren't as intertwined as many Americans think they are. Ideas like reason, fairness, ethics, and justice, on the other hand, are pretty secular. If atheists are truly committed to these concepts, supporting LGBTQ people should be a given.

Judah*, a gay man from Ohio, told me his commitments to science, questioning, and the processes of the universe are key to his identity as a naturalist. He grew up in a fundamentalist home, where he was made to feel so ashamed for being gay that he sought out conversion therapy for himself. Being gay played a major role in his rejecting faith, but even when he was religious, he said he was deeply inspired by the values of love, justice, and truth. "In pursuit of truth I left faith behind," he told me.

Judah said that atheists' desire for a society driven by ethics and reason should be enough to support the cause of LGBTQ equality. I asked him what he would say to an atheist who didn't see the connection between the two.

"I would encourage them to consider what it is to be moral, and to be ethical," he said. "Could they truly say they're ethical if they stand for oppression and injustice, or stand by and allow it to occur? Can they really say they are moral if they allow LGBTQ kids to be bullied to death? I would appeal to their decency, and to their compassion, and their empathy . . . I would challenge them to see if they could justify a world where they expect to be treated equally but LGBTQ people are not."

When Religion Hurts...

"The Word of God"

DANIEL Ashley Pierce had the coming-out experience every young LGBTQ person fears. He also caught part of it on camera.

Pierce is from a Christian family in Georgia. He came out to them in 2014, and a couple of months later, he published a video on YouTube of his family assaulting and berating him for violating "the word of God." Pierce told *HuffPost* he'd prepared the camera because his family was having an intervention of sorts, and he wanted evidence in case it got violent. (The fact that he had that foresight should tell you a lot.)

Pierce was 20 when he recorded the terrifying altercation. The video starts with his family yelling at him for the "choice" he's made. They tell him he's no longer welcome to live in their home, curse at him, and hurl slurs at him, calling him a disgrace and a "damn queer." Eventually, the camera gets shaky as they start beating him, his stepmother punching him in the face as he yells for her to stop.

"No, you can believe that if you want to," someone tells him in the video, "but I believe in the word of God, and God creates nobody that way. It's a path that you have chosen to choose... You go by all the scientific stuff you want to. I'm going by the word of God."[95]

It's hard to imagine any story like this having a silver lining, but Pierce did receive an outpouring of support and used this moment of visibility to give back to the community. Ultimately, he chose not to call the police, but he was disowned by his family. His boyfriend set up a fundraising page to help him get back on his feet and cover his medical expenses. When the campaign took off, raising nearly $100,000 (far more than he needed), Pierce used the money to support Lost-n-Found, the LGBTQ youth organization that helped him relocate when he was in danger.[96]

There's no shortage of stories illustrating how religion has harmed LGBTQ people. It can happen in a number of ways: interpersonally, as when someone like Pierce is rejected because of someone else's faith; institutionally, when laws prioritize "religious freedom" over equal rights; and plenty of rungs in between.

Of all the barriers to full LGBTQ equality, religion is the most aggressively defended. To this day, people ranging from small-town bakers to government officials claim religious beliefs as an excuse to denigrate, delay, or deny equal rights. Some of them get away with it. As people who care about separating church and state, atheists should be outraged that one group's religion can be used to take away another group's rights. But we're more than atheists: we're human beings. That alone should be enough for us to give a damn when someone gets hurt.

Excessive Entanglement

"Congress shall make no law respecting an establishment of religion, or prohibiting the free exercise thereof." We all learned the Establishment Clause in school. It means the government cannot prohibit religious expression, but also that it cannot enact laws that prioritize one religious system over another. That includes belief over nonbelief.

In 1971, the Supreme Court heard *Lemon v. Kurtzman*, a case addressing whether the Pennsylvania Superintendent of Public Schools could reimburse the salaries of private school teachers, many of whom taught at Catholic schools. The Court held 8-1 that the Pennsylvania law violated the Establishment Clause for intermingling church and state unnecessarily.[97]

That case also set an important precedent for how future church-and-state lawsuits would be decided. In their decision the Court established the "Lemon test," a set of three "prongs" that deem whether a law violates the Establishment Clause. For the law to pass the test, "the statute must have a secular legislative purpose, its principal or primary effect must be one that neither promotes nor inhibits religion, and it must not foster 'excessive government entanglement with religion.'"[98]

The law under scrutiny in *Lemon v. Kurtzman* was busted by the "excessive entanglement" prong. It could be argued that this prong of the Lemon test is the one most likely to depend on the whim of a judge's personal opinion. After all, "excessive" is a subjective term. You and I might find it excessive to prominently display the Bible's Ten Commandments at a government building, but others might disagree. Only about 20 legal cases relating to LGBTQ rights have invoked the Lemon test. (One of them, *Barnes Wallace v. City of San Diego,* asked whether San Diego violated the Constitution by leasing land to a Boy Scouts of America-affiliated group that discriminated against LGBTQ people and atheists. The Ninth Circuit Court of Appeals ruled in favor of the city, finding no religious overstep.)[99]

Whether they have faced the Lemon test or not, virtually every LGBTQ issue facing political backlash right now has been attacked by some argument religious in nature. Marriage, kids, transgender identity, the right to buy a cake, for Pete's sake. Some of these issues have been settled—although it doesn't feel safe to assume so under the Trump administration—while others are still in the throes of debate.

Some advocates have assumed the Trump administration won't bother trying to unravel equal marriage because it would take a lot of work to overturn a Supreme Court decision. However, that doesn't mean religious pushback against marriage equality has died down. In 2017, at the annual "Washington: A Man of Prayer" event held at the U.S. Capitol, a Texas Congressman actually wept as he "confessed the sins of our nation" into the microphone. Rep. Randy Weber tearfully apologized to God for taking the Bible out of public schools, for the country's legalization of abortion, and for same-sex marriage.[100]

"Father, we have trampled on your holy institution of holy matrimony and tried to rewrite what it is and we've called it an alternate lifestyle," he cried, literally. "Father, oh Father, please forgive us!"

Though marriage equality is the law of the land, it's far from universally accepted; the number of Americans who support it hovers between 55% and 60%. And even though clerks are required to issue marriage licenses regardless of their personal views on homosexuality, there's no law saying they have to do so kindly.

In 2016, deputy clerk Debbie Allen of Gilmer County, West Virginia allegedly harassed a lesbian couple to the point of tears as they were obtaining their marriage license. The couple said Allen called them an "abomination" and told them God would "deal with them." When they asked her to stop, she told them it was "her religious right to say what she wanted, as long as she issued the license." A family member of the couple called Allen's boss to complain and was told that "her staff did nothing wrong and that the next couple would get the same or worse." The couple filed a lawsuit and won $10,000 in damages, plus a formal apology.[101]

Also, the acceptance and legalization of marriage equality is not an international norm. Marriage equality is legal in about two dozen countries, primarily in the Americas and Europe. By contrast, in much of Africa and the Middle East, homosexuality itself is illegal. In just under a dozen countries, it is punishable by death.[102] (In the first chapter, I spoke about American evangelicals' role in the terrorizing of LGBTQ people in Uganda and elsewhere. The messages we convey about LGBTQ people matter, sometimes on a scale we can't even fathom.)

Back in the United States, marriage paved the way for near-equality when it comes to same-sex parenting and adoption. The last state ban on same-sex adoption—Mississippi's —was only struck down in early 2016.[103] Full joint adoption for same-sex couples is now allowed in all 50 states plus Washington, D.C., and in some two dozen countries as well.

However, in a handful of states, state-funded adoption and foster agencies *are* permitted to discriminate against potential parents based on the religious beliefs of the groups running them.[104] This is a not-so-subtle way of saying that same-sex parents—as well as atheists or other people whose "lifestyles" don't fit a religious agency's idea of the perfect parents—may be turned down, even if they've done nothing wrong.

To make matters worse, anti-LGBTQ conservatives still claim that children need a mom and a dad to succeed, an idea that research has proven incorrect time and time again.[105] But while it's become second-nature for us to tune out the trolls, it's more disappointing when elected officials—whose job it is to *help* same-sex couples—fall prey to those falsehoods.

In Kentucky, for example, family court judge Mitchell Nance attempted to recuse himself from any further cases regarding same-sex parents "as a matter of conscience." He wrote that he would not be able to participate in such cases without the possibility of bias, due to his "conscientious objection to the concept of adoption of a child by a practicing homosexual."[106] (He announced plans to resign a few months later amid ethical concerns about that recusal; the ACLU said these biases made him unfit for office.)

Technically, it was nice of him to bow out so his beliefs won't interfere with a child finding a home, but it's a shame he had to do so at all. Furthermore, could any gay people, even in non-adoption cases, feel like they were getting a fair hearing in Nance's courtroom? We can only hope that other judges who might be experiencing a similar crisis of conscience would make the same decision—to announce their biases publicly and step away from the bench, rather than quietly deny children families for no reason at all.

Works in Progress

Though a few LGBTQ civil rights have been won despite faith-based opposition, many more are still actively threatened by religious bigotry and overstep. Take conversion therapy, for example. Seven states and counting have banned the controversial practice of "ex-gay" conversion therapy, which claims to "cure" people (primarily youth) of being LGBTQ through some combination of talk therapy, religious teaching, and even physical forms of aversive conditioning or other abuse.[107] The concept of conversion therapy has been disproven far and wide; homosexuality is not an illness to be cured, and even if it were, conversion therapy just doesn't work. More often than not it's actually scarring, and it has been connected to higher risks of depression, substance abuse, and suicidality, among other effects.[108]

And still, religious leaders believe it's their right to try to forcibly "convert" LGBTQ young people. In 2015, the conversion therapy provider JONAH (Jews Offering New Alternatives for Healing) was forced to shut down after a jury unanimously decided that the group was committing fraud by claiming they could turn gay people straight.[109] The following year, a group of pastors brought a lawsuit in Illinois over the state's recently-passed conversion therapy ban.[110] The pastors wanted a religious exemption to the law, claiming that homosexuality is "contrary to God's purpose ... [and] can be resisted or overcome by those who seek to be faithful to God and His Word." (It's not, and it can't be.) U.S. District Judge Ronald A. Guzmán dismissed the lawsuit, stating the original law hadn't applied to religious services in the first place. The pastors took this as a victory, and with that, the "religious exemption" crowd won again.[111]

In early 2017, Congressional Democrats introduced the Therapeutic Fraud Prevention Act of 2017, an attempt to ban conversion therapy nationwide.[112] Protecting minors from abuse should be a bipartisan issue. But the Religious Right's influence on the Trump administration—Mike Pence's unclear history as a proponent of conversion therapy, for example— means many LGBTQ activists are less than confident that the bill will go anywhere. (We're fighting for it anyway.)

LGBTQ people's access to healthcare is also unfortunately inconsistent. LGBTQ Americans face a host of health disparities compared to their straight and cisgender counterparts, including higher instances of mental illness, substance abuse, and suicide. And yet, a series of factors prevent LGBTQ people from seeking out the healthcare we need. Patterns like a lack of cultural competency and discriminatory practices by healthcare and insurance providers are serious deterrents.

Religious exemptions to nondiscrimination laws can actually facilitate discrimination in healthcare. In 2001, the LGBTQ legal group Lambda Legal filed a lawsuit against the North Coast Women's Care Medical Group on behalf of Guadalupe Benitez, who was denied fertility treatment because she is a lesbian. Her doctors claimed that their Christian beliefs protected them against providing services that they offered to heterosexual patients.[114] It took seven years before the California Supreme Court ruled in Benitez's favor, determining that "the rights of religious freedom and free speech" do not exempt physicians from abiding by civil rights law.[115]

In an earlier chapter I also talked about a lesbian couple whose pediatrician refused to see their six-day-old baby because of the doctor's religious beliefs.[116] Because Michigan has no law protecting LGBTQ people against discrimination, the doctor's blatant religious bigotry was fully legal.

Even more recently, the Trump administration has indicated that it may no longer enforce a policy that bans anti-transgender discrimination in healthcare.[117] Transgender people (and especially trans people of color) face especially daunting challenges in accessing healthcare. In the 2015 U.S. Transgender Survey, one-third of trans people reported having a negative experience with a doctor related to their gender identity. A higher percentage of trans people than Americans overall rated their health as "fair" or "poor," and 39% of trans people said they were currently experiencing "serious psychological distress," compared to only 5% of the U.S. population.[118] The future of healthcare in the United States is uncertain, but the protections that LGBTQ people secured under the Affordable Care Act are undoubtedly at risk.

The state of transgender health might not be a hot-button issue to mainstream audiences, but transgender people's bathroom use is. As I mentioned earlier, opponents of trans people using affirming bathrooms are not necessarily doing so from a point of religious fervor. They're more often invoking the "bathroom predator myth," or a blatantly false conception of what it means to be transgender and why trans people would want to use the bathrooms they do.

As many trans people will tell you, though, the bathroom debate is about more than just bathrooms. Bathroom access dictates whether transgender people are allowed to exist in public places. Barring trans people from bathrooms sends a message about their dignity and humanity, relegating them to second-class status. And as *Slate*'s Mark Joseph Stern writes, some religious conservatives might find a faith-based argument for denying trans people equal rights, too:

> The Southern Baptist Convention has declared that "gender identity is determined by biological sex and not by one's self-perception—a perception which is often influenced by

fallen human nature in ways contrary to God's design." The Lutheran Church-Missouri Synod insists that the sex we are assigned at birth is "a God-given identity" and that gender confirmation surgery "will only mutilate the body God has given." Pope Francis has suggested that gender transition "does not recognize the order of creation." Most anti-trans religious reasoning falls along these lines: God created us male or female, and we must remain locked into one side of that binary from birth through death."[119]

If more immediately life-threatening issues ever make it to the mainstream conversation—things like discrimination in housing, healthcare, high rates of homelessness, suicide, and familial rejection of trans youth—we've already set a terrible precedent. If religious bigotry can sway the conversation over bathrooms, it's likely to be mentioned when a host of other basic rights are up for discussion, too. (And the reality here is that none of these issues should be questions at all.)

Attempts to legalize discrimination are almost always based on religion. These laws, again referred to as RFRAs (for Religious Freedom Restoration Act), usually say that businesses cannot be penalized for refusing to serve certain customers on the basis of the company's religious beliefs. Laws like this are the spark for many stories you hear about same-sex couples being refused wedding cakes or flowers by conservative bakeries or florists. When he was still governor of Indiana, Mike Pence signed a RFRA into law—but at the last minute, and only after a public outcry put intense pressure on him—added a stipulation banning businesses from discriminating on the basis of sexual orientation or gender identity.[120] Still, pro-LGBTQ businesses and customers saw past the edit and recognized the bill's homophobic origins. Indiana lost $60 million in potential revenue in less than a year when 12 organizations decided not to host their conventions in Indianapolis in part because of the law.[121]

And even though the separation of church and state was supposedly enshrined centuries ago, religion still seeps into public institutions in toxic ways. Take Michael Stack, a special education teacher at San Luis Obispo High School in California. After the school's student newspaper published an edition focusing on LGBTQ issues, Stack wrote a letter to the paper—likely knowing it would be published—explaining that he was compelled to respond because he "didn't want to displease God." In his letter, he quoted a Bible verse stating explicitly that gay people "deserve to die," adding that the Bible is "without error." As if that wasn't abhorrent enough, the school refused to discipline the teacher.[122] Their official response: "A bedrock principle underlying the First Amendment is that the government may not prohibit the expression of an idea simply because society finds the idea offensive or disagreeable."

I wrote about this incident on my personal blog, GayWrites.org. One person commented that because the teacher was known to students and commanded their respect, writing the letter to the newspaper was tantamount to standing up at a school assembly and announcing that teachers could kill LGBTQ students. This is an extreme comparison, but it's not wrong. Imagine how you'd feel if a teacher you were supposed to trust announced that people like you deserved death. Even if they hadn't said your name, you'd feel unwanted, even targeted. Nobody should feel like that, let alone at school.

Luckily, the majority of teachers are not like this. Research from GLSEN, an organization focused on safer schools for LGBTQ students (full disclosure: I used to work there), indicates that 97% of LGBTQ middle and high school students know of at least one LGBTQ-friendly staff member on campus. Sixty-four percent know of at least six, and 41% know of 11 or more.[123] That's impressive.

Still, if something like this had happened at my Florida high school—where I was deeply closeted and teachers never talked about LGBTQ issues—it would have stuck in my memory more than anything else in those four years. Being queer in high school is hard enough as it is without Bible-based death wishes from teachers. Case in point: seven states (not just schools, but *states*) ban teachers from talking about homosexuality in a positive way at all.[124] This can include anything from discussing LGBTQ history like the Stonewall Riots to a teacher sponsoring a student Gay-Straight Alliance club. It should come as no surprise that homosexuality is often banned from school curricula about sex ed—or, as in South Carolina, it's only allowed to be mentioned in conjunction with sexually transmitted diseases.

In less extreme (but still disappointing) cases, some schools ban library books with LGBTQ-related content. Five of the top 10 books banned from schools in 2016 were axed because of queer characters or storylines.[125] That list includes *I Am Jazz*, a perfectly G-rated book by teenager Jazz Jennings about her life as a transgender kid. At one school in Wisconsin, the staff planned a reading and discussion of *I Am Jazz* to support a 6-year-old transgender girl who had recently come out. But they were forced to shut it down because the anti-LGBTQ religious group Liberty Counsel threatened legal action for "violating parental constitutional rights."[126] In this case, members of the community rallied behind the young girl by holding readings of the book in other locations. But not every transgender kid is lucky enough to have that kind of community support.

Last but certainly not least, religion is still a driving force that propels families to abandon their LGBTQ loved ones. According to a 2012 survey of agencies that work with LGBTQ homeless youth, nearly 70% of the young people they serve had experienced family rejection, and more than half had been abused at home.[127] It's a little more difficult to collect data from LGBTQ homeless youth themselves, but an endless supply of anecdotes like Daniel Pierce's story paint a clear picture of how religion affects families' views of their LGBTQ kids.

Rolling Stone published a story in 2014 featuring young people who became homeless after their religious families cast them out.[128] "Highly religious parents" are "significantly more likely" to kick their gay kids out of the house than non-religious parents, wrote reporter Alex Morris:

> As societal advancements have made being gay less stigmatized and gay people more visible—and as the Internet now allows kids to reach beyond their circumscribed social groups for acceptance and support—the average coming-out age has dropped from post-college age in the 1990s to around 16 today, which means that more and more kids are coming out while they're still economically reliant on their families. The resulting flood of kids who end up on the street, kicked out by parents whose religious beliefs often make them feel compelled to cast out their own offspring (one study estimates that up to 40 percent of LGBT homeless youth leave home due to family rejection), has been called

a "hidden epidemic." Tragically, every step forward for the gay-rights movement creates a false hope of acceptance for certain youth, and therefore a swelling of the home-less-youth population.

To me, this is one of the most gut-wrenching side effects of religious homophobia and transphobia: every time we make progress, certain conservative voices will fight back more forcefully than they had before, and our most vulnerable citizens will suffer. Nobody is immune to the harm that religion too often inflicts on LGBTQ people, but some groups are better equipped to handle it than others. For those who don't have supportive families or financial resources; for people who live with the overlapping oppressions of racism, sexism, homophobia, and transphobia; for those who are LGBTQ and also un-documented, disabled, homeless, and yes, atheists—we must fight back harder.

voices   Lisa

Lisa and I met in Nashville, Tennessee, on the first morning of a sever-al-day LGBTQ advocacy workshop. We chatted about our lives over the hotel's continental breakfast around 7 a.m., and even though I'm awk-ward with introductions, her energy and enthusiasm immediately made her one of my favorite people from the weekend.

We didn't talk much after we parted ways from the conference, but she got back in touch when I started asking around for stories of faith and identity. What struck me most about her story was her upfront acknowledgment of the ways some Christians use their faith to demean others, and her commitment to model a more inclusive Christianity.

Lisa grew up in a mixed-denomination Christian home—Methodist and Catholic—and while she went through the motions of Sunday school and a first communion, she says she never learned much about what it meant to be a Christian. Years later, she's settled into both her non-de-nominational Christian faith and her identity as a lesbian, even though it took a while to get there. Here's part of our conversation.

How active are you in church now?

When I first identified as a Christian, I was 29. My best friend, at the time, shared "The Gospel" with me in a way I could finally understand. Before then, religion seemed like it was something for other people. I felt awkward about it because it wasn't something that I was used to. When I came out, I felt like the church would burn down if I walked in.

When I moved back to Arizona in 2012, I came out to myself again. Then, I started the process of coming out to my friends, again. It was important for me to put a face and a name to the issues of marriage equality, so I came out to the majority of people through Facebook. I wrote a note entitled, "Know a Lesbian? Now, You Do." I lost some "friends" and I deleted others. I've been living more and more of my authentic self ever since. Currently, I am active in my prayer life but I do not attend a church where I live or online. I have been too damaged by leaders and others in church to step into a church again. Or, at least for now.

Have you ever faced any kind of conflict, whether internal or external, over being both Christian and LGBTQ?

When I had arranged to [come out to] my mom, we went for a walk in her apartment complex. The first thing out of her mouth was, "You're not pregnant, are you?" I told my mom that I was "gay." She raised her voice as she told me sternly, "That's not the way God intended it!"

Later, when I identified as a Christian, I had a lot of internal conflict. A friend came to me, handed me a book and asked me to read it. She said that God had a better path for me and He didn't want anyone to be gay. I read the part of the book that she suggested. I was confused and hurt. I loved God and I felt that I had finally started becoming my true self. I prayed and asked God to change me if He wanted me to be different, because I didn't know how. I guess this was a more private version of conversion therapy. I no longer attended the "gay" church that I belonged to. I no longer lived as a lesbian. My friend's parents had been "praying" for me. They had called the 700 Club prayer line for me to no longer be gay. Then, CBN wanted to interview me. I refused. I didn't want the world to know my shame.

How do you interpret the parts of Christianity that some people read as inherently homophobic and transphobic?

Just like anything that is written, whether a historic document or someone's post on Facebook, it is best when the time period and circumstances are used as a framework or foundation. When truly examined, there are very few biblical mentions of homosexuality and even fewer that refer to it solely (meaning without also referring to other topics). The Old Testament, in many ways, provided a foundation for the New Testament. It pointed toward the direction and deity of Jesus. When truly examined, I find less negative scriptures about homosexuality or trans identities than about handling finances. There are some sections of scripture that I have studied thoroughly and I honestly believe the church leadership is wrong on their interpretation of those scriptures.

Have you ever struggled with or considered leaving your faith because of something LGBTQ-related?

I have struggled more with the people of my same faith than my faith itself. When people that I have known for years became hateful and hurtful, it was difficult to take. I had to realize how shallow their thinking was. It didn't happen without a lot of tears, though. In those moments, I come back to my purpose. My purpose is to create loving, encouraging and safe places for LGBTQ people, in spite of what some rude Christians may think. I am not misguided in my faith, in my sexual identity or sexuality or my purpose. I am finally living my life more integrated than I ever have. I am embracing all of my identities right now; it is sometimes a frightening process but it is also very liberating.

How do you think religious groups and LGBTQ people can collaborate for social justice, if at all?

If religious groups truly represented their religious foundations, this would be an automatic area of collaboration. Jesus was radical in His day. He was all about social justice and caring for people. At the framework of many religions, the basis rests in concepts of compassion, kindness, helping others. These concepts are needed to carry out the labor of social justice issues. When they are not, we have the chaos that we are living in today.

Making It Better

At the time of this writing, Mike Pence is vice president of the United States. The second most powerful man in the country, supposedly a key adviser to the president and a person with major sway over how our country operates, is on the record saying that marriage equality might bring about societal collapse. He has said that outlawing same-sex marriage should not be considered a matter of discrimination, but an adherence to "God's idea." The president's Cabinet is full of people who share those views, and so is the country. It's frightening.

That said, I want to be intentional about recognizing that not all LGBTQ people are harmed by religion in the same way. For most people in the United States, our circumstances don't compare in any way to the egregious human rights violations taking place in countries like Uganda or Russia.[130] That's not to say our challenges are any less valid because others have it worse; rather, this is an opportunity to reflect on how vast and painful the struggle for equality is across the globe, and to get fired up for a movement that doesn't end in the United States.

Personally, I don't know what it's like to be gravely ostracized by someone you love because of who you are, and for that I am grateful. Sure, strangers have occasionally yelled hateful things when I'm out with my partner. Maybe once a week someone on the internet will tell me I'm going to hell or I deserve to die. But my family hasn't disowned me, homosexuality isn't illegal where I live, I haven't experienced homelessness, and I haven't lost my job for being who I am. In the grand scheme of things, I am lucky.

Countless people in our communities—LGBTQ people, atheists, and others who are abandoned by their families or by society—have not fared as well. Institutionalized religion has the support of some of the wealthiest, best-connected and most influential people in the country. While progress is coming slowly, thousands of people or more are still hurting. Here, atheists have the opportunity to right the wrongs of religious overstep, even if we can't end religious discrimination altogether. (At least not overnight. But we're working on it!)

Those who do have the resources to help must take the opportunity to support those who aren't as fortunate. This can look like donating to groups that work with homeless LGBTQ youth, volunteering your time, working on the ground to support local legislation, or lending your ear (or your couch) to somebody who's gone through a rough time. As people who value secular ideals in society, atheists must do more than just complain when religion is used to harm people. We're all talk unless we take it further by standing at the frontlines to help those who were harmed.

. . . And When Religion Helps

I WISH I'd taken better notes during my internal coming-out process, but I remember being too ashamed to even write it down.

I know that I started to realize I had feelings for other girls when I was 12 or 13, but I didn't have a label for it. (I didn't even know bisexuality was a thing then.) I remember thinking that something about me was sick, broken, and different, and I definitely wasn't ready to accept it, let alone put it on paper. I was terrified of this thing that I felt but couldn't name, so I refused to document it properly. But that didn't stop me from polling the people around me about what they knew, and what they thought of it.

I was in sixth grade when my lunch table started talking hypothetically about homosexuality. My Christian friends—the same ones who were adamant, at the age of 11, that we'd all wait until marriage before having sex—repeated the mantra "love the sinner, hate the sin" every time the topic came up. I don't even remember why it came up at all. Nobody at our middle school was openly gay, and we weren't savvy enough to pay attention to any celebrity comings-out or laws that had been passed. But there must have been a reason I turned to my friend and asked, "Would you think less of me if I was gay?"

Her voice got quiet and she looked away from me. "No," she said. "I'd still love you. I might not change clothes in front of you, though."

All things considered, it wasn't a terrible reaction. (Let's be real. We were all in chorus together. Deciding who to stand next to in the giant group dressing rooms was a big part of our lives.) I didn't think of that conversation as a coming-out moment, either. But the girl was by far my most religious friend up to that point, and she didn't freak out. She was actually kind of nice about it. *Maybe it wouldn't be too bad,* I remember thinking. *Maybe they wouldn't all hate me.* And then I put the idea away for a couple more years.

I haven't talked to that friend, or any of my middle-school Christian posse, in close to a decade. I don't know who among them is pro-marriage equality, or pro-choice, or pro- any of the other social issues that have defined the battle over "religious freedom" in the last few years. But I haven't forgotten my friend's careful consideration of my question from when I was a closeted kid. I've used it to try to think optimistically (though not without reservations) about attitudes of believers toward LGBTQ people.

When I was gathering sources for this book, I found that the people who were most eager to talk to me were LGBTQ people of faith who wanted to share their stories. It's easy and common for atheists to dismiss religion as a monolith that's universally toxic to LGBTQ people. In reality, it's much more complicated than that. We've already talked about just how many people belong to both groups—nearly 60% of LGBTQ people consider themselves religiously affiliated, according to the Pew Research Center.[131] In early 2017, Gallup estimated that there are 10 million LGBTQ Americans. When you consider the two side by side, that means close to six million people in the United States are both people of faith and LGBTQ—about the same number as the populations of Maryland or Missouri.[132]

Growing up, most of us are exposed to religion long before we learn that LGBTQ people even exist. People of faith are likely to have belonged to their religions, or at least *a* religion, since they were kids, sometimes without having any say in the matter. We learn about faith early on and can form a genuine connection with it as children or teenagers. For some people, that's an important relationship to maintain, even if eventually coming out changes the circumstances. And for others, a connection to religion comes later in life, not through childhood rituals but as a result of one's own personal journey and reflection. That's valid, too. No two atheists are identical in how they came to their (non-)beliefs, and neither are any two people of faith.

This is not to say that religious institutions, ideas, and individuals have not caused grave and unforgivable harm to LGBTQ people; they have. Citing religious beliefs is the easiest way to get away with homophobia or transphobia because society tends to bend over backwards to accommodate religion. (Mainstream Christian beliefs, at least—people of Muslim or Jewish faiths likely couldn't get away with what many Christians do.) Kentucky county clerk Kim Davis became something of a martyr for the Religious Right because her refusal to marry same-sex couples stemmed from her religious beliefs. Had she cited a different reason for her actions—"gay people freak me out," perhaps—the response from the Right would have been much more subdued. Unapologetic bigotry isn't as good for PR, you know?

But without making excuses for those who abuse religion, it's important to recognize that LGBTQ people of faith are everywhere, and that they ache under discriminatory laws and hateful ideologies, too. Atheists might not see a logical reason for LGBTQ people (or anybody) to be religious, but plenty of people of all identities find comfort and community in belief.

Faith is way more complex than simply knowing the name of the church where you were baptized before you could talk. It's a personal belief about how the world came to be, how it works, and how you relate to it. It's every person's right to believe or not believe as they choose. And allying with LGBTQ people of faith, who are also likely to be more progressive and may even share atheist or humanist values, can be a productive way for atheists to work toward equality and justice.

Chris Stedman, the gay and atheist author of *Faitheist,* told *Religion News Service* in 2013 that it's possible to critique religious dogma without tearing down people of faith.[133] Instead, he called for an interfaith collaboration between atheists and religious groups, suggesting we have constructive, forward-moving conversations with people whose worldviews we don't share.

"I would encourage anyone interested in building interfaith bridges to reach out to others, to speak from your own experience, and, most importantly, to actively listen," he said. "Be honest, but also be compassionate."

Your capacity to be a good person is not determined by whether or not you believe in God, and your commitment to human rights shouldn't be determined by whether you identify as LGBTQ. Bringing down faith-based bigotry is a massive undertaking. Working with people who *are* connected to religious communities is a great way to do it.

Unfortunately, this vision of collaboration isn't always possible, especially with groups whose anti-LGBTQ hatred goes beyond opposing same-sex marriage. Some religious groups are so open to diversity, inclusivity, and even ideas outside their belief systems that they more closely resemble atheists than evangelicals. But others preach a gospel so vehemently toxic, it advocates murder—and that's hardly an exaggeration. It's nobody's job to play nice with people who seek to invalidate their basic rights, or to try to appease people who condemn their existence. (In the sharp words tweeted by Robert Jones, Jr., a gay, black writer who created a social media community under the name Son of Baldwin: "We can disagree and still love each other unless your disagreement is rooted in my oppression and denial of my humanity and right to exist.")[134]

Throughout this book, I've tried not to characterize religion as inherently harmful; certainly there are atheists on both sides of that argument. There are atheists who believe religion is an obstacle to LGBTQ equality, and others who feel the best path forward is to work with progressive believers who share the same goals. It's my hope that the portrayals of faith in this chapter will make it harder to back up the claim that "religion is always the enemy."

In some cases, religion drives people to say and do heinous, horrifying things. But in others, religion—whether organized or informal—is what motivates people to find community, take action for good, and even join forces around a social justice cause. The answer to supporting LGBTQ people, then, isn't making a blanket judgment about the positive or negative effects of religion. It's working to make sure everyone has access to the same rights, respect, freedoms, and—if they so choose —beliefs.

Affirming Churches
As I discussed earlier, while atheism is more common among LGBTQ people than among the general public, a sizeable num-

ber of LGBTQ people do belong to some sort of religious tradition. Forty-six percent of LGBTQ people reported themselves "religiously unaffiliated" in a 2017 PRRI survey, as compared with 24% of the general population.[135] But 41% of LGBTQ people in the survey identified as Christians, and another 10% as members of a non-Christian faith. To some atheists or even some LGBTQ people, those numbers may seem unbelievably high, especially when it comes to those who belong to more conservative faiths. But for LGBTQ people who feel called to faith, there are more places than ever ready to accept them.

Perhaps the best-known LGBTQ-affirming *and* atheist-affirming church is the Unitarian Universalist Association. Founded in 1961, the church abides by seven Principles that serve as "strong values and moral guides" for members. The Principles emphasize respect, justice, equality, and the freedom to explore. Not a single one of them suggests that you have to believe in God to participate, making the UU a popular congregation for atheists, agnostics, or spiritual ex-Christians who are looking for community without commandments. Built into that framework is unconditional support for LGBTQ people, both believers and non-believers.

One person I spoke with, Philip (not the same Philip mentioned earlier), has been going to a Unitarian Universalist church since 2001. He said he started drifting from religion around the age of 35, feeling that his mainstream church was no longer serving him in the way he needed. The Unitarians provided the community he'd gotten from his former church, minus the theological expectations; it was a safe place for him to congregate with friendly faces without being a believer.

"The Unitarians gave me a sense of freedom to question, explore, and find out what I thought and felt, which is something nobody else seemed to care about," Philip said. "The Unitarian church has always been more about community than beliefs, simply because there is no set creed to follow; we all share different perspectives, and celebrate them."

Philip is also bisexual, and says that the church is open-hearted and nonjudgmental about accepting him for who he is.

"I can go in there with painted toenails," he said, "and no one bats an eye!"

Another UU-goer I talked to, a woman from Ohio named Katie, was raised Catholic, but went through a 15-year period without religion. One day, on her way home from a vacation, she drove by a Unitarian church. "[It was] a religion I had never heard of before. So I googled it, and there was my worldview built right into the seven Principles. No god, no judgment, no dogma, no demands." The UU church's seven Principles aligned with her viewpoints and didn't impose a belief system, so she found the nearest church and stopped by on a Sunday morning. "[I] found community with like-minded folks and I didn't need to put a label on myself," she said. "I met many UU's my first few Sunday services that even after decades of spiritual exploration were still searching, and that was absolutely O.K."

For LGBTQ people of faith looking for a more explicitly belief-centric community, congregations across many faith traditions now make it clear that they welcome members of all sexual orientations and gender identities. In progressive neighborhoods, it's not uncommon to walk by a church or synagogue and spot a rainbow flag waving outside. Some churches state on their websites or even their social media accounts that they welcome all members, regardless of sexual orientation or gender identity.

The website of the GALIP Foundation, a group connecting LGBTQ Christians with resources, includes an Affirming Church Directory. Through the site, you can enter your location and desired Christian denomination and pull up a map of LGBTQ-affirming churches near you. Of course, the tool's usefulness varies based on where you live.[136] Larger states that skew liberal have hundreds of churches in the directory; for smaller, rural states, it's more like a handful.

This makes sense; it's obvious that affirming churches would pop up and thrive in communities with higher numbers of LGBTQ people, and larger populations in general. But it's also important to remember that there are LGBTQ people in every state, and that some of them are also Christian (especially in communities with a heavy religious influence). The more LGBTQ-inclusive churches make themselves known, the more LGBTQ Christians might feel safe coming out to help affirming faith groups grow.

Christianity isn't the only faith tradition with pockets opening up to LGBTQ people. The organization Keshet, for example, was founded in 1996 and works on behalf of LGBTQ inclusion in Jewish life and culture. A website called jewish-lgbtnetwork.com aggregates a roster of LGBTQ-affirming synagogues, support services, and other Jewish groups throughout the United States. LGBTQ-affirming Muslim organizations exist in countries from the United States and Canada to Egypt and Sudan. In 2016, the *Times of India* reported that there were only eight openly gay imams in the world (and another four who are gay, but not openly)—but eight is better than zero.[137] ("If the question is 'do we exist,' of course, we do exist," Daayiee Abdullah, one of those eight, told the *Times*.) There are even groups for LGBTQ members of some of the most conservative Christian faith traditions, like the Mormon Church.

Sahar Ali Deen is the founder of the group OUTMuslim, a mostly online community for LGBTQ Muslims. He created the group to address the lack of LGBTQ Muslim representation around him, something that complicated his own coming-out process. By age 13, he'd come out to his mother and scoured the internet for resources aimed at supporting LGBTQ Muslims. But the coming-out narratives he found didn't necessarily apply to him.

"Almost everything I read was about (and written for) white gay boys, not for brown ones," Deen told me. "I read about rainbows and hugs and exclamations of 'I still love you.' Of course, the stories didn't always end well, but I figured that what I had in common with the happy ones was loving parents that cared about my future. If Mikey and Joey and Scott were in their parents' good graces, surely the outcome wouldn't be so bad for me."

Deen's coming-out didn't go as well as the ones he read stories about online. He endured discussions about the moral dilemmas of sexuality *and* homosexuality, had his internet access revoked and his bedroom door removed. He later decided to create OUTMuslim, where he could invite fellow LGBTQ Muslims to share their stories and build a compassionate community with people from all faith and identity backgrounds.

"I wasn't a Bobby or Justin after all," he said. "When I did realize there were gay Omars like me, and bisexual Alinas and transgender Kabirs who needed to hear stories of other Muslims experiencing similar things, I decided to create OUTMuslim."

As OUTMuslim shows, with the advent of the internet, it's easier than ever to find a network of people who affirm your faith and your sexual orientation or gender identity. Virtually every major religion has some kind of online presence for LGBTQ believers. Some of these are established nonprofits with boards and financial statements, whereas others are informal Facebook or Meetup groups that foster community. While these groups vary in size and status, the fact that they exist proves their members exist: LGBTQ people, some of whom have suffered at the hands of a faith they trusted, who want to connect with others like them who still believe.

Sahar Ali Deen

voices

Sahar Ali Deen and I talked a little over a week into Donald Trump's presidency, when Trump's executive order targeting Muslim-majority countries was in full swing and rumors were growing about how he would address LGBTQ rights. As a gay and genderqueer Muslim, Deen said, he's heard messages for most of his life that his existence isn't plausible. He especially felt that "othering" in the wake of the attack at the Pulse nightclub in Orlando, when it was found that the shooter was Muslim. Launching OUTMuslim and connecting with other LGBTQ Muslims has been one way of tackling that constant denigration, he says; it reconciles the way he feels with what others say about his overlapping identities. Here's a portion of our conversation.

How do your LGBTQ and Muslim identities relate to one another? Do you find that they strengthen or complement each other in any way?

In the past, it felt much more difficult to reconcile these seemingly opposing parts of myself, but at this point in my life it mostly strengthens and empowers me. I recognized at a young age that regardless of the views that my family members, fellow students, or teachers held that I was still a valid, existing human being. When someone said to me, "it's impossible to be Muslim and gay," and I didn't automatically poof out of existence, I figured there must be something wrong in their calculations. Of course it was hurtful to hear these kinds of remarks, but I still was both, and I still was breathing. And I still had goals and needs and opinions. Eventually, living with this kind of awareness gave me a certain type of freedom in knowing how limiting certain ideologies can be. It showed me the danger of blind faith and that my spirituality could not be prescribed by any ideology. I started to understand that identity can be limiting, but it can also be empowering. These are both contradicting views on the idea of identity, but they both hold truth and I didn't have to choose.

Have you ever faced pushback either from Muslim communities for being LGBTQ, or from LGBTQ communities for being Muslim?

I have, and continue to face opposition from both sides for various reasons. This comes from people who are very close to me as well as nameless people on the internet. When I decided to create OUTMuslim I knew I'd have to deal with other Muslims who felt that my support of people who held queer and Muslim identities was blasphemous. At the same time, there were a plethora of LGBTQIA* people who had felt shunned by religion – particularly by some of the mainstream ideologies that have come from Muslim communities. Many of these people would ridicule maintaining faith in Islam or religion at all. From the first day that OUTMuslim has had an online presence, I have received incredibly hateful and vilifying messages from both sides. This isn't to say that I don't receive affirming messages, too. I do feel a sense of community from those who have identified with what OUTMuslim stands for, and I feel their support every day.

On the flip side, it is also a familiar experience to be a target from queer-identifying people as well as cis/straight ones too. The tragic attack at Pulse happened on the morning of the day my city's pride parade was scheduled. I remember feeling scared to attend any of the pride events because of being a Muslim, as well as trying to wrap my mind around what had happened. Just weeks prior to this, someone had left a severed pig's head at the entrance of a local mosque

---

* An extension of the commonly used acronym that adds representation for "intersex" and "asexual."

to express their Islamophobic sentiments. So on a day like Pride, I was nervous about being the target of violence as a Muslim person. There was a rise of groups such as "Twinks for Trump" and "Gays for Guns" on social media, so it felt very unsafe to be a Muslim at this time, even though I shared part of my identity with these people. What was even more upsetting was that this shared queer identity was also historically the target for similar violence.

Have you ever faced any internal struggle over being both LGBTQ and Muslim, and if so, how did you overcome it?

When I heard the news of the Orlando attack, I clearly remember thinking to myself, "If they reveal the name of the shooter, and it's a Muslim name, I am going to be livid." And then they did, and it was, and I was aggravated because it seemed like Muslims couldn't get a break from the media. By default, I would now be in a position where the seemingly opposing identities which had given me much strength and freedom were now going to be put through the ringer. I'd be hearing the words "Muslim" and "gay" and "queer" being spoken by people on TV and on the radio who had no lived experiences of what it was like to be either, or both. This is where having a platform like OUTMuslim came in handy. I could speak up and tell my narrative and give my opinions and share my viewpoints the way that I saw them. I did not want to be painted as a victim, nor as a villain—I just wanted to be seen as a human who was as dumbfounded by the situation as anyone. The OUTMuslim page attracted a lot of media attention and I was able to give statements, and my aggravation somewhat turned into a hopeful sentiment. After my statements were printed and broadcast, the nay-sayers (both Muslim and LGBTQ-identifying) started to send vile and, in some cases, murderous messages. Some of the attacks were directed not only at me but to whatever family I may have too. In the wake of such a horrific attack, these messages were especially distressing.

This made it complicated to continue—was I doing the right thing? I knew speaking up was necessary, but now I was also potentially putting my family and myself in danger. Should I continue? If I stopped the advocacy work to keep my family safe, was I betraying the part of myself to which it was so important to be a voice of change? I can't say I've come to any answers to these questions, but I continue to do the work that feels important. And I continue to feel conflicted about it. I can only keep going, because that's life, I guess.

What is your response to people who try to use the Muslim faith (or ideas they describe as the Muslim faith) to perpetuate homophobia or transphobia, whether in the U.S. or abroad?

We must stop identifying each other through our differences. The cost is too high, and we lose our own humanity when we berate or assail our fellow people. Let us love and cherish one another with the time we're given on this earth. To quote a translation of the Qur'an, *"By time, all humankind is in loss. Except for those who do righteous deeds and advise each other to truth and to patience."*

How can atheists (specifically straight/cisgender atheists) be effective allies to you?

First off, ask. Ask, rather than assume about people's experiences and needs. Also, listen carefully. Often, when someone expresses their struggles, social and systematic forms of oppression start to become visible. As a person who is more privileged because of your gender and sexuality, you have a responsibility to speak up when you witness an oppressive/prejudiced action or remark. This must be consistent in and out of the presence of those who are being marginalized. If you are in the company of friends and let your companion get away with an ignorant remark, the work is not being done. In terms of being an atheist, it is important to remember that your understanding of the universe is not necessarily universal. And others may understand exactly what you do with a different vocabulary, or by using a methodology that is not limited to data and physical observations. Biologically speaking, all human experience is generated within one's own body, using the infrastructure of one's own senses—this makes each individual's scope a very limited one. There are many ways to understand and perceive this world and every person you encounter has just as valid a perspective as you. Radical or violent ideologies are often a result of the politicization of religion, not the religion itself.

What is one thing you want atheists to know about LGBTQ Muslims?

Even though at first sight, it may seem like there are only two genders, some may argue that there are three, five, or ten. Some may argue that there are as many genders as there are people. Perhaps we can look at the idea of religion/spirituality in the same way. There are as many kinds of Muslims as there are people, just as there are as many kinds of atheists as there are people. No one's identity or experience should be limited by a label which you think you understand wholly—you don't. You can only hope to understand and be enlightened by others, just as they may be enlightened by you.

But the Bible Says...

Mainstream Christianity has made clear that adhering strictly to the Bible—or at least one interpretation of it—is not a prerequisite for believing. (Certainly some of the most devout pastors in the country wear mixed fabrics, eat shrimp, and don't stone their ill-behaved children.) But still, too many homophobic conservatives cite Scripture—the Old Testament, no less—as a reason to demean LGBTQ lives, particularly when it comes to marriage, having kids, and (gasp) sex. That can pose an obvious problem for people living at the intersection of being Christian and LGBTQ. Where's the line between respecting the Bible you grew up with and casting it aside for its many faults?

As it turns out, that line is wherever you put it. No two people of faith practice in the same way—including those who are LGBTQ.

Abhishek*, a bisexual Christian, grew up Southern Baptist in North Carolina. He was taught that sex outside of marriage was sinful, but LGBTQ issues and most other social issues didn't come up at his conservative church. He came out in college and joined a church that seemed more affirming than the one he'd grown up with—until he started talking openly about his identity.

"I was surprised to discover that people at church didn't share my beliefs when I discussed them," he told me. "There was a point where a couple of folks from my small group sat me down to basically convince me that God can keep me from giving in to same-sex attraction. I disagreed both with the substance and the relative importance of our disagreement. At least one person believed that 'sin is sin' and that agreement with them was necessary for being a Christian."

Abhishek was ready to put the awkward conversation behind him; he loved the music community at his new church and auditioned to join the praise band. But the church's elders decided it would not be appropriate for Abhishek to play in the church band as an openly bisexual man, even though he'd been helping to clean up after services for over a year. That's when he started to fade from the church; he started participating less and less, and eventually found another fellowship.

Now, he says his affirming faith community plays a big role in what keeps him connected to the church. His church community has many other LGBTQ members and marches in their local Pride, for example, and he plays in the band with the church's blessing. He says he avoids Christian spaces where the vibe might be more homophobic. Right now, he says, the clearest part of his faith is the community it brings him; the rest is fluctuating with time.

"Without my community I find that my faith is not super sustaining on its own. Because my primary interactions with faith are through community and through reading theology, when I'm looking to get strength through my personal relationship with God I often come up short," he said.

"I'm still not super resolved in what I believe, but I'm pretty far from where I was three years ago. In some ways that isn't related to my queerness, because what convinced me was historical scholarship and comparative religions. But I also suspect that I wouldn't have been driven to seek out alternatives if I hadn't felt uneasy about how people who believe in biblical inerrancy treated me as a queer person."

Abhishek's story echoes the ways in which many people experience religion today. As I mentioned earlier, America is shifting secular. But the lines are blurry when it comes to holding beliefs, or even participating in religion, in a way that strays from expectations of that faith institution. (For example, I talked to many self-identified atheists who also attend the Unitarian Universalist church, where some members presumably do believe in God.)

Queer Theology, an online collective of LGBTQ Christians and their allies, tears down the idea that belief must exclude LGBTQ people. One of its founders, Father Shannon T. L. Kearns, told me the group is intended to be "unapologetically Christian and unapologetically queer."

"We wanted a resource that showed the gifts queer and/or trans people have to give to the church," he says.

Kearns, a transgender man and former fundamentalist, is an ordained priest with the Old Catholic Church, a progressive Catholic group that's not in communion with the Church in Rome. He said he's tired of having conversations about the "clobber passages" in the Bible—the few verses that are often repeated as "proof" that Christianity opposes homosexuality.

"The scholars are clear that the Bible does *not* condemn homosexuality and that the verses commonly used against gay people don't mean what they have been interpreted to mean," Kearns says.

"I'm much more interested in the positive. If you look through both the Hebrew and Christian scriptures there is a common thread: A push toward justice for all people that is centered around those who are most at risk and marginalized. God wants justice; a just world where people treat each other with respect and dignity. God wants economic justice. God wants immigration justice. These are not things that we are reading into the text; they are explicit and clear."

Matthew Vines, a Christian LGBTQ activist, makes the same case in his book *God and the Gay Christian.*

"My core argument in this book is not simply that some Bible passages have been misinterpreted and others have been given undue weight," he writes. "My larger argument is this: *Christians who affirm the full authority of Scripture can also affirm committed, monogamous same-sex relationships.*"[138]

Bad Faith

There's a reason many in the U.S. often associate religion with rabid homophobia. It's because the most widely shared stories about the intersection between LGBTQ issues and religion are negative. Protesters at Pride parades hold up signs about God's wrath, and religious groups are usually the first to argue against LGBTQ-inclusive legislation. Some "traditional family" advocates perpetuate vile myths about gay people harming children. Some Independent Fundamental Baptist (IFB) preachers publicly wish death upon LGBTQ people. These actions can be the work of extremist hate groups, but other times, they come from run-of-the-mill Christians who think they're making the world a better place by tearing us down so brutally. You don't have to be a card-carrying member of a hate group to spread hate.

The most famous example of poisonous religiosity is the Westboro Baptist Church, the group best known for picketing at military funerals, college campuses, LGBTQ community events, and anywhere else they're bound to get attention. Westboro's visibility reached new heights in 1998 when they picketed the funeral of Matthew Shepard, a gay college student who was murdered in a brutal hate crime in Laramie, Wyoming.[139] The "church" says of soldiers killed in action that war casualties are God's punishment for America's growing acceptance of LGBTQ people. Usually, they bring signs reading slogans like "Thank God for Dead Soldiers" and "God Hates Fags." (The latter is both their charming catchphrase and the URL for their website.)

Now, it feels strange to bring up Westboro Baptist and their associates in a chapter about how religion can help the movement for equality, but hear me out. The internet loves to speculate about exactly *why* Westboro does what they do. One theory posits that it's all an elaborate scheme to rile people up until someone attacks them, in which case they can sue for assault. Some people hope it's just performance art. Westboro itself says their motives stem from "God's word." They claim to preach a doctrine inspired by the principles of Calvinism and take issue with the message enshrined by (some) churches that "God loves everyone."

"We adhere to the teachings of the Bible, preach against all form of sin (e.g., fornication, adultery [including divorce and remarriage], sodomy), and insist that the sovereignty of God and the doctrines of grace be taught and expounded publicly to all men," reads their website.[140] They boast a record of nearly 60,000 protests since 1991, even with a membership of no more than 100 and as few as 40 people. They claim to be Christians, but it's a kind of Christianity that few people would ever admit to supporting. (Though that doesn't mean Westboro sympathizers aren't out there—they are.)

Though they're loud and visible, aside from the occasional amicus brief, Westboro Baptist doesn't work too hard to actually take rights away from LGBTQ people. Some raging homophobes do. When we're faced with an extremist opponent of this kind, the objective isn't partnership, but just the opposite: radical, intentional othering. Though it may seem counterintuitive, over-the-top portrayals of bigotry can ultimately serve the LGBTQ movement by illustrating what happens when you allow religious homophobia and transphobia to run unchecked.

For example: In 2015, a licensed attorney named Matthew McLaughlin submitted a proposal for a ballot measure in California called the "Sodomite Suppression Act." It called for the mandatory execution of gay people—just for being gay, no other reason—by "bullets to the head" or "any other convenient method."[141] The proposal was hastily struck down as unconstitutional. Years before, McLaughlin had proposed a tamer (but still unconstitutional) measure to make the Bible required reading in public schools.[142] McLaughlin fell off the radar after his proposal flopped, so he's presumably still wandering around California, thinking about other ways he can try to legalize the murder of LGBTQ people. It's scary to think about.

Then there's a long list of pastors who definitely glossed over the "love thy neighbor" part of the Bible, preaching McLaughlin's terrifying vision from the pulpit. Steven L. Anderson is the pastor at Faithful Word Baptist Church, an IFB church designated by the Southern Poverty Law Center as a hate group, where he advocates for the death of LGBTQ people. (He makes clear that church members should never kill gay people themselves, but the government should formally execute them. They can even use a firing squad.)[143]

One of Anderson's disciples is Donnie Romero, the pastor of Stedfast Baptist Church in Fort Worth, Texas. After the shooting at Pulse, Romero said he was praying that the *survivors* of the shooting would also die. He referred to the Pulse victims as the "scum of the earth," and said he prayed "that God will finish the job . . . so that they don't get any more opportunity to go out and hurt little children."[144] In a similar show of despicable rancor, Pastor Roger Jimenez of Sacramento—another IFB pastor—preached that Orlando was "a little safer" after the shooting. "Are you sad that 50 pedophiles were killed today?" he asked in a church sermon uploaded to YouTube. Then he answered his own question: "Um, no, I think that's great! I think that helps society."[145]

And then there are people like preacher John McTernan and televangelist Pat Robertson. They don't advocate for LGBTQ people to be put to death. But whenever there's a major hurricane or tornado, you can count on them to claim that natural disasters are God's way of punishing us for accepting homosexuality. (That's at least two strikes against science, right?)

These talking heads don't exactly make the case for allyship between LGBTQ people and religious groups; quite the contrary. To genuinely kindhearted Christians, they're perfect examples of, "Dude, you're making us look bad." These are anecdotes of religion gone terribly, terribly wrong, moments where a secular approach to social justice is undeniably more constructive.

It's clear to most of us that these extremists don't reflect the views of the majority of people of faith, particularly Christians. (In 2016, 27% of white evangelical Protestants supported marriage equality, as did 64% of white mainline Protestants, 39% of black Protestants and 58% of Catholics.[146]) But even if the hatemongers are a fiery minority, they're still out there, and they hold these beliefs fully and openly. Whether or not they have any influence outside their small circles is up for debate, but it's terrifying to know they exist at all.

So why mention them here?

Because the absurdity of some of these groups *works to the benefit of the LGBTQ rights movement.* To a person who has no familiarity with social activism, catching a glimpse of a Westboro Baptist protest on the nightly news gives a very specific picture of what anti-LGBTQ activists look like: monsters. They intentionally disrespect and even "pray" for more dead soldiers, something that should cross a line for anyone, but especially diehard patriotic conservatives. They're loud. They're rude. And they're not even the worst examples of faith-based homophobia out there.

In some ways, Westboro Baptist Church has *strengthened* the case for equal rights for LGBTQ people. When religious figures go over the top in their theatrical opposition to LGBTQ rights, they can actually turn out more people for the pro-LGBTQ cause. In some cases, it's in the form of activists who plan successful counter-protests, like the Vassar College students who raised $100,000 for the Trevor Project in response to Westboro Baptist planning a protest on their campus.[147] Other times, religious groups come to marches to support LGBTQ people, seeking to convey that some Christians are loving and accepting. (There's no shortage of images online showing Christians at Pride parades holding up signs that read, "I'm sorry for the way my church has treated you.") Finally, Westboro is a caricature of what can happen when anti-LGBTQ ideas multiply and mutate in the name of religion. Religious moderates considering joining the anti-equality brigade may see Westboro Baptist and decide they don't want to be associated with that kind of philosophy after all.

But we're living in a weird and uncertain time. Major victories for LGBTQ people are followed by unthinkable tragedies; certain politicians see equal rights as a threat, so they bite at the heels of our slow-moving progress with ugly determination. It's easy to tell ourselves that violent homophobes like the Westboro Baptist Church and Pastor Anderson are few and far between, but we have no idea how many people they have influenced. And there are certainly elected officials in Washington eager to roll back any civil rights we've achieved.

That's why the secular movement for LGBTQ rights is so critical. As long as religious opposition to equality exists—even if it does sometimes look like an absurdist street fair—someone will use it against LGBTQ people. It could come in the form of a discriminatory law, a hate crime, or a kid getting kicked out of her house, but sooner or later, it will show itself. It's our responsibility not simply to disarm and denounce extremist hate groups, but also to call out any moment when religion is used to deny LGBTQ people equal rights. And though it seems contradictory, sometimes the publicity of radical religion gets more people fired up about the cause—in a good way.

Building Bridges

In 2014, the Supreme Court ruled that the town of Greece, New York, could open public legislative sessions with sectarian prayer.[148] A lawsuit had been brought by two women, one Jewish and one atheist, who argued that meetings almost always opened with explicitly Christian prayers, alienating non-believers and members of other religions. While groups like the ultra-conservative Family Research Council praised the decision, David Silverman, president of American Atheists, called for atheists and people of minority religious groups to work together to oppose the ruling.

"That's what we have to do, not only organize the atheists, but the Satanists, the Scientologists," he said in a talk at Stanford University. "We as atheists have the responsibility to urge them and push them and get them in there to get their prayers."[149]

Religious overstep can take many forms. The prioritization of one belief system—let alone the acceptance of religion interfering in politics—is just one of them. In the United States, belief is considered in higher regard than non-belief, and Christianity is prized above all other religions. All schoolchildren automatically have Christmas Day off of school, for example, whereas the same schoolwide recognition is not always given to Jewish and Muslim holy days. But for a more terrifying example, consider the hellfire that was the 2016 presidential election. Donald Trump was endorsed by members of the Ku Klux Klan, who claimed he alone could restore the country to its status as a "White Christian Republic."[150] His vice president, Mike Pence, had previously suggested marriage equality would signal the collapse of society, attributing his beliefs to "God's idea."[151]

It's not a coincidence that these two ideas are gaining momentum at the same time, or even that they ran on the same presidential ticket. It's intentional, strategic, and dangerous. White supremacy, dominant Christianity, and the oppression of LGBTQ identities are inextricably linked; enabling one is passively endorsing the other. Consider the executive order on immigration Trump signed in his first full week in office.[152] In four of the predominantly Muslim countries named in the original order—Iran, Sudan, Yemen, and Somalia—homosexuality is punishable by death.[153] Sending LGBTQ refugees back to those countries effectively puts an expiration date on their lives.

Defending the rights of LGBTQ people to live and love freely, then, isn't only about marriage equality and workplace rights. It's about shattering the forces that preach racism and xenophobia in the same breath as "religious freedom." It's about challenging systems that give some groups more power than others. It's about basic human decency.

In light of Trump's election, the Holocaust-era poem by Pastor Martin Niemöller made the rounds again, symbolizing our collective need to support one another:

First they came for the Socialists, and I did not speak out—
Because I was not a Socialist.

Then they came for the Trade Unionists, and I did not speak out—
Because I was not a Trade Unionist.

Then they came for the Jews, and I did not speak out—
Because I was not a Jew.

Then they came for me — and there was no one left to speak for me.

If atheists don't defend our allies in the struggle against religious persecution, who will defend us when we're targeted next?

It's also important to point out that you don't have to support religion in order to support LGBTQ people of faith. Once more: *you can oppose religion and still want basic human rights for LGBTQ people who are religious.* Just like conservative judges should be able to keep their anti-marriage-equality beliefs private while making decisions based on the (secular) rule of law, atheists who are strictly opposed to religion can do the work of supporting their fellow humans, even if they don't agree with how those humans live their lives. In fact, it's crucial that they do.

In a 2012 article for *Salon*, writer Adam Lee wondered if atheists can partner with religious progressives on social issues. It's a fine line to walk; as atheists, many of us want to acknowledge the harms religion has inflicted, or even oppose religion in its entirety. That position can absolutely inform an atheist's stance on civil rights, but it's not an excuse to degrade or demean anyone who disagrees. Instead, we should focus on big-picture issues that benefit us all: getting religion out of government, securing equal rights for all, and ensuring that science and reason, rather than arbitrary morals, inform policy decisions.

"We [New Atheists] believe that society will be more just, more prosperous and more peaceful when elected officials can set policy based simply on a reasoned weighing of the evidence, and not appeals to scripture," Lee wrote.[154] "Thus, our claim is that by weakening the power of religion, both religious liberals and secular humanists stand to gain.

"Will it drive people away to attack their deepest beliefs? Our answer is that, whatever they say they believe, people respond to passion and conviction, not to artful diplomacy or rhetoric watered down for political expediency."

I asked a few LGBTQ people of faith how atheists, especially straight and cisgender atheists, can be helpful allies, as well as what they want atheists to know about LGBTQ people of faith. Earlier, Sahar Ali Deen, the gay Muslim who started OUTMuslim, answered that question with an insightful call to listen, respect differences, and keep an open mind. Others agreed with him.

Abhishek, the former Southern Baptist, emphasized that there are multiple interpretations of religion—Christianity in particular. "I think one way atheist allies can help is just by being familiar enough with both the pro-queer and anti-queer sides of Christianity, especially if they didn't grow up in a religious household, so they can better support us as we interact with those in our families and community," he said. "I also think there's space for solidarity. I know many atheists have struggled to 'come out' to religious family, and knowing that many of us religious queer folk also have had similar experiences could be powerful."

Brandon, the Christian transgender teacher featured earlier in this book, told me some of his strongest allies are cisgender, straight atheists. "I believe that their atheist beliefs give them the strength to accept my queer/trans authenticity as a truth," he said. "Their intelligence and thought process appeals to me and is very similar to my own religion. Cis/het atheists are more like me in my queer/trans Christianity than most people would realize."

Lisa, interviewed earlier about being a Christian lesbian, wants atheists to know that she is content in both her identities. "I would want atheists to know that I am solid in my faith and I am solid in my sexuality," she said. "I don't struggle with my faith. My struggle rests with the Christian extremists, who are unfortunately very vocal. In my understanding and study of my faith, they truly do not represent the Christianity that centers on Jesus as the focal point."

And Bryan, the Catholic transgender man who feels called to be a priest, echoes her strongly. "I am not oppressed," he said. "I do not need to be freed from the Catholic Church. I am a devout man who really can make a difference in my community. I would not feel freer without religion. I have tried it and I felt lost and alone without it. Please do not pity me or look down on me. I know the Catholic Church is imperfect, but it is mine and I love it deeply."

Atheists sometimes think that fighting religion indirectly means supporting LGBTQ people. However, religion isn't always the bogeyman; sometimes, it's what gives solace to LGBTQ people who are oppressed in so many other ways. Attacking religion cannot be our core strategy in achieving equal rights.

We have to acknowledge that there are a lot of religious allies working toward the same goal: true equality. Even if atheists believe religion and LGBTQ rights are logically incompatible, many Christians strongly disagree and their actions show it. We can't be short-sighted enough to lump all religious believers together when we criticize faith-based homophobia.

For every Kim Davis, there's a Dr. William Barber, the head of the NAACP in North Carolina, who brings together Christians in the fight for civil rights. For every Westboro Baptist Church clone, there's an emergent Christian church with a gay pastor who wants to make life better for everyone.

LGBTQ people of faith are atheists' allies. We may have theological disagreements, but we must be willing to focus on our commonalities to achieve a larger goal of equality. Religion doesn't always lead to homophobia. Sometimes, faith really can be the driving force for good.

What Allyship Looks Like

Speechless in Tampa

MY YOUNGER brother, Arthur, is my best friend. He's tall, friendly, and funny. He's heterosexual and cisgender and one of the best support systems in my life. He figured out that I was queer before I was ready to tell him, but didn't force me into a conversation I didn't want to have. Today, we have matching equal sign tattoos. (Actually, that's not true. His is bigger.)

When Arthur was in middle school, my mom got a phone call that he had kicked one of his classmates—hard. The kid had apparently taunted Arthur by calling me a lesbian. I hadn't settled on any identity yet and certainly hadn't told anybody, but "lesbian" was still a bad word in our circle. My brother thought he was defending me against the gravest of insults.

The taunter got a swift kick in the shin. Arthur got suspended. My mom and I both cried that he had been violent. There was no discussion about the intricate details of what motivated it.

Fast-forward about ten years. I'm extremely out and newly engaged. Arthur and I both have plenty of queer friends, and we talk about LGBTQ issues with our family regularly. One night, he called me to tell me about a classmate in his master's program.

"She seemed like a nice person and we were all hanging out," he told me, "when she suddenly said, 'I just hate gays. I just think gays are disgusting and shouldn't exist.'"

The young woman was from a country where homosexuality is illegal, and she delivered the lines without flinching. Arthur was stumped on how to respond. I was shocked that a young person in a university setting would say something so awful, especially unprompted. Where had that come from? Did she expect a group of twenty-somethings to agree with her?

Not totally sure what I would have done in that situation, I told Arthur that this was his chance to "come out" as a person with a queer family member, to stick up for me and every other LGBTQ person he knows and loves. Presumably this person didn't have any LGBTQ friends (that she knew of). It was the responsibility of her straight and reasonable friends, then, to tell her those kinds of statements were unacceptable. At the very least, I said, he had to realize that she wasn't the type of person he should develop a friendship with. That kind of toxicity is a dealbreaker.

Arthur talked to her later after he'd taken some time to think it through, and she didn't offer much of a response. (Though she did tell him she also didn't believe in interracial marriage and child-rearing, so she had way more going on than either of us was prepared to address.) They both graduated from the program, I glared at her at the commencement ceremony, and they'll probably never see each other again. Que sera sera.

My brother's classmate seemed pretty normal... until she wasn't. Her outburst of spontaneous homophobia caught everyone off-guard, and in the moment, she got away with it. I'll never know what inspired her to say what she did when she did, but we know that she felt comfortable saying it. In speaking out so explicitly against an entire group of people, this person made one of three assumptions: first, that the people around her would agree with her (or at least be indifferent); second, that someone might object, but she would face no consequences; or third, that she could handle the repercussions because she held those convictions so strongly. None of those options is heartwarming.

I'm proud of my brother for following up with this young woman in a thoughtful way, and for checking in with an actual LGBTQ person about how to do it. That's the thing about supporting a group you're not a part of; in order to make a real, productive impact, you have to follow their lead. There are plenty of ways to be a bad ally, like patting yourself on the back for doing the bare minimum, or thinking you know what's best for someone else without asking them first. But there are also lots of ways to be a good one.

Truly supporting LGBTQ people and other marginalized groups in your day-to-day life can take a little bit of work. You might find yourself staring down biases you're not comfortable acknowledging, or having to challenge assumptions you took for granted. But I promise it's worth the effort. Remember that concepts like reason and logic are fundamental to most atheists' understanding of the world. And standing up for your fellow humans in their time of need is the only reasonable thing to do.

Allies and Accomplices

In social justice circles, particularly in the LGBTQ world, there's a lot of discussion about what it means to be an ally. The most basic definition of "ally" is a person who supports the cause of a marginalized group to which they do not belong. In that sense, heterosexual people can be allies to LGBTQ people, but gay, lesbian, and bisexual people can also be allies to transgender people, white LGBTQ people can be allies to LGBTQ people of color, and so on.

But there's more to allyship than that. Simply expressing tolerance of a group of people who are different from you shouldn't merit a celebration in one's honor; it's an act of basic human decency. And it's dangerous for people to think that passive allyship—support from a distance—is enough to make a difference.

That's why preferred definitions of the word "ally" commonly include one key word: *active.* True, active allies—sometimes called *accomplices*—express their support for different groups even when doing so isn't convenient or comfortable. They advocate for their marginalized peers when they aren't in the room, and prioritize the voices of those peers when they are. An ally doesn't take the microphone from you on your behalf; they hold it up for you.

So what does it look like to be an *active ally* to LGBTQ people, regardless of their beliefs?

A crucial part of being an ally is defending a person or group whether or not they're present to hear it. This is a principle that can apply to anyone; it's the grown-up equivalent of not letting the school bully talk about your friends behind their backs. So why is it so difficult to put into practice in adulthood?

Many of us have grown up around people who didn't take kindly to difference—those who are leery of races, religions, sexual orientations, and identities they aren't familiar with. Or maybe we have friends who don't care one way or the other, but who drop casual racism or homophobia into otherwise tame conversations. ("No homo," anyone?) If you say something challenging them, you run the risk of being ridiculed yourself. If you're straight, maybe they'll accuse *you* of being gay, and you'll have to explain both that you're not *and* that it would be OK if you were. (And that just sounds exhausting.) Or maybe you *are* gay (or bi, or trans, etc.), but you don't want to be "one of *those* gays." You don't want to ruffle feathers or ask your friends to behave any differently just because you're at the table. We all want to be liked. It's normal.

Don't get trapped in that mentality. It's *important* to ruffle feathers for these reasons, whether you're LGBTQ or not. These intimate moments with friends and family are where the best learning can happen. If an acquaintance of yours witnessed a conversation where someone put you down—for being an atheist, for your race or upbringing, for something that makes you different—you'd want them to do the same on your behalf. Hopefully, they would.

Then there's the advocacy component of allyship. Here, I'm speaking specifically to the straight, cisgender atheists reading this. Being outraged at the government isn't fun. We don't protest or hold rallies for the hell of it; we'd much rather live in a world where everyone respects everyone and we don't need to flood the streets in rage and fear. Unfortunately, we aren't there yet. And while there are more openly LGBTQ people than ever before, we can't do it alone.

That's where we need help—from people of all identities and religious backgrounds, but especially from atheists who share our concerns about religious overstep and irrational policymaking. If your LGBTQ friends are up in arms about a new law, elected official, or Cabinet appointee, find out why. Do your homework. Think through the implications that certain policies could have for LGBTQ people—plus atheists, people of faith, people of color, poor people, and so many others—and get mad, too. Sign the petitions we post on Facebook. Donate to our causes, if you can spare it. Follow our lead and ask how you can help; we generally know what we're doing.

Come to marches with us, if they're not designated as LGBTQ-only spaces. (Those are necessary sometimes; having a place to heal and plan with others who share your experiences is vital.) Call the governor, your state legislators, and your Congresspeople and voice your concerns, if that's what the moment of the movement calls for. So many times, the most egregiously anti-LGBTQ laws are also an assault on the freedom from religion, like the "license to discriminate" laws that have emerged in dozens of states. Those are atheist issues, too.

Finally, you cannot be an effective ally without holding empathy in your heart. When news of the shooting at the Pulse nightclub in Orlando broke, people with ties to the communities most affected—LGBTQ people, Latinx* people, even Orlando residents, to an extent—had reason to react more strongly than others. As the death toll on television climbed, did you text your LGBTQ friends to ask how they were doing?

I was out of the country at a cousin's wedding the day Pulse happened, which was a privilege and a curse. Shock and grief had hit us all like a punch to the gut, but I was still far away from the epicenter of the heartbreak. Without a community of LGBTQ friends around to grieve with, it didn't feel as real. It hit me completely a few days later, when my future wife and I came across Amsterdam's gay rights monument by accident. It was piled high with flowers, candles, letters, and rainbow flags. We sat at the monument for 15 minutes, heavy with reality, absorbing the messages of love that had poured out from 4,500 miles away. Certainly the thousands of gifts at our feet hadn't come only from LGBTQ people.

It's unfair to assume that every LGBTQ person will feel severely traumatized by a tragedy like Pulse, but many of us did. After the high-profile suicide of Leelah Alcorn, a transgender teenager who said her parents sent her to Christian conversion

---

* The word "Latinx" has recently come into use as a gender-neutral replacement for "Latino" or "Latina." The -x suffix is used because it is non-gendered, fostering more inclusion for people who don't identify with the male or female identities implied, respectively, by "Latino" or "Latina."

therapy, public support for trans youth soared on platforms like Twitter and Tumblr.[155] Eyes turned to caring for North Carolina's LGBTQ community after HB2 was passed. Calls to LGBTQ suicide hotlines spiked after Donald Trump's election.[156]

These moments represent sadness and solidarity in the aftermath of anti-LGBTQ violence—whether literal, political, or societal—and they're crucial to supporting LGBTQ people. When something happens that harms one of us, many more of us will feel its effects resonate. During and after these moments, check in with your LGBTQ friends. Invite them over. You don't have to assume the worst, but be genuine and kind. "What awful news today. Are you doing OK?" will suffice.

Empathy also shouldn't be exclusive to times of mourning. Before the Supreme Court ruling, I would text my family in a group chat whenever another state legalized marriage equality. They celebrated with me every time, never letting the news get old or sending canned responses. Heterosexual friends and family listened to my rambling thoughts about the state of the movement, bought me books they never would have picked up otherwise, asked my opinion on the LGBTQ news of the day, and sent me articles about topics they knew I'd be interested in. Every one of those actions was another way of saying, "I support you."

Of course, it's key to remember that your LGBTQ friend has a life, interests, and values beyond their sexual orientation or gender identity. You don't want to tokenize your friend, play into stereotypes, guess their interests based on one factor of their identity, or assume they want to date your only other gay friend. (Thanks for offering, though!) There's a difference between "I thought you might like this article because you were talking about the subject the other day" and "I thought you might like this article because you're gay."

But in general, making an effort at all is really, really important. Whether it's celebrating a positive development, lending support after a tragedy, or just engaging in conversations that wouldn't normally pertain to you, showing up matters. After Pulse, LGBTQ people knew who would be there for them to help sort out their feelings. Remember, the collective "LGBTQ community" is made up of millions of LGBTQ individuals. We all relate to our identities and to the movement differently. If you strike up a conversation about it with us, we might have more in common than you think.

Ashton P. Woods

Ashton P. Woods is a founder of the Black Lives Matter movement's Houston chapter and co-chair for the Black Humanist Alliance, a secular group under the American Humanist Association. He describes himself as unapologetically Black (capitalization intended), same gender loving (a term coined by activist and writer Cleo Manago specifically for Black gay men, lesbians, and bisexual people), HIV-positive, and atheist, identities he brings into every space. We talked about how identity-based social justice groups have failed to include everyone in their work, and what they can do better.

You're very intentional about declaring yourself as Black, same gender loving, HIV-positive, and an atheist all at once. Why is it important for you to be upfront about all of those identities?

It's all about comfort. So many times we're worrying about making people comfortable in our space, and a lot of people don't like rejection. So when I say those words or use those descriptors, that's me showing my whole self and being honest about who I am and not being here for your comfort. The purpose of me saying those words is that I know it pisses people off, because they're like, "You don't have to say that, no one cares." But you do care. You do care, because I wouldn't have to say it if you didn't.

Does that happen often?

Yeah. I have people that don't invite me to events or don't welcome me because I'm an atheist. That goes to show you the bias of feeling like you have to fit in with certain terms of heteronormativity: this mainstream whitewashed couple who lives in a white house with 2.5 kids, just like the straight people do, saying, "Hey, we're just like you." Except that's not representative of all people within the LGBTQ community across the spectrum. Especially because a lot of us are people of color. And then what you find is that there are people who are left out on the fringes.

Can you give me some examples of how you've been left out of mainstream organizing?

Folks will come back to me and say I wasn't invited to this event because I'm an atheist and people aren't ready to deal with me bringing that to the table. A lot of people are believers and just don't want me around them. It's not like I walk around with a stylized "A" on my forehead or a pentagram on my chest. But I tend to call people to the front and say, "You need to be more inclusive." I don't try to say what they believe in is not real. I just say that there are people with other beliefs. People don't like being called out. Aside from that, I'm pro-Black and a founder of the Black Lives Matter Houston chapter. A lot of people just see me and think, "He's a big Black man, I'm afraid of him." And that's why they exclude me. There's this big Black man who's aware of these intersections and is not afraid to call them out despite the fact that they're afraid. They don't like that at all.

Are there other ways these different groups have been resistant to your participation?

Each and every group has a bit of fuckery within. I'm not an ex-Christian. I was really raised religionless. But I've found that a lot of people in the atheist community, especially white men, tend to be homophobic as hell. They left their belief [in God] behind, but kept all the fucked-up beliefs that come along with it.

Like within the LGBTQ community, there's still white men and women who are racist as hell. Being LGBTQ doesn't make you any more or less racist. Then there's the misogyny. As far as in the Black community, we deal with a lot of misconceptions about the Black Lives Matter movement and who is a Black Lives Matter activist versus just being activists who happen to be pro-Black. And getting pigeonholed into this thing where you're [either] an LGBTQ activist or you're a BLM activist. Well I'm both, actually, because I'm Black and I'm LGBTQ. And I'm not going to let you make me choose. [The Black Lives Matter movement] and organization was founded by three Black women with their own unique intersections, one who is bisexual and one who is a lesbian. So there has to be a recognition of people in their fullness.

How can allies work to foster that inclusion in different activist groups?

For me, it's not about allies. I like to be allies with other people, but the best way to be an ally is if you're white or straight or part of any other group, organize people who identify like you. Teach them. And then when you come across people you claim to be an ally to, listen, take notes, and then take that back to those people you're supposed to be teaching. You shouldn't be organizing with me. You should be organizing with people who look like you, to be honest. Because you're really doing a disservice if you're just with me marching around the street, and you're not teaching your fellow white folks, "Hey, you can't say that and here's why," when you're in a room alone with those people.

I'm a cisgender man, but I do have a lot of trans friends and I support the trans community. But when there's a transgender person in the room who can talk about being trans, I'm going to shut up and I'm going to listen. Then when I'm in a room full of people who are cisgender and they say something stupid, I can correct them and say, "Here's what this really is, and if you actually want to know more I can bring in someone who's trans who can tell you their story." You break the seal by correcting them and then by bringing someone in the room who can speak for themselves. I think I'm looking more for accomplices as opposed to allies. Accomplices don't care what they may lose in the process.

How can all of these different groups work together to bring about positive change?

People misinterpret that as, "Oh, all of us should just merge together." No. When I do my work with Black Lives Matter Houston, that's a specific thing with Black folks because Black folks know what Black folks need. And I don't need to paint that with whitewashing or allyship. That's why there's groups like SURJ [Showing Up for Racial Justice, a group specifically mobilizing white people in the fight for racial justice]. Allies should be organizing themselves. Now, if we come together and work together on things? That's great. But when we do that, we all have our own lanes that we work in. There was a protest I went to, and this white woman was hugging police officers. And you know, people don't understand how offensive that is to somebody like me. So when we come together, I always ask people to be mindful of what they're bringing into the room and what they're bringing to the table.

Onward

The principles of good allyship are not exclusive to LGBTQ people. Everybody wants someone to have their back. Historically, it's been difficult to get people to show up for causes that they think don't affect them—think not only LGBTQ rights, but immigration, racial justice, and other issues that primarily impact only a few groups. It's time for that to change.

Throughout this book I've tried to ask one big question that shapes how people respond to social movements: Is there anything inherent to atheism that would compel an atheist to participate in the LGBTQ rights movement? The atheists I asked were pretty evenly split, and it seems like the answer is both yes and no. Atheism does not require any set of political or social beliefs. It does not command a stricter commitment to free speech or freedom of religion, it does not center on a group of like-minded believers, and it has no guidebook. Atheism is the absence of belief in any gods. Full stop.

But even though atheism itself doesn't intrinsically support any social justice movement, many atheists do. Atheists support abortion access and opposed the war in Iraq in higher numbers than believers, and were early advocates for marriage equality. And the many of us who are both LGBTQ and atheist have a personal stake in what happens next. There's serious power there—political *and* social. We should be harnessing it.

As for shared values and ideas: atheists reject the idea of acting in accordance with the wishes of a higher power. Therefore, they make their decisions based on what's best for them and, in an idealistic world, the people around them. Atheists may see people as accountable to one another rather than to a god. That should breed compassion and a commitment to helping each individual live their life with agency and self-determination. For LGBTQ people to recognize our full potential, we must not be encumbered by bigoted, religiously-influenced laws and social mores that dictate what we can and cannot do. Atheists should care about that.

I asked Katie, the Unitarian Universalist from Ohio interviewed earlier, for her thoughts on atheists' reasons to support LGBTQ people. I loved her answer.

"To me, there is absolutely nothing about being an atheist (using the simplest definition of not believing in a deity) that would compel someone to also join social movements," she said. "But there can be something about your personal reasons for being an atheist that can lend itself to participation in social movements. If what brought you to atheism had elements of being against any form of discrimination, then that might be what connects you to the LGBTQ movement. Humans don't just wake up one morning and are atheist; something led them there. That something might also lead them to social movements."

That push toward social movements can extend far and wide to encompass other causes. For example: the attack on reproductive and abortion rights is hugely tied to religious overstep. In *Burwell v. Hobby Lobby Stores, Inc.*, religious business owners won the right to deny certain kinds of reproductive health coverage based on their own beliefs. If the Republican Party has its way, reproductive health and women's rights may be set back decades. Here, too, atheists of all genders and reproductive systems have the opportunity to step in and speak out. My body, my choice—not the Bible's, not Paul Ryan's.

The LGBTQ movement doesn't exist in a vacuum. Neither does atheism. A principle called intersectionality, coined by civil rights advocate Kimberlé Williams Crenshaw, posits that each of us lives with overlapping social identities—our race, religion, ethnicity, gender, sexual orientation, socioeconomic status, and so on.[157] These identities each carry their own degrees of privilege or disadvantage, and they're linked in shaping how we experience the world.

For example: One person I spoke with, Dorianne Emmerton, is white. Her partner and their young son are black. She has been an atheist since she was a teenager, but says she doesn't spend a lot of time in atheist circles because of the normalized racism and sexism that sometimes flourish there.

"As you go about your daily life, it doesn't matter very much if you're an atheist or not," she said. "It matters to BIPOC [black, indigenous, and people of color] people that they are at least subconsciously judged on sight by every new person they meet. It matters to me very much that I have to constantly justify my relationship, my family, I have to assess whether or not it is safe to behave as a couple in public, that I have to expend the time and money to adopt my own son because he's not biologically related to me. It matters to trans folks to get misgendered, harassed, and subject to violence on a regular basis."

This is another theme that came up in several of my conversations with atheists from many different backgrounds: a particular brand of atheism that ignores or even belittles the oppression of other groups. Emmerton referred to those who participate in this phenomenon as the "Dawkins Bros": predominantly white, male atheists who idolize other white, male atheists like Richard Dawkins, overlooking or even repeating these icons' controversial opinions.[158]

"I think all right-thinking people have an obligation to support LGBTQ people, and I think atheists should support all those who are oppressed by religion, including LGBTQ people, women, and people of other religions/cultures/races," Emmerton said.

Atheists taking the plunge into social justice work must do so through an intersectional lens; that is, with the mindset that LGBTQ people hold an infinite number of identities and will not all benefit from the same solutions. I've talked a lot about marriage equality in this book, as it's undoubtedly the LGBTQ rights issue that's received the most attention and the most hatred from religious groups in the past decade. But once again, marriage isn't the end of the road for LGBTQ people; far from it. Marriage equality doesn't address homelessness or anti-trans violence or conversion therapy. Yes, legal recognition can lead to more awareness and more societal support; no, it doesn't do much for those who are already victimized in other ways.

Furthermore, the LGBTQ movement as a whole—including any atheists who join in—must do more to show up for other movements. Deep-rooted prejudices like racism and sexism fuel hatred against other groups, too, and tackling those biases will mean a better, more just world for all of us. Black Lives Matter is an LGBTQ issue because LGBTQ people are black, too. Islamophobia is an LGBTQ issue because LGBTQ people are Muslims, too. Just like four million people live at the intersection of being LGBTQ and atheist, millions more experience life with more than one identity that casts them out from the straight, white, Christian male norm. We can't look out for our LGBTQ *or* atheist community without showing up for everyone's right to be their whole selves.

Social justice movements have never been more visible, and right now, they're sorely needed. Under the current presidential administration, many of us have something to lose. And now, more than ever, our overlapping, intersecting, sometimes conflicting identities matter. They determine how much we may be targeted in the years to come, and they affect who may listen to us when we have something to say. If the LGBTQ movement and others are going to make it, it will be because people from all walks of life showed up loudly and proudly. We can't do this alone, nor do we want to. Everyone's got something to bring to the table, and there are plenty of seats.

The Personal Is Political

What Happened in Houston

LATE in the evening on November 3, 2015, the city of Houston became a little less safe.[159]

For a year leading up to that day, LGBTQ rights advocates had worked tirelessly to promote the Houston Equal Rights Ordinance (HERO), a measure that would have protected Houstonians against discrimination on the basis of sexual orientation and gender identity, among other traits. The ordinance had been approved by the Houston City Council a year before, but a group of conservative pastors launched a campaign to repeal it. And after a court battle, another round of voting in the City Council, and lots of signature-gathering, a referendum on HERO made it to the November ballot.

Early on in the campaign, it looked like the anti-HERO side was losing. Their credibility took a major hit when it came to light that they might have falsified signatures calling for referendum.[160] But they bounced back when they found a talking point that stuck: HERO would allow transgender people to use public bathrooms that correspond with their gender identity.

Trans people's rights to use the bathrooms that match their identity have been contested nationwide; I mentioned trans student Gavin Grimm's court case earlier.[161] But it's not a hard concept to allow people to decide for themselves what bathrooms they should use—we let cisgender people do it all the time without checking their birth certificates or asking what their bodies look like. Still, when transgender people ask reasonably to use the correct bathrooms, anti-trans activists claim they want to commit a crime. (Never mind that more Republican politicians have been stopped for sexual misconduct in public restrooms than trans people. You don't see anybody trying to kick them out en masse, though.[162])

Yet even though we know that trans people exist, and even though it's been proven that using affirming bathrooms helps trans people be happier and healthier, and even though trans people face much higher risks of violence in bathrooms than cisgender people, conservatives from across the belief spectrum still perpetuate harmful narratives that liken transgender people to sexual predators. That's exactly what opponents of HERO did.

When the anti-equality brigade saw the opportunity to focus on a singular issue—one that many Americans are unfamiliar with—they grabbed it and ran with it. They referred to HERO as the "Proposition 1 Bathroom Ordinance," even though the part about bathrooms was marginal compared to the other rights it would have enshrined (like protection from being fired from your job because of your race, religion, or sexual orientation). HERO opponents plastered signs around the city that read "No Men in Women's Bathrooms." They ran a horrifically inappropriate ad that showed an adult man following a little girl into a bathroom stall and closing the door behind him.[163]

It worked. Only 39% of people in Houston voted in favor of the ordinance; 61% opposed it. HERO was repealed by a landslide.

Its defeat signaled a sharp turn from the upward progression of the LGBTQ rights movement in the United States. Marriage equality had been legalized months before, more public figures than ever were coming out and speaking up about equal rights, and the movement for transgender equality had picked up blazing momentum in very little time. This moment was a definitive failure not just for LGBTQ people, but for all those who value diversity and respect.

The campaign against HERO was an outlier in the archive of anti-LGBTQ campaigns because it relied relatively little on religious ideology. Back in 2008, when Californians enacted Proposition 8 by a slim margin, religious arguments defending "traditional marriage" fueled virtually the entire campaign. Bigotry wrongly justified by religion is one of the LGBTQ movement's greatest enemies, especially considering the deep influence (and deep pockets) the Religious Right wields.[164] But the anti-HERO effort was different.

HERO failed because anti-equality activists scared uninformed audiences into false beliefs about transgender people.

They crafted fear-mongering narratives claiming that sexual predators would take advantage of the law to prey on girls and women, and they deliberately withheld information about what HERO actually did. Pro-LGBTQ activists worked hard to counter the lies, but they were ill-equipped to take on such a sharply emotional message.

Slate's Mark Joseph Stern wrote:

HERO opponents told a compelling (if totally false) story: Radical liberal elites wanted to let perverts and maniacs into public bathrooms, and conservatives needed to step up to protect women. Proponents of the ordinance had no compelling counternarrative except to explain why this talking point was mendacious. In the end, the more gripping narrative won the day, as it usually does in these kinds of fights. In fact, there is a riveting counternarrative to the bathroom myth—but the LGBTQQ* community hasn't really learned how to tell it.

This narrative is simple. Being trans is not a mental illness. Gender dysphoria, the sense that one's gender doesn't align to one's sex, is a mental illness—one that is cured by transitioning genders. A transitioned or transitioning person, in other words, is a healthy person, one who is finally able to live their authentic self with dignity. The more society accepts trans people and acknowledges their true gender, the healthier and happier trans people will be. Granting equal bathroom access is a fundamental part of that process.[165]

This is not to say religious beliefs played no role in HERO's defeat. For one, the campaign to put HERO on the ballot was led by a group of pastors. Conservative speakers touted their strict belief in God's creation of man and woman as reason to oppose the ordinance. Former governor and GOP presidential candidate Mike Huckabee called on voters to "show your support for your own Biblical beliefs" by protesting the bill. But it was ultimately secular scare tactics about "men in women's bathrooms" that convinced a majority of Houstonians to vote against HERO. As a result, thousands of people lost civil rights.

The anti-HERO camp outright lied about transgender people and the effects of the ordinance. On the flip side, atheists are among the strongest advocates for fact-based approaches to

---

* An extension of the acronym that adds a second Q for "questioning."

public policy; we support critical thinking and oppose policies born out of faith and fear. Atheists and humanists had every reason to be a big part of the conversation on HERO from the beginning, but didn't seem to make a dent in the public debate.

This doesn't mean atheists were nowhere to be found. For one local group, the Humanists of Houston, openly supporting the HERO campaign was the first time they had taken a public stance on a political issue. I spoke with Benita Malone, the group's vice president, about why Humanists of Houston got involved.

"The HERO campaign is directly aligned with our mission," she told me. "As a Humanist group, we do not merely hold a naturalistic worldview based on reason, but are also concerned with living ethical, meaningful lives with concern for our fellow human being."

About a year before the official vote, Malone said, she and another board member met at her house to check petitions circulated by the anti-LGBTQ, anti-HERO side, in case any signatures were suspect. She later started attending meetings held by Houston Unites, the coalition supporting HERO, and cross-posted their events so Humanists of Houston members could attend. "It is the goal of Humanists of Houston to be open and accepting of everyone," Malone said.

Just a few months after HERO's defeat, the Kinder Institute's 35th annual Houston Area Survey found that 73% of Houstonians considered it "very important" to pass a non-discrimination law.[166] Then-mayor Annise Parker, who is openly gay, told the Kinder Institute she believed the virulent opposition to HERO grew from the Religious Right's personal vendetta against her.

"We are home to some of the largest mega-churches in America. . . . They've been stirring that pot for a long time. They were like, 'Here's proof. We told you she had this secret gay agenda,'" she told them. But Houston was, at the time, the largest U.S. city to have elected an openly gay mayor. And statistics showed that the pro-HERO movement had actually pulled ahead of its opposition in the weeks leading up to the vote.[167] Pair that with Kinder's findings—that most

Houstonians do believe in equal rights for LGBTQ people—and HERO's defeat didn't add up.

It's crucial to remember that HERO didn't extend rights only to transgender people; it protected against discrimination on the basis of 15 characteristics, including traits like race and religion.[168] Just as the ordinance barred anti-LGBTQ discrimination, it protected atheists from being denied equal treatment because of their non-belief (no small thing in Texas), or African Americans for the color of their skin. But the ordinance was framed by opponents as a "bathroom bill," an idea that many people simply couldn't relate to without clear, compelling examples of what it means to be trans. Instead, said HuffPost writer Michelangelo Signorile, "many average people interviewed on the street thought the ordinance was all about allowing 'men' to use women's restrooms."[169]

Mark Joseph Stern offered three possible next steps for Houston's LGBTQ community to rebuild after the loss: "Debunk the lies, then debunk them again, and again, and again. Confront the fear. Convey a simple message simply." For atheists, this approach to education and discussion is textbook.

Because religion played only a small role in HERO's opposition, defending the ordinance didn't require anyone to change their belief systems. (Some HERO advocates even cited their faith as reasons to vote in favor of the measure.[170]) Instead, it called for basic education about the issue of fairness and equality. HERO would have protected all citizens from discrimination—transgender people, yes, but also Christians, atheists, people of color, veterans, elderly people, and countless others whose narratives were omitted from the conversation altogether. HERO failed because of misinformation and flawed reasoning, two areas atheists are more than equipped to address.

For a city that is home to so many mega-churches and die-hard conservative Christians, Houston does have an atheist population, even though it's a minority. Between 2009 and 2011, the group Houston Atheists saw its membership double in size, to about 1,400 people.[171] The Humanists of Houston Meetup Group had more than 3,000 online members as of mid-2017.[172] And according to a study from the Pew Research

Center, as many as 20% of Houstonians reported having no religious affiliation.[173] Certainly many of Houston's religious "nones" showed up to the polls that Tuesday to defend equal rights, but there's no way to know for sure how many atheists participated in the pro-HERO campaign.

Whether or not atheists played an active role in trying to uphold HERO, the measure's defeat sent a nasty message about the right to live, love, and believe freely in Houston. On November 3, lies triumphed over reason. The LGBTQ community's loss was atheists' loss, too.

Election Night

Let's set the scene: It's November 8, 2016, the night Donald J. Trump defied so many polls and pundits to be elected president of the United States, and I don't have a plan.

Technically, it's early in the morning on November 9. My fiancée of six months is an editor at a news website, so she's at the office glued to one screen as I'm home alone glued to another. Midnight passes, then 1, 2, and well after 3 a.m. before she comes home. Hillary Clinton's team sends her supporters home from the Javits Center. Trump gives his victory speech before it's officially been called. I'm in shock.

Neither of us can sleep. Instead, we talk until well past 4 in the morning about whether we should get married earlier than we planned, in case this hyper-conservative new administration decided to repeal marriage equality. We're both working full-time, I'm in graduate school, and we don't have a ton of money. The original plan was to have a long engagement, giving us time to save up, plan ahead, and enjoy the process. She works with a dozen freelancers who get health insurance through the Affordable Care Act. At the time, I work at an HIV/AIDS organization that's largely government-funded. What next?

Our reaction, raw and real as it was, was self-centered. Marriage equality may be at risk under the Trump/Pence administration, but it's a harder target than an unsettled issue like transgender rights, for example, or broader issues like immigration or climate change. The ongoing debate over *Roe v.*

Wade, 40-plus years later, shows that some issues may always be controversial enough to draw the ire of religious conservatives, Supreme Court decision or not. Maybe marriage equality would never have full public support, but hopefully it would fade from public scrutiny. It was becoming clear that we'd have more work to do.

A few days after the election, my future wife and I regrouped. We wouldn't rush to get married right now, we decided, because marriage equality was probably safe for the time being. We'd focus our energy on supporting our Muslim and black and transgender and Latinx and undocumented and disabled and uninsured friends. And if the new administration so much as mentioned the possibility of undoing marriage equality—well, that's when we'd call our parents to apologize and rush to the courthouse.

In the days following the election, analysts, journalists, and lawyers scrambled to figure out which of Trump's campaign promises he could constitutionally keep and which were out of the question. In his post-election interview with *60 Minutes*, Trump said that marriage equality is "already settled," implying that he wouldn't prioritize rescinding it.[174] Trump claimed to be an ally throughout his campaign, and some pointed out that he was less openly homophobic and transphobic than many of his hardline Christian opponents. His first few months in office, however, proved futile any efforts to give him the benefit of the doubt. (After all, he chose notorious homophobe Mike Pence as a running mate; who was he kidding?)

The political issue that had religious extremists most riled up for a while—marriage equality—has been resolved. But conservative religious groups are still the loudest opponents of related issues, such as same-sex couples' right to have children. And now there are opportunities for them to invade other civil rights battles, like the fight for transgender rights or protections for LGBTQ students in public schools. The defeat of HERO demonstrated how you can harm the LGBTQ community without necessarily invoking religion. This messaging and political outreach to conservative Americans with little knowledge of the LGBTQ rights movement will only continue.

As anti-equality advocates dwindle in number, their messages are changing, and they're finding other ways to permeate the legal system with bigotry.[175] Atheists who fought to keep religion out of politics shouldn't abandon the cause now—in fact, this should be a moment to double down on the work.

If their numbers are decreasing, then why does it seem like homophobic talking heads are getting more and more airtime? The downside to heightened visibility for LGBTQ people is an awakening of bigotry that never had the opportunity to manifest before. LGBTQ rights were rarely a major talking point in elections before the 21st century, if they were mentioned at all. But in 2016, the first election after the nationwide legalization of marriage equality, these issues were part of the conversation from the beginning. That gave bigots a chance to speak out, too.

The Democratic Party championed LGBTQ rights throughout its 2016 platform, including a fierce defense of marriage equality, condemning the epidemic of violence against transgender people, calling for comprehensive federal non-discrimination protections, and committing to supporting the rights of LGBTQ people internationally.[176] But they may have anticipated that conservatives would push back on the basis of religious freedom. To that end, they wrote: "We support a progressive vision of religious freedom that respects pluralism and rejects the misuse of religion to discriminate."

In contrast, the Republican Party laid out a platform that decried same-sex marriage, spoke against same-sex couples raising kids, and hinted at the promotion of conversion therapy. They referred to the Supreme Court's marriage equality decision as the work of an "activist judiciary," falsely claimed that children are better off with a mom and dad than with same-sex parents, and opposed penalties for businesses that discriminated based on religion.

Republicans enlisted the help of Tony Perkins—who heads the Family Research Council, designated an anti-LGBTQ hate group by the Southern Poverty Law Center—to craft the platform, presumably the pieces about religion and LGBTQ issues.

The GOP platform dedicated almost a whole page to religious freedom, with special emphasis on one particular quote: "We pledge to defend the religious beliefs and rights of conscience of all Americans and to safeguard religious institutions against government control." Maybe the more moderate forces on the GOP's platform committee didn't push back harder against all this because they assumed it would be moot after Hillary Clinton won. But we know how that worked out.

After a period of unprecedented progress for LGBTQ people under Obama, Republicans won. Suddenly, the White House filled with people whose views more closely matched Perkins' and Pence's.

In the past few years, some Republicans have tried to suggest that homophobia and transphobia are *not* guiding principles of their party. The most recent election season, however, annihilated that mask entirely. The GOP platform made it clear that cementing LGBTQ people as second-class citizens was—and is—a priority. And even if you think the platform carries little weight, in the first months of his presidency, Trump took several actions supporting those goals, like weakening workplace protections for federal LGBTQ employees, removing Obama-era guidelines protecting transgender students at school, and nominating conservative Neil Gorsuch to the Supreme Court. So much for calling himself gay-friendly.

Unfortunately, there's also such a thing as wanting to be an ally (supposedly) and failing. A prime example is the Log Cabin Republicans, a "Republican organization dedicated to representing LGBTQ conservatives and allies" with a 30-year history. The very concept of the Log Cabin Republicans is contentious, especially as the modern-day GOP becomes more visibly homophobic and transphobic. It's sometimes argued that you cannot be both a Republican and a supporter of LGBTQ rights in the 21st century; today's Republicans have practically built their brand on opposing equality. Groups like LCR disagree, citing shared stances on issues like national defense and the economy as reasons to vote GOP.

But is allying with the Republican Party the way to go for people who actually support equal rights, especially those who are LGBTQ themselves? Right now, it doesn't sound like it's working. Another Republican LGBTQ group, GOProud, dissolved in 2014. That group was famous for taking virtually no position on most LGBTQ issues and appointing notorious bigot Ann Coulter as an adviser. (I don't get it either.) When the Republican Party released its history-making hate platform in 2016, the Log Cabin Republicans made a statement about the toxicity of the platform... but nothing about it changed. (Surprise.)

That's why it was big news when LCR *didn't* endorse Donald Trump for president. Trump's misogyny and racism will surely make the history books, but he said little about LGBTQ rights while campaigning. On the other hand, LCR had previously endorsed Mitt Romney[177] and John McCain,[178] who weren't as homophobic as the 2016 GOP lineup but also didn't have shining track records on LGBTQ rights.[179]

You have to wonder: Would LCR have endorsed a nominee like Rick Santorum, who once compared marriage equality to 9/11?[180] Or Mike Huckabee, who lamented the "ick factor" of same-sex relationships?[181] (Right back at you, Mike!) Mitt Romney was an outspoken opponent of marriage equality, but the organization declared its members "Americans first" and endorsed him "despite [their] disagreement." LCR endorsing virtually *any* of the major Republican candidates in 2016 would have meant backing vocal homophobia and transphobia. Was it just Trump's particular brand of contempt that was too much for them? Or would 2016 be the year when LCR finally said that a Republican who doesn't support equal rights isn't the right Republican for them?

Finally, while the Log Cabin Republicans didn't endorse Trump the candidate, they seem pretty on board with at least some of his initial actions as president. In January of 2017, LCR praised Trump for saying he wouldn't alter an executive order protecting LGBTQ federal workers from discrimination. The group said nothing when, two months later, Trump actually did take action to make those protections harder to enforce.

When the Department of Education revoked Obama-era guidelines protecting transgender students, LCR asked Education Secretary Betsy DeVos and Attorney General Jeff Sessions to reconsider, but they also continued to endorse DeVos on their website. Log Cabin strongly denounced Trump's attempted ban on transgender people in the military, but also invited Carly Fiorina, who has a history of opposing LGBTQ non-discrimination laws, to headline their 40th anniversary celebration a few months later.

Some big-picture issues like religious freedom laws are still up in the air, and Trump's administration will play a big role in what happens in the future. We'll see what role (if any) Log Cabin plays when those debates come to fruition.

And for the record, I asked LCR for an interview to hear their take on all of this. They never responded. (Surprise again!)

There are atheists whose views parallel those of the Log Cabin Republicans, too. In early 2016, Hemant interviewed some atheists about why they were voting GOP that year. One person said they were willing to overlook Ted Cruz's religious fundamentalism for his views on the Constitution. Another said they agreed with Trump's plan to defund Planned Parenthood, but at the same time appreciated Trump acknowledging how many women Planned Parenthood serves. The quote that most terrified me read, "I really dislike the religious side of the Republican Party but at least they like firearms which can be used to defend my non-religious views."[182]

Like Log Cabin's existence, these ideas seem counterproductive and contradictory to me. How can you oppose religious overstep, but vote for its biggest proponents? It's a reminder that correlation isn't causation, and that being an atheist doesn't come with prescribed political views. It also shows that those of us who do feel strongly about social causes shouldn't take other atheists' agreement for granted.

Perhaps it's possible to hold conservative viewpoints on some political issues and still be an ally to LGBTQ people. But right now, the modern-day Republican Party doesn't make sense as a place to do it. And herein lies another reason for atheists to join forces with the LGBTQ rights movement: no matter who you voted for or what party you traditionally align with, the Trump/Pence administration has put the separation of church and state in grave danger. Supporting LGBTQ rights, in this exact moment, is one avenue for fighting against the excessive entanglement of religion and government.

Abby Stein

I first interviewed Abby Stein back in 2015, about a month after she came out to her Ultra-Orthodox Hasidic Jewish community as a transgender woman.[183] Abby's story is especially interesting because she's the descendant of a founder of Hasidic Judaism, Rabbi Yisroel ben Eliezer (also known as the Baal Shem Tov). In Hasidic Judaism, strict roles prescribe how men and women "should" behave, and being transgender definitely doesn't fit into them. Abby told me that she didn't know different gender identities existed until she was 19. She thought she was crazy for feeling the way she did.

Abby left the Jewish faith formally a few years ago for what she called "philosophical and ideological reasons," but she's still maintained cultural ties to the community. She also writes about her experiences with gender, religion, philosophy, and atheism on her blog, The Second Transition.[184] Her family hadn't taken the news of her coming-out well when we first spoke, and she told me they weren't doing much better when we talked more recently. We discussed her experience of coming out twice and her take on why atheists are natural allies to LGBTQ people.

Can you tell me how you identify on both the religious spectrum and the LGBTQ spectrum?

> I identify as a woman of transgender experience. Religious-wise, I usually say I'm philosophically atheist and spiritually or culturally involved with [Judaism].

Can you talk more about the relationship between those two? Did being an atheist help you figure out you were trans, or vice versa, or neither?

> For me, it was definitely interrelated. I lived in a community without trans people, and I got to a point where I knew there's this part of my identity, mainly gender, which everyone disagrees with. To me, atheism was an outlet to explore my identity. I ended up learning about trans people, learning about transition, and so on. I feel like they were very strongly intertwined. There are a lot of overlaps be-

tween coming out as an atheist in a community that is very cult-like and coming out as trans. From people saying, "What the hell are you talking about, this doesn't make any sense," to people saying, "You're evil, you're the devil," and so on. The backlash I have gotten for being trans is somewhat amplified back from what people get for being atheist.

Did people really tell you that you were the devil?

Yeah, I get that all the time. I was Satan, and the devil, and all the words they used for it.

Were any of the people who said that close to you?

One of my brothers actually reached out to me once after coming out. He used an Aramaic term for Satan. And I replied, "Thanks for the compliment."

That's heavy.

Yeah. But I don't take it as an insult at all. It's whatever. It's a joke. It's like when religious people, especially Christians, start claiming that atheists worship Satan. I'm like, what the fuck. I don't worship Satan, that's not the point.

Should atheists support the LGBTQ rights movement because of their atheism?

Definitely. I think we're all people that have been discriminated against. Atheists are one of the most discriminated-against groups today. There still hasn't been a single member of Congress that was openly an atheist. It's considered political suicide to be an atheist. There's definite discrimination on a broader spectrum. The validity of it is being questioned, just like a lot of other minority identities. And we can really gain a lot by working with each other. For an atheist who is also queer, that ends up making it a lot harder for them in every form. [For example,] if they grow up in a conservative family, they'll have enough on their plate for being queer, and if they're also atheist they get all this other baggage of discrimination. So there's a lot of overlap.

Do you think that if you had been only trans or only an atheist, but not both, that your family and your community would have reacted better?

Only an atheist, definitely. I mean, they reacted negatively, but the fact is that it wasn't as big of a [deal] as being trans. If I would have been just trans, in my community specifically, it's a lot more cult-y. You have to fit in more. They don't have an understanding of trans people. I'm visibly trans. I think it might be a bit different than being just an atheist. For me, to some extent, being an atheist while leaving the community and transitioning was too much.

How can an atheist who is straight and cisgender be an ally to you?

Just by putting themselves out there and saying, "We are allies." Not just being a cis, straight ally, [but] being an ally *because* they are atheist, saying, "We know what it's like to be a minority. We know what it's like to get hate for our identity." In addition, it would be really good to have more support groups for LGBTQ people that are run by specific nonreligious organizations. In general, I even find that a lot of queer people end up being really spiritual. So for people who don't believe in God, they don't feel comfortable in a lot of these spaces. It's important to have a humanistic LGBTQ support group, or specifically atheist. I think it's also important to be aware that trans people come in all different forms, which includes all different forms of religious communities. Know that people who are not just atheist but have an additional minority identity really struggle. They need more support.

Resist, Resist, Resist

Now that LGBTQ issues are (back) up for political debate, especially more controversial topics like transgender and youth rights, their opponents are ready and prowling.

Internet-famous conservative Christians like activist Laurie Higgins and preacher Michael L. Brown, who didn't talk much about transgender people until recently, are suddenly out in full force. They rile their supporters by googling pro-trans-rights articles and attacking the subjects and authors mercilessly—not necessarily the most effective strategy for enacting policy change, but definitely one that stirs their readers. Trans people have been around for much longer than they've held space on the Democratic Party platform, but it's only recently that they have become a major talking point.

But ignorance is no longer an option. From *Orange is the New Black* to Caitlyn Jenner, transgender people are undeniably visible in a mainstream way. So are other faces of the greater LGBTQ rights movement, and their opponents. Modern-day Anita Bryants amass followers quickly online, and it can be hard to keep up.

For example, notorious internet troll Milo Yiannopoulos, who was raised Catholic but says he also has Jewish heritage, gives plenty of fodder to anti-LGBTQ violence on the Right. He's a gay man who openly harasses women, black people, transgender people, and others—often in the name of free speech, doing it just because he can. In an interview with *Nightline*, Yiannopoulos said he was "doing God's work" by racially harassing comedian Leslie Jones until she quit Twitter.[185] And to podcast host Joe Rogan, he said that "everywhere that doesn't have a strong Christian heritage is a fucked up place with bad morals."[186] Nice.

Ultimately, nobody should be responsible for justifying their existence to other people. Nobody. That's where active allyship comes in. It's not enough to *not* support people like the Log Cabin Republicans and Milo Yiannopoulos; it takes openly *defending* LGBTQ people, sometimes to strangers and sometimes to your closest friends, in order to make an impact. As I've said before, atheists have much to gain from a society that embraces LGBTQ rights: lesser influence from religion into politics, a stringent commitment to civil rights, and, of course, benefits for the many people who identify as both atheist and LGBTQ.

LGBTQ people have been fighting for decades, but we can't do it alone. It's time for atheists to join the fight, entirely and intentionally. Both our groups will be better for it.

Learning From Each Other

Why Organize?

REBECCA Vitsmun looked oddly calm as she stood before the image of her destroyed home, wearing a plain grey t-shirt and holding her fidgety toddler, Anders. It was 2013, and a tornado had ravaged Vitsmun's town of Moore, Oklahoma, killing more than 20 people and devastating more than a thousand homes and businesses. She was nearing the end of an interview with CNN anchor Wolf Blitzer, discussing how she and her family had managed to escape their home just before the storm hit. That's when Blitzer posed an awkward question that, to him, may have just been a way to end the segment on a high note.[187]

"You're blessed. Your husband is blessed. Anders is blessed," Blitzer told her on air, as Anders babbled and played with the microphone. "I guess you gotta thank the Lord, right?" Blitzer asked her. "Do you thank the Lord for that split-second decision [to leave]?"

Looking down at her son and then back at Blitzer, she replied, "I'm actually an atheist." They both laughed as Blitzer fumbled to recover from his well-intended faux pas. But she relieved him, adding, "We are here, and I don't blame anyone for thanking the Lord."

The atheist community's response to Vitsmun's televised "coming-out" was astounding. An online fundraiser called "Atheists Unite," started by comedian Doug Stanhope, raised more than $125,000 for Vitsmun's family to rebuild their home. She joined the Foundation Beyond Belief to launch its Humanist Disaster Recovery Teams, the first humanist-focused volunteer program providing relief after disasters like the tornado in Moore. Glenn Beck claimed the entire interview was a setup, while atheist publications welcomed Vitsmun's commentary.[188] Before too long, it seemed like everybody had seen the clip of the "Oklahoma atheist" who'd survived a tragedy against the odds—and didn't credit God for it.

On the "Atheists Unite" Indiegogo page, Stanhope wrote: "It's important that our community shows that we have your back when you come out publicly as an atheist. Let's show the world that you don't need to believe in a god to have human compassion nor does all charity fall under the banner of religion. The impact of getting Vitsmun and her family properly housed by the atheist community will do far more good than sitting in bars or chat rooms mocking people of faith. Like religion, free-thinking will be more easily spread through compassion and decency."[189]

The unified response to Rebecca Vitsmun's coming-out is a testament to the collective power of the atheist community—when the community wants to unite. It's also a perfect example of how organizing around a cause always comes back to one central theme: real people with real stories. Whether you're trying to pass a law or to convince your aunt that gay people aren't sinners, characters are simply more compelling than facts and figures. If you want someone to join your cause, you've got to show them the real faces behind it, not just spout statistics at them.

Before we talk strategy, though, there's another big question to be answered: is atheism a cause around which to organize? Many would argue no. Actively seeking others to partake in your belief system is a major tenet of universalizing religions, something atheism is clearly not. The largest universalizing religion is Christianity, particularly Mormonism, Evangelicalism, and other denominations that skew conservative. Buddhism and Islam fall under the universalizing umbrella as well. By its very nature, atheism is not a religious system, but a lack of one. (As the joke goes, atheism is a religion like "off" is a TV channel.) Atheism can be experienced and explored in groups and societies, but unlike major religions tied to houses of worship, congregations, and denominations, it's not grounded in a *community* of like-minded believers—or non-believers, as it were. There are exceptions to that, as we see from the local atheist communities that have been created in cities across the country, but most atheists aren't members of those groups. For that reason, it might not make sense for atheists to actively organize around atheism as a social cause.

However, whether atheism sets out to "recruit" or not, certain goals and ideals commonly accompany non-belief. The end of faith-based discrimination, the separation of church and state, and policies based on reason and evidence are valid ambitions for millions of people regardless of their religious affiliation, but they're especially resonant for atheists who feel strongly about the issues. (Not every atheist agrees on them, of course—there are anti-choice atheists, anti-gay atheists, and others who disagree with these ideas on their own philosophical grounds—but by and large, atheists skew liberal on social issues.) These concepts also come up during more targeted attempts at policy change, such as when we rally together against anti-abortion laws or discriminatory "religious freedom restoration" laws. Therefore, contributing to *existing* social movements—those which embody Humanist ideals, whether intentionally or not—from a secular lens is a valuable way for atheists to join forces.

There's also something to be said for bolstering public acceptance of atheism. While the number of atheists in the United States is on the rise, non-religious Americans are still a minority, especially compared to Christians—22.8% compared with 70.6%, according to the Pew Research Center's Religious Landscape Study.[190] Public perception of atheists also runs low compared with other religious groups. An analysis of Pew data found atheists are viewed "more coldly" than Jews, Catholics, and evangelical Christians in the United States; Christians especially hold unfavorable views of atheists.[191] "Atheists themselves are rated positively by atheists and agnostics, and they receive neutral ratings from Jews and those who describe their religion as 'nothing in particular,'" Pew reports. "Atheists are rated much more negatively by other religious groups." (For what it's worth, atheists also rated evangelicals a chilly "28" out of 100 on average.) Much of the LGBTQ rights movement also has focused on visibility, awareness, and public acceptance. Atheists who care about how they are perceived by the outside world (surely not an insignificant number of us) could find it worthwhile to work with and learn from LGBTQ activists fighting a similar battle.

There may be room for both—supporting progressive human rights causes while simultaneously promoting and defending atheism and its accompanying ideas. Even if it's not atheism itself that atheists should rally around, leading with atheist-friendly ideas like rationality and reason can bring about justice for many different groups and causes. The LGBTQ rights movement is one such cause, but atheists' call for a just, rational society can power other movements, too. And the way to do it is by finding stories that resonate with people — stories like Rebecca Vitsmun's. Telling an average American that everyone deserves the freedom of religion is dry and impersonal. But introducing them to a perky, resilient mom and her squirmy toddler who survived a natural disaster? That's sure to have an impact.

The Power of Stories

The concept of storytelling for a cause brings us back to Proposition 8 in California in 2008, when only three states (including California, briefly) had legalized same-sex marriage.[192] As awareness of the measure to ban marriage equality grew, the Religious Right painted a bombastic image of what would happen if marriage equality was legalized: innocent children learning about same-sex marriage at school, good Christians going to jail for speaking out against equality, and heterosexual marriages mysteriously invalidated. It was obviously fictional, bordering on the absurd. But the pro-equality side failed to home in on compelling stories that could counter the Religious Right's narrative of fear.

Marc Solomon, a leader in the marriage equality movement and the founder of the organization Freedom to Marry, has spoken extensively about the precise, multifaceted strategy it took to legalize same-sex marriage. In his book *Winning Marriage: The Inside Story of How Same-Sex Couples Took on the Politicians and Pundits—and Won*, Solomon dove into the topic of campaign messaging.[193]

A veteran of the movement, Solomon described the hesitation he felt during the clash over California's Prop 8. Though the fight for marriage had already been brewing for decades, organizers fine-tuned their messages as the movement grew more and more visible. Solomon hadn't been working on the anti-Prop 8 campaign directly, but even from a distance, he knew that the pro-marriage equality commercials weren't right. Most of the ads looked like "typical political spots," he wrote. They emphasized changes to the Constitution and un-equal treatment, rather than telling the stories of real people affected by the law. Solomon wrote:

> Given that the burden of proof was on us, our side needed to make the most emotionally compelling case we could. However, that's not what I thought we were doing. The arguments we were using in the ads appealed to the head; protecting the Constitution, highlighting the support of key electeds, and protecting fundamental rights in the abstract. They didn't elicit emotions. Our opponents were masterful in conjuring up fear about what would happen to society, to the institution of marriage, and to the family if gays were al-lowed to marry. The only antidote to fear was love, empathy, connection, and an appeal to people's better angels. That required using real people talking poignantly about why marriage was important to their family—their parents, their children, and themselves. If we didn't evoke those emotions in a powerful way, I felt we'd be in serious trouble.

In the book's afterword, Solomon wrote out a list of the top lessons he'd learned in the marriage equality fight that can be applied to other social movements. "Convey a bold, inspira-tional vision," he wrote. "Focus on values and emotions. Meet people where they are."

Storytelling worked for the marriage movement because it humanized a cause many Americans weren't quite familiar with. If you're not gay, bi, or another non-straight identity, it's hard to identify with the pain and stigma of being singled out for your sexual orientation. But most anyone can understand the desire to fall in love, care for your family in times of need, and build a life without fear. A good lawyer could craft a mov-ing legal argument for marriage equality from a constitutional perspective, but nothing compares to seeing the faces and hearing the voices of a family that just wants to stay together. When Obama announced his support for marriage equality, the former constitutional law professor noted that he was moved by the same-sex couples he had come to know.

Do these persuasion techniques apply to atheism? Is athe-ism a social movement? Again, it depends on who you ask. But whether atheism is considered a movement, a cause, a community, or merely a word for non-belief, there is value in knowing how to bring about respect and tolerance for groups that fall outside the majority. To garner widespread acceptance, atheists need to find their story.

For some atheists, that might not be the most intuitive approach. We tend to lean toward the objective over the subjective, facts over feelings. One of the first things they tell you in journalism school is that three anecdotes don't make a trend. I'm also not saying that stories are a stronger indicator of the truth than data (no alternative facts here!) or that the right spokesperson can convince people to radically alter their beliefs. Rebecca Vitsmun's baby is adorable, but that doesn't make her opinion more correct than yours. Rather, storytelling puts a face to an issue, making it more relatable and memorable. You can sympathize with a person more than with an aggregation of statistics.

Take Herb Silverman, founder of the Secular Coalition of America. In 1990, Silverman ran for governor in South Carolina as a write-in candidate, knowing that atheists were technically not allowed to run for public office. A provision in the state's constitution read that "persons who deny the existence of a Supreme Being" were unqualified for public service.[194] He lost the race, so the provision remained in place, but he didn't stop fighting. Two years later, he applied to be a notary public — but lawmakers denied his application because he crossed out the words "so help me God" in the application oath. Silverman filed a lawsuit that went all the way to the South Carolina Supreme Court, where the judges ruled the provision unconstitutional.[195]

You wouldn't need to know Silverman personally to understand the significance of his political run. He saw an injustice in the law, brought awareness to it, and eventually righted it. Calling attention to yourself like that takes guts, whether you're a South Carolina atheist fighting for political inclusion or a same-sex couple in Utah fighting for marriage equality.

In a 2012 article for *Alternet*, Adam Lee wrote that religious progressives have more in common with atheists than with the

Religious Right, and that the fast-growing number of atheists in the United States could bring about huge social changes. One key tactic, he wrote, is to provoke a sense of compassion and shared human experience, rather than convince conservatives to interpret the Bible in more liberal terms.

"The major progressive movements that have overcome religious opposition—women's suffrage and civil rights being two examples from recent history, with gay rights moving along the same trajectory—didn't do so by offering a more convincing reinterpretation of the Bible (Dr. Martin Luther King Jr. notwithstanding)," Lee wrote. "Instead, they won out by emphasizing a sense of identity, a narrative that resonated emotionally with the broader public, and a demand for fairness and justice previously denied to them. These are all things that the secular movement has to offer."

Come Out, Come Out—Or Don't

In an earlier chapter, I talked about the pressure that both atheists and LGBTQ people can face in coming out to their loved ones. It's a big decision. There are the obvious, very real risks of being rejected by your family, and we've addressed those somewhat. But even if all goes well, there are other outcomes to consider.

When you're the only person of a certain group that somebody knows, you run several risks, from being tokenized as the spokesperson for that community to worrying that everything you do will support a stereotype they have in their head. When I came out, a family member asked me (maybe jokingly, maybe not) when I was going to cut all my hair off. That's virtually impossible to respond to—how do you combine "we don't all do that" and "it's OK to do that" into a single defense of your individuality?

The considerations for coming out as LGBTQ and as an atheist are similar. Dan Barker, a co-president of the Freedom From Religion Foundation, was a preacher before he came out as an atheist. In his book *Godless*, he writes about sending a letter to his community sharing the news and the array of responses he received.[197] Some of his colleagues and friends questioned his decision, said they would pray for him, or told him they were saddened and disappointed. One said there was nothing meaningful about his newfound non-belief, while another suggested Barker was "hurt and bitter." These are all responses that LGBTQ people hear every day when they decide to come out to friends and family.

The Reddit group focused on atheism has a special section, as I mentioned earlier, dedicated to coming out. This is the advice offered to young people who aren't sure whether to take the plunge:

> If you do decide to "come out," then consider that "atheist" has many evil, hateful connotations to religious people. It's right up there with "Satanist." You might be able to reduce the amount of flak you get by choosing a label for yourself that has a similar meaning but is less controversial. Please consider using an alternative such as "agnostic" or "humanist" or "non-religious," which does not carry quite as much baggage.
>
> There's also another approach: You could say "I've lost my belief" or "I don't know what to believe any more" or even "God doesn't speak to me any more." Asked if you are an atheist, you could say "I don't know."
>
> This makes you look less like a monster and more like a victim. You'll be subject to sympathy rather than anger. You won't be kicked out. But you run the risk of having folks work really hard to bring you back to God.

This is interesting, difficult advice. It presupposes a terrible reaction from loved ones—which is possible, if you're from a deeply religious family—but it also suggests changing, omitting, or strategically rewording some details about yourself in order to elicit a less extreme response. A version of this happens in LGBTQ circles, too. I've known more than a few people who came out to their families as bisexual, even though they identified as gay or lesbian, because they thought that might soften the blow. (Doing this sends a harmful message about the validity of bisexual identities, but that's a whole other story.) When I came out as bi, I definitely deployed that messaging subconsciously, chock-full of internalized homophobia and biphobia: "I like girls, but don't worry, I can still end up with a guy like I'm *supposed* to!"

If you've ever had to share a big, difficult secret about yourself with a loved one, you can relate to the awful feeling that builds up in your chest for the minutes, hours, and days before you tell them. You don't want to hurt anyone. You don't want anyone to think differently of you. Your mind flashes to the worst-case scenario, where you might lose your family, your reputation, or even the roof over your head. And if you share something personal about yourself that's markedly different from the people around you and that you can't change—your beliefs, your sexual orientation, your gender identity—the stakes are undoubtedly higher. You can't decide what they'll do about it or how they'll respond. You know there's nothing either of you can do to "fix" it. And you can never take it back.

National Coming Out Day, recognized each year on October 11, marks the anniversary of the second March on Washington for Lesbian and Gay Rights and celebrates the community's right to live out in the the open. Online, it's celebrated with a flurry of Harvey Milk quotations and "Come out, come out, wherever you are" memes in *Wizard of Oz* colors. But each year, messages also circulate reminding young people *not* to come out unless they are sure they'll be safe. When teenagers email me to say they're desperate to come out to their families but worried about the repercussions, I run through a quick checklist: Are you certain that you won't get kicked out or physically harmed? Are you certain that you'll still be financially supported? Do you have a place to go and a plan for survival if you do get kicked out? Is there at least one person in your life whom you know will continue to love and support you?

If you can't answer "yes" to all of these questions, I tell them, hold off until you're completely self-sufficient. That weight will stay on your chest a little longer, and it's a heavy burden to carry—no one should have to choose between their safety and their authenticity—but if laying low means a guaranteed place to sleep for a few more years, it's a trade-off you have to make.

When I came out to my mom—by accident on my way to a Pride parade, no less—it didn't come up again for close to a year. When my grandmother found out a little while later, she didn't speak to me for three months. My coming out experience didn't feel easy at the time, but it was a walk in the park compared to the thousands of LGBTQ kids who are disowned, abused, thrown out of their homes, or worse after opening up about who they are. (And for the record, my family has come around a hundred times over, and they're supportive as anything now—not all families get there.)

Coming out sucks sometimes. There's no way around it. And it's unfair and irresponsible to tell young LGBTQ people, young atheists, or anyone else that their identities aren't valid unless they're out to the whole world—especially before they're ready for it.

But let's say you've run through the worst-case scenarios, and you're pretty confident everything's going to be OK. Then what?

For one, you could be making a positive, perhaps surprising difference in a lot of people's lives. As early as 2009, polling from Gallup indicated that people who knew a gay person were more likely to support same-sex marriage.[198] Knowing someone gay helped politicians like Ohio Republican Sen. Rob Portman and even then-President Obama change their minds on marriage equality (at least according to their public statements). And while public support for same-sex marriage is greater now than it was then, the idea still applies. Pew data from late 2016 showed that Americans who know a transgender person are more likely to support transgender people's right to use the public bathrooms that match their gender identity than those who do not.[199]

Similar conclusions have been drawn for atheists. In the 2014 study mentioned earlier, Pew found that "knowing someone from a religious group is linked with having relatively more positive views of that group."[200] At that time, people who personally knew an atheist rated atheists an average of 50 on a 0-100 scale of warmth and personability. Those who didn't know an atheist rated them an average of 29.

If that sounds like a lot of pressure, don't stress. The hard part is almost over! As a person who's about to share something significant and personal about yourself, your only job is to speak your truth and take care of yourself. If your news is received with confusion or concern, it helps to be patient. You may have to answer questions you're not thrilled with, but you can do so at your discretion. Your family may appreciate information that helps them understand where you're coming from, but you're not required to provide it. You have the right to your boundaries when it comes to coming out, and it's OK to assert a limit as to what you want to talk about. (This is also a good time for a reminder that coming out should happen on your own terms, and that nobody but you can decide when you're ready!)

Remember the guidance from Reddit: it's a good idea to know what you'll do if the worst case scenario happens, just in case. But hopefully you won't need it; many families are eventually supportive. Accepting that your kid (or sibling, or parent, etc.) is different than you thought she would be is a different process for everyone, but there are more resources than ever that can help family members go from apprehensive to affirming. And if all goes smoothly, you may have just added a couple more supporters to the movement for equal rights. Great job!

On the flip side, when somebody comes out to *you*, you have a responsibility to respond with love and affirmation, even if you don't totally understand. The best advice I ever heard for what to say when someone comes out to you boils down to three short sentences: "I love you. Thank you for telling me. Can you tell me more?" Affirm that you're a safe person to talk to and that you support them no matter what—trust me, hearing that never gets old. Ask your questions respectfully. Prioritize listening. Coming out is scary no matter how many times you've done it, and everyone deserves to be heard.

Coming out is more complicated when you have to do it more than once, or for multiple identities, as I mentioned before. Gay and atheist, bisexual and transgender, nonbinary and agnostic—you get the picture. Identity is multifaceted, and there are lots of ways you can throw your family for a loop with an identity they weren't expecting. But evidence abounds that visibility can help normalize marginalized groups and even bolster public acceptance. Plus, there's a good chance it'll make you feel better, too.

voices   **D. S.**

In July of 2015, D. S., an agnostic gay man in Los Angeles, sent a group of his friends a six-page document about his thoughts on religion and invited them to respond. He said he got good feedback on it and invited me to read it as well.

"When my little mountain village in Vietnam was destroyed by the Viet Cong, the story goes, I was first taken to a Buddhist orphanage," he writes. "But because my Montagnard people were apparently Christian (and helping the Americans), I was then taken to a Christian orphanage, so even as a baby unable to speak, religion was exerting itself on me.

"Similarly, my adopting father said as a kid in southern Indiana he spent more time in church than he did out of it, and he had seen how religion had affected people in both good ways and bad, so he made the conscious decision in raising me to not subject me to that, to let me discover religion on my own, and for this I am eternally grateful to him."

D. S. and I talked about why people get involved in social justice causes (spoiler: mostly because they know someone who belongs to that group). We discussed coming out in both atheist and LGBTQ spheres, ways atheists can organize, and why visibility matters more than ever.

Which did you recognize first, your gay identity or agnostic identity?

My father who adopted me was raised in a very religious small-town environment, and thankfully consciously chose to not raise me that way, so I never had to wrestle with that or come out as agnostic. But I definitely had to come to terms with being gay. Living in Los Angeles makes both much easier. I think being gay, agnostic, or even Asian in a small town is really hard.

Does being agnostic influence your perspective on LGBTQ issues?

Being gay influences my perspective on LGBTQ issues. If I weren't gay, I'd have to know a close family member, friend or coworker to care. I think the same is true for agnostics and atheists. When gays came out, they were told to not to make such a big deal about it, this "choice" they made. But, hello, religion is a choice; there's no genetic predisposition to a particular faith; it's not in your DNA. Yes, you get it from your parents because it's total social conditioning. Only when family members, friends, and co-workers saw the discrimination gays faced did they care, too.

Do you think atheists and LGBTQ people share common goals or values?

Yes, and maybe atheists could learn from the struggle and progress of LGBTQ people: from Stonewall to marriage equality, in one lifetime; from drag queens to [Apple CEO] Tim Cook. I think atheists have an important role in America, to remind everyone of the importance in separation of church and state. People in power never understand their privilege until it's thrown in their face, be it white privilege, male privilege, heterosexual privilege, or Christian privilege. People advocating for "freedom of religion" only mean Christianity, and don't want or care about Judaism, Islam, Buddhism, or atheism.

How should atheists advocate for themselves?

For atheists to get up to speed, they're going to need to "come out," and have the whole host of organizations: anti-defamation leagues, campus support groups, legal defense teams, primetime TV characters, Yellow Pages directory, etc. Atheists need a "victim" whom people can identify with and champion. Everyone loves Spock because he was so logical—someone like that. Even though atheists fall under the protected class of "can't discriminate on the basis of religion" (or lack thereof), discrimination happens.

Do atheists have to know someone LGBTQ in real life in order to care about LGBTQ issues?

People only care about issues if they know someone who's affected by them, be it atheism, cancer, homophobia, Islamophobia, racism, etc. When I was coming to terms with being gay, I think my dad's biggest concern was that I, as a guy, would end up wearing dresses and makeup, because that's the gay stereotype he knew.

At this point in time, I think LGBTQ people are doing OK. Life isn't perfect, but at least you can talk about them in public. People can name a few and have a general understanding of their issues, like marriage equality, adoption, employment discrimination, etc. The same may not be true for atheists. People can hold negative opinions about them because they don't personally know any (or maybe the ones they know are the basis for their negative opinions).

And what are atheists' issues? Are they under attack, or are they the ones doing the attacking? "We don't believe in God, and we want everyone else to stop believing in God" may not be a winning strategy. The focus should be on what atheists do believe in: freedom of religion and from religion, separation of church and state, that our public schools should not teach creationism, and that our laws should not favor one religion over another.

Finding Your People

The natural next step after coming out and declaring yourself is finding your place in your community, whether it consists of atheists, LGBTQ people, both, and/or the other identities that mean something to you. Obviously, this part is optional. We won't revoke your Gay Card for missing Pride or your Atheist Card for not hanging out with other atheists. But finding people who share your experiences can be validating and freeing —and also lead to real change.

Before Barack Obama was elected president, politicians like Sarah Palin and Rudy Giuliani mocked him for his background as a community organizer.[201] Then-vice presidential candidate Palin quipped that her experience as a small-town mayor was "sort of like a community organizer, except that you have actual responsibilities." (Obama won by almost 200 electoral votes.) Community organizing has a rich history of connecting people with politicians, citizens with decision-makers. In the social justice world, it's also a key way to reflect on how different communities are faring and take action to make the changes they need.

At a previous job, I was lucky enough to work with Tea Sefer, a Chicago-based community organizer who has been working in social justice for about a decade. Sefer, who uses the singular pronoun "they," started organizing around LGBTQ issues in high school. They have since worked on issues like immigration reform within the Bosnian diaspora, and contraception and abortion access in communities around the country.

I asked Sefer to walk me through what it's like to organize for the first time. Well, technically, I asked them what to do when something in the world pisses you off and you want to do something about it.

"The point of community organizing is that it's people coming together around a specific issue," they said. "If it's something that just bothers you, and doesn't actually affect a larger community, and the thing that you're fighting for doesn't necessarily improve people's lives or their access to resources, then you don't really have a goal in mind. You just want to get on a soapbox and talk.

"Narrow it down, figure out what your specific goal is and what the problem [is]. And then make sure that the impact that you're implementing is actually going to improve people's lives."

A big part of setting those goals, Sefer said, is talking to other people about the issues they are facing and what kinds of changes would alleviate those issues. Once you've identified a solvable problem—say, a local law that enables discrimination —that's when you start to mobilize. It's also critically important to look for people who are already working on those issues, and to join forces with them if you can.

"If there's already people doing the work, always join someone else first," they said. "When you're trying to start your own ship while there's other ships already working, all you're doing is making yourself learn the lessons that those people have already figured out. Don't reinvent the wheel."

The great thing about the atheist and LGBTQ overlap is that we're already collaborating. Earlier, I talked about how Humanists of Houston helped out during that city's campaign for LGBTQ rights. Major atheist groups publicly state that LGBTQ equality is crucial to their vision of justice, morality, and individual freedom. And again, there are simply so many of us who belong to both groups that it would be absurd not to take advantage of our combined knowledge, networks, and experiences.

"Community organizing isn't just about achieving goals; it's about the real grassroots [idea] that we are family and we're in this together and we're fighting for each other's rights," Sefer said. "Especially for marginalized communities and communities that have faced a lot of oppression, hatred, and violence, I see organizing as a way to harness our collective power. And that is [a form of] healing, also."

Since Donald Trump's election, this idea of organizing as a means of healing seems more pertinent than ever. Minority communities are hurting under Trump's policies, proposals, and bizarre Twitter outbursts. In the first few months of his presidency, marches championing women, science, Muslims, transgender youth, and even tax transparency drew millions of protesters in hundreds of cities. There are books, websites, and Facebook groups dedicated to helping us figure out what to do next while taking care of ourselves in the process.

On January 20, 2017, I donated $20 to Planned Parenthood and another $20 to the ACLU. The day after Trump's inauguration, I went to the Women's March in New York City with a sign inspired by the musical *Hamilton.* ("Rise up!") The week after that, I went to a protest of Trump's executive order on immigration with a sign that said "Queer Atheist Against Muslim Ban." The week after that was the anti-Trump protest led by LGBTQ organizers, and I skipped that one because I was emotionally and physically drained.

Sometimes it can feel like in order to be a "good" LGBTQ person (or atheist, or activist of your choice), you have to stretch yourself so thin for the cause that you're barely functional in the other parts of your life. But that's not a sustainable way to do advocacy work, Sefer told me. It's acceptable, even necessary, to pace yourself in order to keep your movement thriving. Change doesn't come in the span of a weekend; it can take years of work.

"I view my organizing work as something I'm going to do for the rest of my life, so I do it in a way that's sustainable for me," Sefer said. "I don't show up to every protest or rally, I can't do everything. With brand new organizers and people who are very excited about an issue, they have to make sure that they're committed to that issue not for the next three weeks or six months, but for at least a year or two if they're trying to get real change to happen.

"We don't change quickly. And our systems don't change quickly. But realizing that you have that power and actually can impact things is rad."

Harvey Milk was famous for many things, among them his disdain for closets. "Burst down those closet doors once and for all, and stand up and start to fight." "If a bullet should enter my brain, let that bullet destroy every closet door."

When Milk was assassinated in 1978, he didn't take every closet door with him. But his idea that declaring yourself to the world can change everything has resonated with generations of activists who followed him. Coming out to yourself, coming out to others, and joining forces with your community to make a difference — this is the outline of how LGBTQ people have fought for equal rights for decades. And atheists can follow this same path in their own quest for justice, whatever that may look like.

This is an important moment to reflect on what Ashton Woods, the Black Lives Matter Houston activist interviewed earlier, had to say about allyship and *accompliceship.* You don't have to belong to a group to advocate for the rights of that group, but you do have to respect your role in the movement. If you find yourself inspired to join a social justice cause, look around the room where the core of your work is taking place. What have you set out to do? Who is leading the conversation? Are you working on behalf of someone who's not in the room, and if so, how do you get them there?

The LGBTQ movement has made incredible strides toward equal rights and social acceptability. While atheists don't have the same obstacles to overcome, many of us understand what it's like to be stigmatized and share similar views on issues surrounding religion and politics. We need to follow in the footsteps of Rebecca Vitsmun and Herb Silverman and Jessica Ahlquist — who feel comfortable enough to talk about their atheism publicly — in order to build relationships, explore our common ground, and frankly, get shit done.

By advocating for the kind of society we'd like to see, and modeling the sort of atheist we wish the stereotype would become, we can make lasting positive changes — for our community and for those around us.

Frequently Made Arguments
—And How to Respond

Welcome to New York

I TAKE the train every weekday from the borough of Brooklyn, New York, into Manhattan for work. On any given day, there's a small chance I'll encounter a subway preacher.

You can't tell who they are when you board the train. It's not like when you see someone eating a burrito at eight in the morning and decide to stand on the other side of the car; there are no visual cues. Subway preachers come in all shapes and sizes, ages and genders, and certainly all different decibel levels. Some walk quietly through the aisle, handing out informational postcards about their Lord and Savior Jesus Christ. Some stand in the corner, telling us that God loves us, every one, no matter where we come from or who we voted for. The boldest parade through the cars, loudly proclaiming that we will all burn for our sins.

Usually when this happens, I just turn up the music in my headphones and look the other way. I consider myself a pretty forthright person when it comes to calling out my friends and acquaintances on their bullshit, but I haven't worked up the courage yet to do the same with a stranger. For one thing, you never know who you're talking to. The vast majority of subway preachers are harmless, if not for their interruption of my daily listen to the *Hamilton* soundtrack. But even in a supposed liberal haven like New York City, there must be at least one proselytizing passenger who's ready to start a fistfight over the word of God. As luck would have it, if I ever decided to talk back to one of them, I'm sure that'd be the one I found. (Just you wait.)

The more pressing issue is that you just don't accomplish much by talking back to a subway preacher. What's the point? Are you going to change his mind and inspire him to trade in his Bible for *The God Delusion*? Is she going to give you a hug and tell you she's actually a closeted bisexual? Really, what's your endgame?

A lot of the time, we talk back to make ourselves feel better, or maybe to blow off some steam, like we're doing a good deed for the sake of inflating our own egos. In the face of an increasingly hostile political climate, though, it's becoming more and more important to defend those communities who are disproportionately targeted, whether by an aimless subway preacher or by the president of the United States.

But let's be honest: the people who need confronting usually aren't subway preachers. (And unless you're one of the few people he follows on Twitter, you're not going to get in touch with the president.) The people you need to talk to aren't one-off protesters at Pride parades or trolls on YouTube or anonymous accounts on Twitter. They're the people close to you whose attitudes force LGBTQ people to live in fear and shame: your friendly aunt, who says she loves her child too much to let him be transgender; your aging grandfather, who says there's no room for queers under his roof; your college roommate, who thinks lesbians are hot, but insists that marriage is between a man and a woman.

These are the people whose homophobia and transphobia we often let go unchecked. We love them, or they're family, or they don't know any better—whatever the excuse, we find a reason to let it slide time after time, even when the things they say aren't just hurtful and hateful, but blatantly, scientifically false.

There are also the nameless but familiar faces we see every day who need reprimanding. Employees who make snide comments to trans people, restaurant patrons who taunt the same-sex couple sitting next to them, and, yes, sometimes even the subway preacher on the 5 train. Hate can happen anywhere.

Herein lies the key question: When someone spouts bigotry and cites religion as his excuse, should you intervene?

If you're LGBTQ, it's your call. But if you're straight and cisgender, yes. Almost without question, yes. The exception is if your immediate safety could be compromised. This is a legitimate threat in lots of public confrontations with strangers, but less so when you're talking to your own friends and family; you're probably not going to get kicked out of your house for having a gay friend, the way you might for actually being gay.

Why the double standard? I'll give a couples of examples.

As I was wrapping up this book, the website Lifehacker published an interview with the Rev. James Martin, a Jesuit priest and author of a book about building bridges between Catholic and LGBTQ communities titled *How to Talk With Religious Conservatives About LGBT Rights.* (Perfect timing, right?) Reporter Leigh Anderson asked Martin how to speak to someone who's intolerant of LGBTQ people about these issues.

"I would propose *not* talking to them and actually listening to them," Martin replied. "Frequently these conversations are 'how do we talk *to* these people or how do we talk *at* these people?' The presumption is that we're doing the talking (which is very American), instead of us actually listening to them."[202]

Speaking for myself, that kind of patience can feel impossible in some conversations. In the handful of talks I've had with people who were unapologetically, explicitly anti-gay, I had a hard time articulating anything in response, let alone thoughtfully considering where they were coming from. When a friend of a friend says that people like you are disgusting and sad, you're caught off guard. And when I first read the interview with Rev. Martin, I was worried I hadn't been compassionate enough in writing this chapter—that I hadn't left enough space to hear people out. It can be really hard to navigate that sweet spot. You want to affirm the humanity of the person across from you, but you also want to avoid the unfiltered venting of someone who bemoans your existence.

In a film by Shakti Butler called *Cracking the Codes: The System of Racial Inequity,* Joy DeGruy, a black woman, tells a story about going to the grocery store with her sister-in-law, a biracial woman whom DeGruy says looks white.[203] When DeGruy reaches the checkout line, the white cashier asks her to present two pieces of ID before she can pay for her items—something she hadn't asked of DeGruy's sister-in-law just minutes before. DeGruy's sister-in-law asks the cashier why only DeGruy was asked for ID—something DeGruy could not have done without further marginalizing and calling attention to herself as the stereotypical "angry black woman," DeGruy says in the film. When her white-appearing sister-in-law steps in, though, other white customers notice how DeGruy has been wronged and come to her defense as well.

"She pointed out the injustice, and she, as a result of that one act, influenced everyone in that space," DeGruy says in the film. "But what would've happened if [I as a] black woman had said, 'This is unfair, why are you doing this to me?' Would it have had the same impact? [She] knew that she walked through the world differently than I did and she used her white privilege to educate and make right a situation that was wrong."

I bring this example up for a reason, knowing that it's shallow and unfair to compare the LGBTQ rights movement to the movement for black civil rights; the two struggles have vastly different histories. However, there is a universal lesson to be learned when it comes to using your societal advantages—say, your standing as a heterosexual person—to connect with people who don't want to hear it from minorities. Just as some white people tune out when people of color talk about racism, some straight people don't want to hear from LGBTQ people about homophobia and transphobia. (Political correctness! Special snowflakes! Go back to Tumblr! [Insert your dull Twitter comeback of choice here.]) That's one place where atheists can be allies; even if you don't believe in the god that the person sitting across from you worships, you can connect with her as a fellow straight person and go from there.

Once you've committed to chiming in, what comes next? There are a handful of vaguely religious arguments that opponents of equality tend to fall back on; in the next few pages, you'll find go-to responses for them. If you can familiarize yourself with the reasons conservatives' core arguments are unsound and unhelpful, you'll be well-positioned to help defend the rights of LGBTQ people in the future.

These suggestions are meant to guide conversations with people in your life who may never have thought about LGBTQ issues from anyone's perspective but their own—that is, if they've thought about these issues at all. Sometimes these folks mean well; sometimes they really, really don't. Modify your tone and visible rage levels as needed. If you can, assume the best of intentions.

It also needs to be said that when it comes to a topic this charged, it's hard, if not impossible, to get people to change their minds. Research suggests that when someone holds a belief closely, there's no real way to change their mind, and telling them that their opinion is wrong might make them cling even harder to it.[203] That doesn't mean it isn't worth speaking up, though. When you say something, you remind people that their words have consequences. But more importantly, you show your LGBTQ friends and family members that you've got their backs in an uncomfortable or threatening situation. Maybe you can't talk your aunt out of taking passages from Leviticus literally, but calling her out on her comments sends a strong message to your gay younger sibling (or cousin, or uncle, or whomever) that someone in the room supports them.

Finally, feel free to go off script if that's what feels right. You know your aunt, grandpa, or roommate better than I do; think about what kinds of messages would resonate with them. Stories are more convincing than facts, especially if the person you're speaking with knows someone affected by these issues (which they almost certainly do, even if they don't know it). And remember that nobody likes to be yelled at (although some people totally deserve it).

These tips are just a starting point. Adjust and adapt them as necessary. And if you want to use these answers to sass a preacher next time you're on public transit? That's on you.

"The Bible Tells Me So"

You'd think Bible-centric arguments would be the easiest to dismiss in broad-reaching conversations about civil rights, since not everybody believes in the Bible. Unfortunately, this text and its infinite interpretations are too often cited as justifications for discrimination, intolerance, and even violence. But that doesn't mean those verses are correct, current, or even universally agreed-upon. There are many translations of supposedly anti-LGBTQ passages in the Bible, and just as many interpretations of whether the Bible takes a stance on homosexuality at all.

WHAT THEY SAY: "The Bible says homosexuality is sinful."

THE ANALYSIS: There are a couple of passages in the Bible that seem to comment on men sleeping with other men. Scholars have debated these verses for years, often referring to them as anti-LGBTQ "clobber passages," and have yet to come to a consensus. For starters, their original text does not always make the verses' intentions clear. A site called Stop Bible Abuse, written by Sean Isler and published by St. John's Metropolitan Community Church in Raleigh, explains that the sheer number of translations into many languages illustrates how murky the passages are. The most literal translations don't make much sense in our current understanding of language, sexual behavior, and identity.[205]

"If translated word for word," the site explains, "Leviticus 18:22 is roughly 'You shall not lie with (adult) man beds (plural noun) a woman/wife (singular noun).' . . . Continuing the unfortunate misuse of (English) grammar, the verse could be interpreted to produce 'You shall not lie with a male [in the] beds of a woman,' which is to say that if two men are going to have sex, they cannot do it in a bed belonging to a woman, i.e., which is reserved only for heterosexual intercourse."

Rev. Martin also said in the Lifehacker interview that homosexuality isn't the only type of sexual relationship that the Bible seems to condemn. "In Church teaching, *any* sex outside of marriage is sinful," he says. "That also includes straight people who are living together before marriage, which no one seems to bat an eye at." The Bible also condemns divorce, but most conservative Christians don't judge divorced people a fraction as harshly as they do LGBTQ people. And perhaps most telling is that there are countless books, articles, and other forums debating the very issue of homosexuality in the Bible, meaning there's no universal Christian perspective on this topic.

That said, most non-Christians (atheists in particular) are probably not interested in countering the Bible with a deeper look into the Bible; after all, we don't accept the authority of any of it. Therefore, the most important non-scriptural argument to make here is questioning the intentions of Christians who tout some extreme verses of the Bible as sacrosanct while completely ignoring others. The shellfish and mixed fabrics parallel has been beaten to death, but it's still true; the Bible condemns these things too, but nobody gets up in arms about outlawing them. If your interpretation of Leviticus calls on you to support hating (or murdering) gay people, why not follow every other obscure, outdated detail in that book and the rest of the Bible, too? The answer is because it's usually not about the Bible. Rather, homophobic Christians cite the Bible as a means of justifying their bigotry, which is usually rooted in disgust.

HOW TO RESPOND: "The Bible says a lot of things, but that doesn't mean we abide by all of them. It's pretty unreasonable to selectively follow some passages of the Bible and not others —especially when the ones you're choosing are the most hateful. After all, you wouldn't execute a child who doesn't obey their parents (Exodus 21:15), would you?"

BONUS: Like all literature, the Bible is open to interpretation, and that means there's a way to find queerness in it. Some scholars have written that the Bible contained one or even two same-sex couples. In the Hebrew Book of Samuel, the heroes David and Jonathan are extremely close friends whose relationship may or may not contain notes of homoeroticism, depending on who you ask. Likewise, the story of Ruth and Naomi is one of deep love (platonic or otherwise) between two women, which some have interpreted as queer in nature. Take that, Leviticus.

WHAT THEY SAY: "Being transgender is a sin."

THE ANALYSIS: Biblical arguments against transgender people are fairly new to this debate, as trans people and trans issues have only recently come into mainstream awareness. The Bible decidedly does not say anything specifically about transgender people. Some conservatives claim that because "God made Adam and Eve," we should assume gender begins and ends at those two. And one verse, Deuteronomy 22:5, decries cross-dressing, which is not the same thing as being trans. But queer Christian scholars have said that it's a stretch to glean a condemnation of transgender people from either passage.[206]

For example, Father Shannon T.L. Kearns of Queer Theology writes: "One could make the argument that in these times the lines between 'men's' and 'women's' clothing is blurred to be pretty much meaningless. You could also make the argument that as a transgender man it would be against my nature to wear women's clothing and so therefore I am abiding by the command."

But Kearns also says that bickering about the subtext of different verses is not usually productive, and it might be more effective to focus on what the Bible *does* say about gender. "As we read throughout Scripture there is a large number of affirming passages for trans and gender non-conforming people. We find righteous women warriors, a wonderful passage in Isaiah about Eunuchs being given a name and a family, Jesus' words of affirmation towards Eunuchs, the man carrying a jar of water in the Passion narrative, the Ethiopian Eunuch in Acts, and much more."

HOW YOU RESPOND: "The Bible doesn't specifically say anything about transgender people. More importantly, it expresses support for the ways people of all genders contributed to society, and it celebrates people who don't conform to gender norms."

"Think of the Children!"

Nobody likes to be told how to raise their kids. Instead, it's wiser to encourage people to empathize with other children and families. Even people who disagree with LGBTQ "lifestyles" would probably still say they want the best for LGBTQ people's children. With enough time, hopefully everyone will agree that what's best for kids is a supportive home, a loving heart, and an open mind, no matter the genders of their parents.

WHAT THEY SAY: "Kids need a male and a female role model at home."

THE ANALYSIS: This doesn't make sense. This line of thinking implies that there are certain roles and traits that can be espoused only by a mom or a dad. That's never been true, and we've never been more aware of it than now; moms can go to work, dads can run a household, women can be outspoken and strong, and men can be sensitive and nurturing.

Shortly after Massachusetts upheld same-sex couples' right to marry in 2003, Brad Sears and Alan Hirsch, who researched sexual orientation law and policy at UCLA, penned an article for *The Village Voice* anticipating anti-gay attacks rooted in the one-mom-one-dad trope.[207] "Insisting on gender-based role modeling makes sense only if there are viable models of gender to begin with," they wrote. "We want all parents to model compassion, responsibility, independence, and good citizenship. These virtues are androgynous."

HOW YOU RESPOND: "Why? Men and women are both capable of teaching kids good values and life lessons. Raising a child is not inherently male or female. And besides, being raised by two moms doesn't mean a boy will never meet an adult man, and vice versa."

WHAT THEY SAY: "Talking about LGBTQ people with children is inappropriate."

THE ANALYSIS: Kids are coming out as LGBTQ at younger ages than ever, marriage equality has made it easier for same-sex couples to start families, and LGBTQ people have never been more present in media and pop culture. And still, this bump in visibility is a drop in the bucket compared to the images of heterosexuality that kids are bombarded with every day, from prince-and-princess fairy tales to sex-fueled commercials for body spray. Talking about LGBTQ people with kids—positively, of course—opens them to worldviews they may not have known about before. It encourages them to be kinder and more accepting. And if down the line, they realize that they fall somewhere on the LGBTQ spectrum, their lives will be infinitely easier if they've grown up around positive conversations about people like them, rather than the shameful and humiliating slander that so many previous generations endured.

HOW YOU RESPOND: "Kids should grow up learning to respect everyone, and that includes LGBTQ people. There's nothing inappropriate about being LGBTQ — even many conservative churches admit that — just like there's nothing inappropriate about a man marrying a woman or the existence of multiple genders. LGBTQ people are just like any other people that kids interact with on a daily basis. They deserve kindness and respect, from kids and from everyone else."

BONUS: Some conservative parents claim that if they tell their children about same-sex couples, their kids will ask how gay people have sex. First, this is ridiculous; no child who watches a happily-ever-hetero Disney movie is thinking about how Prince and Princess Charming get it on. Second, these conversations should always be age-appropriate. That's a given. If your kid is too young to be told about the graphic details of heterosexual sex, don't give them the specifics of gay sex, either.

WHAT THEY SAY: "Gays can't reproduce, so they shouldn't be together."

THE ANALYSIS: Welcome to the twenty-first century: People couple up for reasons other than baby-making. Relationships provide emotional support and human connection; sex can provide intimacy, an assortment of health benefits, and—we're all adults here—it's fun. Plenty of factors can keep people from having children, from health reasons and age to personal preference. The childless-by-choice life is appealing to more and more people—even Christians,[208] who are traditionally more likely to have kids than people of other faiths or the non-religious.[209] And though their bodies can't make a baby together, many same-sex couples choose to have kids in other ways, from IVF to surrogacy to adoption (say, from one of the heavily religious states with high rates of teen pregnancy).[210]

HOW YOU RESPOND: "Lots of couples can't reproduce—elderly people, infertile couples, people with assorted health conditions—and lots of people who can reproduce choose not to. We don't allow straight couples to be together based on their plans for having kids. Pinning that requirement on same-sex couples isn't fair."

WHAT THEY SAY: "Kids with gay parents have worse lives than kids with straight parents. I read a study about it!"

THE ANALYSIS: A 2012 study by sociologist Mark Regnerus claimed that being raised by a same-sex couple causes poorer outcomes in children.[211] Unfortunately for Regnerus, his research methods were irreparably flawed. An internal audit of the study from the journal that published it described it as—and I quote—"bullshit."[212] Regnerus' university later distanced itself from the study for a host of reasons.

For example: Regnerus supposedly interviewed "just under 3,000 respondents, including 175 who reported their mother having had a same-sex romantic relationship and 73 who said the same about their father." But Regnerus didn't take into consideration whether the respondents had actually been raised by a same-sex couple; he defined "lesbian mother" and "gay father" as any person who had a same-sex relationship after having a child, no matter how long the relationship lasted. (According to a scholar who examined the peer review process for Regnerus' paper after the controversy blew up, this alone should have immediately disqualified the study from publication.) Only two—literally two—respondents in the study had lived with lesbian parents for their entire childhoods.

Furthermore, the peer reviewers who accepted the paper were found to have biased connections to the research; some of them had even served as paid consultants.[213] The study stated that it was funded in part by the Witherspoon Institute and the Bradley Foundation,[214] both of which have ties to the anti-gay National Organization for Marriage.[215] Internal documents also later showed that funders wanted the study published before the Supreme Court ruled on marriage equality.[216] Luis Tellez, the president of the Witherspoon Institute, is on the record as saying that "we are confident that the traditional understanding of marriage will be vindicated by this study as long as it is done honestly and well."[217]

All of this was damning for a paper that was already under fire for its methodology. News of the paper's many faults spread quickly, and before long, hundreds of professors and medical organizations denounced it. The last straw came when the

University of Texas, where Regnerus conducted his study as a faculty member, announced it would not stand by his work.[218]

"Dr. Regnerus' opinions are his own," the school wrote in a statement.[219] "They do not reflect the views of the Sociology Department of the University of Texas at Austin. Nor do they reflect the views of the American Sociological Association, which takes the position that the conclusions he draws from his study of gay parenting are fundamentally flawed on conceptual and methodological grounds and that findings from Dr. Regnerus' work have been cited inappropriately in efforts to diminish the civil rights and legitimacy of LBGTQ [sic] partners and their families."

Conservatives continue to use the Regnerus study as a means of arguing against same-sex marriage and families, but the claim lacks any credibility. As for the *real* data behind the issue: Studies both preceding and following Regnerus' failed attempt at science have found the *opposite* conclusion to be true: the children of same-sex parents do *just as well* physically, mentally, and emotionally as kids with a mom and a dad.[220] Case closed.

HOW YOU RESPOND: "You must be referring to the study by Mark Regnerus! That study was debunked so many times and by so many people that the researcher's own university formally distanced itself from the project. In fact, plenty of scientifically sound studies have shown that kids do just as well with same-sex parents as they do with a mom and dad."

WHAT THEY SAY: "The Gay Agenda is trying to convert my child!"

THE ANALYSIS: There's a famous saying that turns the Gay Agenda conspiracy on its head: "If you don't like gay marriage, blame straight people. They're the ones who keep having gay babies." Truly, you don't need a scientific study to know that most LGBTQ kids come from straight parents. While science hasn't nailed down the precise balance of nature and nurture that determines your sexual orientation, the consensus is that it's not a choice, and it's definitely not based on who your parents are. You can't "convert" a child from gay to straight through therapy, and you can't convert them from straight to gay with repeated exposure to the Village People. It just doesn't work that way.

And on that pesky Gay Agenda that everyone keeps talking about—I'm not going to tell you such an agenda doesn't exist, because it totally does. It's just not the one radical conservatives are telling you about. The basic Gay Agenda is pretty damn American, despite how many traditionalists are terrified of it: like our forefathers, all we want is life, liberty, and the pursuit of happiness. We want to be able to walk down the streets safely, go to work and school and the doctor's office as our real selves without fear, love our partners and grow our families in whatever way works for us, exist in public knowing we won't be hurt or harassed or ushered out of a restaurant bathroom, and generally be left alone to do our thing.

The LGBTQ rights movement is fueled by an infinite number of people, identities, and life experiences. We hardly agree on whether there is a singular Agenda at all, but we *can* agree that we all deserve to be treated with respect and kindness, no matter how we identify. (And truthfully, it doesn't matter to us whether your kid is gay or straight.)

HOW YOU RESPOND: "That is neither possible nor useful. It is physiologically impossible to convert a child to any sexual orientation or gender identity; they are the way they are, and that's that. The only Gay Agenda I know of is the movement of people fighting for equal opportunities, justice, and the right to live their lives peacefully and free from harm or stigma. Anyone can support that cause, whether they're gay or not."

"It's a Sickness!"

By definition, illness is unhealthy, and it can often be prevented, treated, or cured. Being LGBTQ doesn't fall into any of those categories. Some hard-right religious conservatives can't imagine what it would be like to be LGBTQ, so they jump to the idea that it's a horrible disease they're lucky enough not to have caught. Not quite.

WHAT THEY SAY: "Being LGBTQ is a mental illness."

THE ANALYSIS: Homosexuality was included in the DSM
—the *Diagnostic and Statistical Manual of Mental Disorders*, a
routinely revised guidebook published by the American Psychiatric Association defining criteria for different mental illnesses—until 1973. The other APA, the American Psychological Association, announced their support for the removal of the
classification two years later. "Homosexuality per se implies
no impairment in judgment, reliability or general social and
vocational capabilities," they wrote at the time, "[and mental
health professionals should] take the lead in removing the stigma of mental illness that has long associated with homosexual
orientation."[221]

The history of the mental classification of transgender people is more complicated. For years, transgender identity was
listed in the DSM under "gender identity disorder."[222] A GID
diagnosis meant that a person identified with a gender other
than the one they were assigned at birth; simply being trans
was enough to be classified as having GID. But in 2013, the
DSM removed the listing for GID and replaced it with "gender
dysphoria," which pathologizes not trans identity itself, but the
distress that sometimes (but not always) accompanies it.

This was an important moment because it created a distinction between identity and experiences, an unusual approach for
the DSM. In an article for *LiveScience* about the change, science
journalist Wynne Parry wrote that when a person is depressed,
their unhappiness is a symptom of that depression. The DSM's
new description turns that pattern on its head, Parry wrote.
Transgender people's distress is not a side effect of being trans,
but of the societal stigma, pressure, and discrimination that
trans people face and may internalize. LGBTQ people do face
disproportionate rates of mental illness and suicide, but again,
these effects are not caused by their identities; they're linked to
high rates of discrimination and bias that LGBTQ people must
often endure.[223]

To make a long story short: Reputable medical associations
agree that being LGBTQ is not a mental illness. Any distress
that accompanies it isn't because of a person's *identity*; it's because of the societal forces that continue to tell LGBTQ people
there's something wrong with them.

HOW YOU RESPOND: "Major medical associations would disagree with that point. Being LGBTQ doesn't cause harm to that person or anyone else, it doesn't require any treatment, and it doesn't get in the way of a happy, healthy, productive life."

WHAT THEY SAY: "Transgender people are delusional."

THE ANALYSIS: Again, widespread data collection on transgender people is pretty new. But the research we have so far indicates that, yes, being trans is a real thing. In 2013, researchers in Spain found that transgender people's brain structures more closely resembled the brains of people with their gender identity than of the gender they were assigned at birth.[224] Another study from 2016 found positive mental health outcomes for trans kids whose families supported them in their transition.[225]

Lead by Dr. Laura Case, researchers at the University of California, San Diego looked at the real-time experience of gender dysphoria, or the feeling that your body doesn't match who you are.[226] Case's team conducted an experiment where they consensually tapped the upper breasts of transgender men and nonbinary individuals who wanted to remove their breasts surgically and measured their brain activity at the same time. Compared with cisgender women who went through the same procedure, the transgender men and nonbinary people had a rapid, reduced response in the part of the brain that distinguishes between the self and others. "The brain is not identifying this sensation as 'me' as much as it is other parts of the body—and it's alarmed by it," Case told the *Daily Beast* in 2017.

In the study, Case also noted that it may not be worth it to try to narrow down transgender identity to a science, writing that "scientific reductionism is unlikely to yield a simple explanation for a phenomenon as complex as gender identity." But what this and other preliminary research does suggest is that trans people aren't "faking it," and that they fare much better when embracing their true selves.

Finally, while research helps us to contextualize and "prove" this information, we should never discount the validity of simply listening to and trusting transgender people's experiences and accounts. Research is an extremely valuable tool, and it should serve as another way to amplify the voices of transgender people.

HOW YOU RESPOND: "Plenty of research has shown that being transgender is a valid identity, and that trans people are the healthiest and happiest when society allows them to live as the gender with which they identify. And besides, if they aren't hurting anyone, who are we to decide how someone else should live?"

WHAT THEY SAY: "Sexual orientation can be changed through therapy, especially when you're young."

THE ANALYSIS: This is one of the most dangerous myths out there, and it's still perpetuated by countless conservatives across religions even though it is entirely false. Conversion therapy, also known as reparative therapy or ex-gay therapy, involves using a range of tactics to try to "change" a person's sexual orientation or gender identity (though the latter happens less frequently). Conversion therapy methods can include a medley of cognitive, behavioral, and psychoanalytic techniques.[227] Some of the most violent forms of conversion therapy have included aversive conditioning, like inducing electric shocks, vomiting, or other types of pain while showing patients homoerotic images.

Conversion therapy is commonly thought of as a form of abuse, and it can lead to horrible outcomes for patients, especially youth. A 2009 report by the American Psychiatric Association found that undergoing conversion therapy can increase risks of depression, substance abuse, and suicidality. That means parents who force their kids into conversion therapy overlook the possibility that their child will *die* for an unsubstantiated promise of a "normal" kid. The APA has also said that there's no reason to believe conversion therapy works. And it should go without saying that even if it did work, it would *still* be cruel; there's nothing wrong with being LGBTQ, and there's no excuse to put someone through that kind of physical, psychological torment, especially a child who's at the will of their parents' decision.

Upwards of a dozen major medical and youth organizations have taken public stances against conversion therapy. A handful of states and localities ban conversion therapy, and more have similar bills in the works. Personal accounts of people who have experienced conversion therapy are gut-wrenching to read. Sexual orientation cannot be changed through conversion therapy, and it's time we stopped trying.

HOW YOU RESPOND: "I'm concerned that you think so. Conversion therapy is considered harmful, unethical, and ineffective by virtually every major medical organization in the country. Its tactics are tantamount to abuse or even torture, especially for kids. There's nothing wrong with being LGBTQ, so conversion therapy is actually just a violent way of trying—and failing—to solve a nonexistent problem."

"First Amendment! First Amendment!"

Ever since the early rumblings of the movement for marriage equality, religious conservatives have looked for a way to opt out. Citing the First Amendment, they claim that society's slow-growing respect for LGBTQ people is a violation of their rights to religious freedom. The irony is that nobody has asked them to disavow their religion and embrace marriage equality or other LGBTQ rights—nothing about our personal rights to belief and expression has changed. As the saying goes, "If you don't like gay marriage, don't get gay married."

However, we still have to follow the law, even if we don't agree with it. If your business provides services for weddings, you must provide those services equitably to all engaged couples. If you treat customers differently based on their gender identity, that is discrimination. And if society calls you out for being a homophobe, that's not a First Amendment violation; it's just deserts.

WHAT THEY SAY: "Same-sex marriage suppresses religious freedom."

THE ANALYSIS: Religious officials have never been and will never be forced to participate in same-sex marriages if they don't want to. Secular institutions (like, say, the government) are a different story—if you're working with the public, you have to treat everyone in the public equally. It's that simple.

HOW YOU RESPOND: "Whose religious freedom is being oppressed? If you have a religious opposition to marriage equality, you don't have to personally accept it. But not everyone shares your beliefs. You wouldn't want to be forced to change your life based on someone else's religion; LGBTQ people shouldn't be treated differently because of beliefs they don't subscribe to."

WHAT THEY SAY: "People have the right to run their businesses however they want, even if that means discriminating against LGBTQ people."

THE ANALYSIS: The Civil Rights Act of 1964 bans privately-owned places of public accommodation—restaurants, stores, banks, etc.—from refusing service to people on the basis of their race, color, religion or national origin.[228] Unfortunately, there is not yet a federal law preventing such discrimination against LGBTQ people. As of this writing, about 20 states and many cities and localities have their own non-discrimination laws.[229]

The gist of these laws is that you can't treat customers differently based on who they are; as a public-facing business, you must provide the same services to all your customers. Contrary to what Breitbart headlines might suggest, there's no such thing as a "gay wedding cake." It's just a wedding cake; if you sell it to different-sex couples, you have to sell it to same-sex couples, too. A business owner who feels so strongly about the issue that she'd change her business model can stop selling wedding cakes altogether to avoid the "problem" of same-sex couples asking for them. Privately, you can believe anything you want. Publicly, you have to play by the rules.

In states that haven't yet banned public accommodations discrimination, it's still a good idea not to discriminate against any customers. If a customer sues, victories in recent legal cases suggest the discriminatory business owner is likely to lose. Word travels fast when it comes to LGBTQ people being mistreated in public, and anybody can leave a Yelp review trashing a business with a homophobic reputation. The First Amendment doesn't protect you from the reactions of citizens who disagree with your bigotry. Plus, treating everyone with kindness is the right thing to do. Isn't *that* in the Bible somewhere?

HOW YOU RESPOND: "People have the right to their own private beliefs, but anyone operating a business that's open to the public is required to follow non-discrimination laws while on the job. Working with the public means you agree to treat members of the public equally; to do otherwise is unkind and unfair."

"It's Just Icky"

Okay, maybe this isn't explicitly faith-based. But it's not uncommon for people to claim religious opposition to LGBTQ rights when what they really mean is they think it's gross. If you suspect that's what's going on, don't be surprised if one of these cop-out answers comes up, too.

WHAT THEY SAY: "It's just not natural."

THE ANALYSIS: If it happens naturally, it's natural. Full stop.

LGBTQ people don't choose our identities. There's no exam or application; no spreadsheet to map the costs and benefits; no fingers crossed that you'll get a letter from an owl on your 11th birthday. Every person realizes it differently, at a different time, and through a different process. Most of us accept it and keep living our lives. That's the definition of something happening naturally. For those who say that homosexuality is man-made (perhaps as part of that same Gay Agenda), that's also incorrect. Same-sex mating and pairing behaviors have been seen in more than 1,500 animal species—though that's not necessarily the best way to convince a homophobe that we deserve equal rights.[230]

Ultimately, though, the argument about whether it's "natural" isn't the right one. We respect people who belong to a different faith than the one in which they were born. We accept people who wear eyeglasses and dye their hair and wear sunscreen and get tattoos, even though none of these things are natural. It shouldn't matter where a person's unique traits come from. Our true selves ebb and flow over time; some parts of ourselves have been there all along and others show up with time and experience. Being LGBTQ is something that most of us believe happens naturally. But even if it didn't, it would still be worth respecting.

HOW YOU RESPOND: "Why not? It occurs naturally; nobody does anything to 'become' LGBTQ. Some people are left-handed or red-headed. Those things aren't unnatural; they're uncommon. There's a difference."

WHAT THEY SAY: "I guess you can be gay, but you don't have to shove it down our throats."

THE ANALYSIS: Aside from the sweet irony of buttoned-up conservatives using the phrase "shove down our throats," this argument is no better than telling LGBTQ people that we shouldn't exist at all. Telling someone they can be LGBTQ as long as they're quiet about it enforces that there's something to be ashamed of. It tells us that we're not worthy of being seen in public.

If anything is being "shoved down our throats," it's heterosexuality. Virtually every fairy tale, cartoon character, and sitcom family is headed by a straight couple (or a single parent who used to be part of one). But the minute a Disney Channel show included one lesbian couple—several years after the legalization of same-sex marriage, no less—some conservatives flipped out and accused the network of "pushing an agenda."[231] (Decades of programming featuring only straight people sounds way more like an "agenda" to me.)

LGBTQ people have existed for as long as people have existed. For much of that time, we've been at best overlooked and at worst violently erased. After all this time, we deserve to do what straight people have always had the right to do—kiss in public, wear the clothes that make us feel good, hold our partner's hand without fear. If those basic activities feel like homosexuality is being shoved down your throat, find a way to adjust your gag reflex.

HOW YOU RESPOND: "What do you mean by that? It's hardly forcing anything to allow LGBTQ people to be seen and acknowledged in public; that's a pretty basic right. Straight people are everywhere—we see countless images of straight people, straight couples, and straight families every day. Why shouldn't LGBTQ people be allowed the same public visibility that straight people are?"

 voices   **Audrey White**

When I started polling my personal networks for stories about faith and LGBTQ identity, there was one person I was hoping would want to participate, and I was in luck. I'm fortunate to know someone like Audrey White, a brilliant, queer twenty-something in Texas who grew up in and still belongs to the Presbyterian church. Audrey, who uses the singular pronoun "they," is a writer who frequently covers LGBTQ topics like bisexuality, gender, and the overlaps between queerness and religion. I was eager to talk to them in my research for this book, and as expected, I learned a lot in our exchange.

What has your experience as a queer person of faith been like overall? Have you ever faced any kind of pushback from religious circles for being queer or from queer circles for being religious?

I have had a relatively positive experience being a queer person of faith. Growing up, I never heard anyone at my church say anything negative about LGBTQ people, and I think I always instinctively knew that religious justifications for homo-, bi-, and transphobic violence and discrimination weren't theologically sound. They didn't sound like the Gospel I knew. I definitely absorbed some of the hatred and discrimination from the larger church and from publicly anti-gay Christians, but once I came out I let all that poison seep away. I wouldn't say I have experienced pushback from queer friends for being a person of faith, but I rarely bring up my faith in queer spaces unless they are specifically queer Christian spaces. If my queer friends say things or make jokes that are anti-Christianity, I'm certainly not going to correct them—usually they have a point.

I actually am reckoning with the question of how to openly be a person of faith among queer and trans people who have been harmed and oppressed by Christians and churches, because the last thing I want to do is bring up bad memories or fears for other people. However, among my friends I will speak openly about teaching Sunday School and positive experiences I have with my faith. I think one of the most productive things I can do is demonstrate that faith is a positive part of my life and demonstrate Christ's love in my life by being a loving, compassionate, radical person in struggle and solidarity with queer and trans people, people of color, poor people, women seeking reproductive care, and other people who are oppressed by the church.

How do you reckon with moments where religion is used to oppress LGBTQ people? For example, what's your response to folks citing the Bible as a means of anti-LGBTQ persecution?

I'm just so over it. I know I can't be "over it" because it is still actively happening, but I have worked so hard to ground myself in affirming, queer and radical theologies that I have very little patience for oppressive and homophobic theologies. The reality is, scripture is a tool that can be used in many ways. It's funny, conservative Christians want to accuse queer-and-trans-affirming Christians of cherry picking the parts of the Bible that we like, but they do the exact same thing—their cherry-picking is just mainstreamed so they can pretend that's not what they are doing. Everyone seeks scripture and theology that feels affirming, inspiring and relevant to our individual selves and communities. I am pretty open to hearing diverse interpretations of scripture, but [Robert Jones, Jr.'s] famous quote comes to mind: "We can disagree and still love each other unless your disagreement is rooted in my oppression and denial of my humanity and right to exist."

In what ways are your LGBTQ and faith identities connected, if any? Are there ways they strengthen or complement one another?

My queer and Christian identities are absolutely and intrinsically linked. I believe that I am a beloved creation, fearfully and wonderfully made. My queerness is a fundamental part of my experience as a human being, so that means my queerness is a beloved part of me in God's eyes. Both my queerness and my faith push me to work for justice, to center myself in love, and to destroy man-made systems that oppress people and deny us the right to live into the fullness of God's promises for us.

Do you see a role for atheists in the LGBTQ rights movement, whether or not they identify as queer?

I believe that everyone who is willing to center queer and trans people, especially trans women of color, in their work for LGBTQ rights has a place in the movement. Of course someone's faith or atheism is going to drastically inform their worldview, and those identities may inform the approaches, context or specific work. For example, because I am a Christian, I plan to get a dual masters in divinity (so, I'll go to seminary) and social work with the goal of working with queer and trans people who are being harmed by the church. For example, I might become a caseworker who works with conservative Christian parents of queer and trans youth to help provide logistical, material and theological assistance so those homes can become stable for the youth and reduce instances of homelessness. My Christian background makes me uniquely positioned to do that kind of work. And if atheists feel similarly inspired and equipped to be in struggle with queer and trans people, then I hope they will absolutely join us!

What Comes Next?

The Future Is . . . Sometime

IN THE fall of 2014, when judges were striking down one same-sex marriage ban after another with unprecedented momentum, my friend Brian posted something on Facebook along the lines of "How long until it's legalized nationwide? Now taking bets." An assortment of his friends chimed in with guesses, some genuine and some facetious. "Two weeks." "A year." "A few more months, probably." "Never."

It didn't seem possible. When my then-girlfriend and I had first daydreamed about getting married, it wasn't legal yet in Illinois, where we met, or Florida, where we'd both grown up. She moved all over the South as a kid, and we talked about how we could never go back there once we were married because our rights wouldn't be guaranteed. If we had to rush our future child to the hospital, one of us might be denied entry. If something happened to one of us, they might not believe us when we said we were a family. It wasn't worth it.

Then marriage equality happened, and it didn't fix everything, but it made us feel like we'd gotten a little closer. The sea of red and pink equal sign profile pictures as the decision loomed almost made it feel like we were reaching a turning point, like maybe it would be smooth sailing from here on out. But that would have been naïve. The anti-equality crowd came out in full force after the decision, spurred by the enormity of their setback. Some of them gave up and moved onto the next battle, but others continued to attack marriage equality, many under the guise of religion.

And the thing is, we're still not equal. Far from it. In nearly two dozen states, it's still legal to fire someone for being LGBTQ. Religious conservatives are fighting mercilessly to defend conversion therapy.[232] As many as 40% of homeless youth are LGBTQ. Transgender women of color are being murdered in the streets at all-time high rates. Some of the most powerful people in the country believe—and say as much out loud—that we are fundamentally lesser than everyone else. If secularism is meant to champion reason, equality, and morality, why should secular Americans accept a world in which elected officials call us subhuman and get away with it? (Republican State Rep. Rick Brattin of Harrisonville, Missouri said on May 8, 2017, "When you look at the tenets of religion, of the Bible, of the Quran, of other religions, there is a distinction between homosexuality and just being a human being." He didn't apologize for implying LGBTQ people weren't fully human and has so far kept his job.)

Looking to history doesn't offer much comfort either. The Civil Rights Act was passed half a century ago, but institutional racism thrives even at the highest levels of government. Women are still fighting for equal treatment under the law, from the wage gap to simple bodily autonomy, and yet the president of the United States is on record saying of women that "you have to treat 'em like shit." Legislation and time have not eradicated the long-held prejudices that render women and people of color societal underdogs, and there's no guarantee that the steps we've taken toward LGBTQ equality will enact lasting changes in attitude, either. As of this writing, many of the laws and ordinances discussed in this book face uncertain futures, with LGBTQ people not knowing whether their rights to live and work freely will ever be restored. HB2 in North Carolina was replaced with a version that still doesn't protect LGBTQ people against discrimination. Houston doesn't have a new non-discrimination ordinance to replace HERO. More than a hundred anti-LGBTQ laws were on the docket in dozens of states as of early 2017.[233]

It's idealistic to think that LGBTQ people, religious minorities (including atheists), and others who are disadvantaged under the current system will ever be considered fully equal by the people at the top. Centuries of evidence suggest it can't be done. Even being LGBTQ doesn't preclude you from being a bigot; see, for example, the gay Republicans who spent a luxurious night in New York mercilessly mocking transgender women,[234] or the well-documented examples of racism permeating some LGBTQ community spaces.[235] (It seems LGBTQ people still have work to do in our own circles, and perhaps we always will.)

But that doesn't mean we aren't making progress toward that lofty goal. Every inch forward makes someone's life better, even if isn't enough to eradicate inequality and save the world entirely. LGBTQ-inclusive laws aren't thrown together in vain as a "politically correct" gesture; they have a measurably positive impact on real lives—and therefore on society at large.

A handful of examples: Some states and adoption networks don't allow unmarried couples to jointly adopt children.[236] That means marriage equality makes it easier for same-sex couples to give kids in need a loving home. Being allowed to transition leads to better mental health outcomes for transgender kids.[237] That means trans-inclusive school policies make it a lot easier for them to be their happiest, healthiest selves. Bias and discrimination are linked to worse physical and mental health for LGBTQ adults, too, and some (transgender people especially) are likely to avoid public places for fear of how they may be treated.[238] How can someone be a productive, tax-paying, economy-stimulating member of society if they're terrified about where to pee?

Atheists have a history of staring down discriminatory laws and negative associations, too. Throughout this book, we've seen examples of atheists facing aggressive distrust and resentment from large swaths of the population, even though the majority of laws that targeted us are long gone. Societal prejudices against atheists continue to this day. We've dealt with this kind of treatment for ages. We should understand and defend those who face it now.

There are religious conservatives who will tell you that the changes brought on by inclusive laws are a bad thing—that it's better for children to be shuffled around foster homes than settled with parents who love them, or better for transgender people to live miserably in one gender than happily in another. (Remember that these and other LGBTQ civil rights do not harm *anybody*—not the kids, not disapproving adults, not the sanctity of marriage, not religious freedom. There are literally no cons—just some life-changing pros.) Those people are allowed their beliefs, but their lack of compassion is astounding.

And if one day, we live in a world where it really is okay to be gay, we may still find ourselves defending the civil rights of minority groups. In the 2016 election, for example, LGBTQ people didn't bear the worst of conservative bigotry; that ire was aimed primarily at immigrants or those perceived to be immigrants, especially Mexicans and Muslims. If the United States is consistent about anything, it's our ability to scapegoat, to find a group we despise and somehow blame them for the decline of civilization. Maybe one day we will have a president who's an atheist, LGBTQ, or both, but it's incredibly likely that old prejudices will remain (Obama's election certainly didn't signal the end of racism), and others will have risen to new prominence.

Though more progressive people of faith are coming out of the woodwork, organized religion still has the power to harm. It isn't going away anytime soon. Even still, atheists' and LGBTQ people's allyship with one another shouldn't be based on the severity of the injustices we face. As groups with up-close-and-personal knowledge of how bigotry—faith-based and otherwise—can inflict unfathomable pain, it's on us to carry that understanding into future generations. We'll never forget those who called us and our families less than human, or the lawmakers who suggested our existence was an affront to society. Even if "it gets better" one day, we'll remember how it used to be. Let's use our unique, overlapping history to call out injustice when we see it and do everything we can to stop it. Let's teach our kids and their kids about what we and our forebears lived and died through. We can't promise them it will never happen again, but we can swear to them that we won't sit quietly by and watch.

I was wrapping up an interview for this book when the person I was talking to asked me a question: What was the most interesting thing I had learned throughout this process? I couldn't narrow it down. Virtually everyone I spoke to had something fascinating to say, and I learned something from everyone. I'm an atheist, but not hyper-involved in the atheist world, and so I don't think about social justice issues from an atheist lens as often as some others do. Similarly, I'm very involved in the LGBTQ movement, but I have no personal experience seriously navigating religion as a queer person. Even with the knowledge I had coming into this project, I had a lot to learn.

One thing I noticed right away is how so many of us feel like we have something to defend—our religion or lack thereof, our gender identity, who we love, how we dress, whether and how we participates in politics. People across faiths, genders, and sexual orientations sometimes speak about those identities assuming someone in the audience opposes their very right to live that way. For many of us, that instinct comes from experience. Every one of us who belongs to a marginalized group—atheist, LGBTQ, queer person of faith, person of color, a member of a minority religion—has likely had to do some amount of advocating for their humanity. Some experience it more harshly than others, but when it comes down to it, that's exactly what coming out is: telling the world you're something other than what they might have believed, and making the case for why you're still worth loving.

It's also fascinating—and at times heartbreaking—to consider how our confidence and comfort levels have changed so drastically in the course of a couple of months, and how they will continue to do so with each and every tumultuous news day. I started writing this book when Barack Obama was in the White House and finished it in the first few months of Donald Trump's presidency. (And by the time you read it, who knows?) In that time, we've seen policies on religious freedom, LGBTQ equality, and other social issues introduced, struck down, challenged in court, and protested in the streets. It took all of one early morning tweet to put the inclusion of transgender people in the military in serious doubt. Key statistics have changed between when I started and finished this project (which made the editing process tons of fun), and I'm sure that it won't be long before many of the numbers in this book are hopelessly outdated. Still, I hope this book has provided more than just a comparison of data. Like I said earlier, personal lived experiences are much more telling of what the world is like, and those memories stick with us even when statistics change.

More than anything, I'm amazed at the different ways people express themselves, and I'm grateful that so many people shared those pieces of themselves with me. There are perhaps no expressions of the self more intimate than who we love and how we believe. These truths guide every decision we make and inform how we move in the world; they can steer our sense of morality, determine the people with whom we surround ourselves, and force us to make hard choices about what we'll sacrifice to build a life that's most meaningful. Our beliefs ground us and our loved ones lift us up. It's hard to fathom our sense of self without them, and there's immense power in sharing them with the world around us.

I hope that we're advancing toward a society where these differences are celebrated, not shamed, though there is evidence that suggests the opposite. In the dawn of the Trump administration, we're certainly on the cusp of some sweeping social changes, though it's too soon to tell whether they'll be revolutionary or reactionary. It's easy to repeat the call to "be the change you wish to see in the world" during uncertain times, and much harder to follow through on it. But complacency is no longer an option. Now is our moment to model the world we want to live in, the world we want to leave behind, the world we wish we'd had all along.

Parting Words

The stories and ideas I heard in researching this book can't be summed up in one inspirational sentence or pithy catchphrase. It wouldn't make sense if they did. Identity is not one-size-fits-all, and while the people I talked with were all generally committed to the well-being of their fellow person, all had different reasons for wanting to do good.

In an earlier chapter, I spoke with Audrey White, the queer Christian writer who attributed their commitment to activism partially to their faith. "Both my queerness and my faith push me to work for justice, to center myself in love, and to destroy man-made systems that oppress people and deny us the right to live into the fullness of God's promises for us," Audrey said. So, too, is the case for many LGBTQ Christians and other socially progressive people of faith.

I think back to what Sincere Kirabo, the social justice co-ordinator for the American Humanist Association, said to me about the AHA's stance on social justice causes like LGBTQ rights: "Humanist philosophy is little more than feel-good rhetoric if its ideas aren't implemented to engage in social change actions that improve unjust conditions within society that negatively impact quality of life."

And finally, there's Katie, one Unitarian Universalist I spoke with, who had a simple answer for why atheists should support LGBTQ people. "Should they participate solely because they are atheist? No. Should they participate because respect and compassion for all human beings is the right thing to do? Yes."

I imagine most readers of this book will identify more with the latter two statements than the first one, but maybe not. I don't know you. Your beliefs and values are yours alone. You can be a force for good in the world regardless of where you come from and what you believe.

What I do hope you've taken away is this: The number of ways you can infuse kindness into the world is impossibly high. We can all find the space to be better to one another, push back against abuses of power and privilege, and reach out to support those around us in times of crisis and calm alike. Take the time to figure out how you can best make the world a little friendlier for the people around you, and all our communities will be better for it. That's worth believing.

Resources and Further Reading

The following is a list of organizations, campaigns, and other resources where you can learn more about LGBTQ issues and how they overlap with (non)belief. This is only a small selection of the hundreds of groups working on the ground to make it better; for local opportunities, reaching out to your nearest LGBTQ community center is always a good place to start. Each group's description below is in its own words.

Atheist, Humanist, and Secular Organizations

American Atheists is the premier organization fighting for the civil liberties of atheists and the total, absolute separation of government and religion. atheists.org

The **American Humanist Association** stands as the voice of humanism in the United States, striving to bring about a progressive society where being good without a god is an accepted and respected way to live life. americanhumanist.org

Black Nonbelievers is a non-profit fellowship of nonbelievers headquartered in the Atlanta area that is dedicated to providing an informative, caring, festive and friendly community. blacknonbelievers.wordpress.com

The **Center for Inquiry** strives to foster a secular society based on reason, science, freedom of inquiry, and humanist values. centerforinquiry.net

Ex-Muslims of North America advocates for acceptance of religious dissent, promotes secular values, and aims to reduce discrimination faced by those who leave Islam. exmna.org

Foundation Beyond Belief is a humanist charity that promotes secular volunteering and responsible charitable giving. foundationbeyondbelief.org

The **Freedom From Religion Foundation** is the nation's largest association of freethinkers (atheists, agnostics) and has been working since 1978 to keep religion and government separate. ffrf.org

Hispanic American Freethinkers is a non-profit educational organization serving as a resource and support to all Hispanic freethinkers. hafree.org

The **Secular Coalition for America** is a nonprofit advocacy organization dedicated to amplifying the diverse and growing voice of the nontheistic community in the United States. secular.org

The **Secular Student Alliance** empowers secular students to proudly express their identity, build welcoming communities, promote secular values, and set a course for lifelong activism. secularstudents.org

The **UU Humanist Association** strives to promote and extend the use of rational inquiry without supernatural considerations, followed by compassionate action in all human interactions. huumanists.org

LGBTQ Organizations

Believe Out Loud is an online community that empowers Christians to work for justice for lesbian, gay, bisexual, transgender, queer, intersex, and asexual (LGBTQIA) people. believeoutloud.com

BiNet USA is America's oldest advocacy organization for bisexual, pansexual, fluid, queer-identified and unlabeled people. binetusa.org

CenterLink is the community of LGBTQ centers, existing to support the development of strong, sustainable LGBTQ community centers and build a unified center movement. lgbtcenters.org

Family Equality Council connects, supports, and represents the three million parents who are lesbian, gay, bisexual, transgender and queer in this country and their six million children. familyequality.org

GLAAD is the world's largest LGBTQ media advocacy organization, tackling tough issues to shape the narrative and provoke dialogue that leads to cultural change. glaad.org

GLSEN creates safe and affirming K-12 schools for all students, working to ensure that LGBTQ students are able to learn and grow in a school environment free from bullying and harassment. glsen.org

The **Human Rights Campaign** is the largest national lesbian, gay, bisexual, transgender and queer civil rights organization in the country. hrc.org

Keshet is a national organization that works for full LGBTQ equality and inclusion in Jewish life. keshetonline.org

Lambda Legal is a national organization committed to achieving full recognition of the civil rights of lesbians, gay men, bisexuals, transgender people and everyone living with HIV through impact litigation, education and public policy work. lambdalegal.org

Lambda Literary believes lesbian, gay, bisexual, transgender and queer literature is fundamental to the preservation of our culture, and that LGBTQ lives are affirmed when our stories are written, published and read. lambdaliterary.org

The **LGBTQ Humanist Alliance** is an extension of the American Humanist Association that operates at the intersection of humanism and social justice to advocate humanist education, LGBTQ cultural competency, and community outreach. lgbthumanists.org

The **National Center for Lesbian Rights** (NCLR) has been advancing the civil and human rights of lesbian, gay, bisexual, and transgender people and their families through litigation, legislation, policy, and public education since it was founded in 1977. nclrights.org

The **National Center for Transgender Equality** is the nation's leading social justice advocacy organization winning life-saving change for transgender people. transequality.org

The **National LGBTQ Task Force,** the country's oldest national LGBTQ advocacy group, advances full freedom, justice and equality for LGBTQ people. thetaskforce.org

Out & Equal Workplace Advocates is the world's premier nonprofit organization dedicated to achieving lesbian, gay, bisexual, and transgender workplace equality. outandequal.org

OutServe-SLDN is the association for actively serving LGBT military personnel and veterans, a non-partisan, non-profit, legal services, watchdog and policy organization dedicated to bringing about full LGBT equality to America's military and ending all forms of discrimination and harassment of military personnel on the basis of sexual orientation and gender identity. outserve-sldn.org

PFLAG unites people who are lesbian, gay, bisexual, transgender, and queer with families, friends and allies. pflag.org

Services & Advocacy for GLBT Elders (SAGE) is the country's largest and oldest organization dedicated to improving the lives of lesbian, gay, bisexual and transgender (LGBT) older adults. sageusa.org

The **Sylvia Rivera Law Project** works to guarantee that all people are free to self-determine their gender identity and expression, regardless of income or race, and without facing harassment, discrimination, or violence. srlp.org

Trans Lifeline is a non-profit dedicated to the well being of transgender people, including a hotline staffed by transgender people for transgender people. translifeline.org

Trans Women of Color Collective (TWOCC) is a national organizing collective led by trans women of color created to uplift the narratives, leadership, and lived experiences of trans and gender non conforming people of color. twocc.us

Transgender Law Center works to change law, policy, and attitudes so that all people can live safely, authentically, and free from discrimination regardless of their gender identity or expression. transgenderlawcenter.org

The **Trevor Project** is the leading national organization providing crisis intervention and suicide prevention services to lesbian, gay, bisexual, transgender, and questioning (LGBTQ) young people ages 13-24. thetrevorproject.org

Acknowledgments

"The doing is the thing. The talking and worrying and thinking is not the thing. That is what I know. Writing the book is about writing the book." —Amy Poehler, "Yes Please"

I am a worrier and a thinker, and it's a miracle I let myself finish this book at all. I am indebted to the brilliant Amy Poehler for writing the mantra above, which kept me going when I thought I could never possibly write this book the way I wanted to. A few words of thanks for those who kept me motivated throughout that long, sometimes grueling process:

Kaitlyn, for your endless love, for keeping me grounded, for taking care of me, and for holding onto my too-big dreams when I feel like letting them go. I can't believe I get to marry you. And I can't wait to edit the next one together.

My mom, for being my first editor and fiercest champion; my dad, for the boundless optimism and cheerleading; my brother, for making me a better person every day; and my grandmother, who asked to read my writing long after she stopped reading books.

Hemant, for being a supportive editor, collaborator, idea-bouncer-offer, and the most patient person in the world. Absolutely none of this would have been possible without you.

Tracey and Arthur, for your creative genius and immense support in putting the final product together.

Gabby, for being a mentor and role model in all things creative, change-making, and community-building. Also for the bacon, egg, and cheese bagels. Forever work wives.

Shirley, for asking how the book was going every single time we crossed paths over the course of a year and a half. You held me accountable in the best possible way.

Lexi, Claire, and Stephanie, for really and truly believing I could do it and reminding me to be proud of myself. Meghan and Nathan, for pet play dates, constant encouragement, and day-making group texts. Brian, an A+ boss, creative collaborator, and friend. Christine, for asking great big questions that made the book better in the eleventh hour.

The teachers and professors who taught me to research, interview, write, edit, and tweet my heart out: Marcus, Ms. C., Nannis, Michele, Doug, Shonali. You're the greatest.

Every person who checked in throughout this process and offered their support, kind words, interested questions, and the occasional snack or drink; there are too many of you to name, and I am impossibly lucky for it.

I owe so much to the dozens of people who lent their stories to this project, sharing details of themselves we so often reserve only for our trusted confidantes. Talking to all of you showed me what community and love really look like, and you added insights I could never have come up with on my own. Thank you. A bonus shout-out to everyone who put me in touch with their friends (or friends-of-friends, or friends-of-friends-of-friends...) in order to add more voices to the book. I'm so grateful.

Finally, we couldn't have realized this project without the support of hundreds of backers on Kickstarter, whose confidence and generosity made all the difference. Thank you to those donors who gave at the $100 level or more: AJ Strauman; Alan L. Hann; Alice Ashton; Alice Cichon; Allen H. Leung; Brandon D. Conley; Brian G. Murphy; Bruce Lang; Cameron Crombie; Catherine and Jack; David Compton, MD; Don D.; Dr. Jon Cleland Host; Gideon Laungayan; Guest 1068172091; Jake Martinez; Jeff Mackey; Jonas S. Green; Joseph R. Benke; Linda Yancey; Michael Cahill; Rift Vegan; Robert Dillenbeck; Tessa Juste; Thomas Shaffer; and Tyler Williams. We are so grateful.

This has been nothing shy of an adventure. I hope it's the first of many.

References

Introduction

1. McKinley, Jesse, and Kirk Johnson. "Mormons Tipped Scale in Ban on Gay Marriage." *The New York Times.* November 14, 2008. Accessed August 12, 2017. http://www.nytimes.com/2008/11/15/us/politics/15marriage.html

2. Campbell, David E., John C. Green, and J. Quin Monson. *Seeking the Promised Land: Mormons and American Politics.* Cambridge University Press, 2014.

3. Jones, Robert P., and Daniel Cox. "Religion and Same-Sex Marriage in California: A New Look at Attitudes and Values Two Years After Proposition 8." PRRI. 2010. http://www.prri.org/research religion-proposition-8-and-same-sex-marriage-in-california/

4. "Hurricane Sandy Blamed On Gays, Obama And Romney By Preacher John McTernan." *HuffPost.* October 29, 2012. Accessed August 12, 2017. http://www.huffingtonpost.com/2012/10/29/hurricane-sandy-gays-same-sex-marriage-obama-romney_n_2038781.html

5. Blinder, Alan, and Richard Pérez-Peña. "Kentucky Clerk Denies Same-Sex Marriage Licenses, Defying Court." *The New York Times.* September 1, 2015. Accessed August 12, 2017. https://www.nytimes.com/2015/09/02/us/same-sex-marriage-kentucky-kim-davis.html

6. "Religious Landscape Study." Pew Research Center. 2014. Accessed August 12, 2017. http://www.pewforum.org/religious-landscape-study/

7. Mehta, Hemant. "Jamie Raskin, Not-So-Openly Humanist Candidate from Maryland, Wins U.S. House Race." *Patheos.* November 8, 2016. Accessed August 12, 2017. http://www.patheos.com/blogs/friendlyatheist/2016/11/08/jamie-raskin-not-so-openly-humanist-candidate-from-maryland-wins-u-s-house-race/

8. "Congress shall make no law respecting an establishment of religion, or prohibiting the free exercise thereof..."

9. Dockterman, Eliana. "5 Things Women Need to Know About the Hobby Lobby Ruling." *Time.* July 1, 2014. Accessed August 12, 2017. http://time.com/2941323/supreme-court-contraception-ruling-hobby-lobby/

10. Liebelson, Dana, and Molly Redden. "A Montana School Just Fired a Teacher for Getting Pregnant. That Actually Happens All the Time." *Mother Jones.* February 10, 2014. Accessed August 12, 2017. http://www.motherjones.com/politics/2014/02/catholic-religious-schools-fired-lady-teachers-being-pregnant/

11. "End the Use of Religion to Discriminate." ACLU. Accessed August 12, 2017. https://www.aclu.org/feature/end-use-religion-discriminate

12. Millhiser, Ian. "When 'Religious Liberty' Was Used to Justify Racism Instead of Homophobia." *ThinkProgress.* February 27, 2014. Accessed

August 12, 2017. https://thinkprogress.org/when-religious-liberty-was-used-to-justify-racism-instead-of-homophobia-67bc973c4042/

13. "Bob Jones University Drops Interracial Dating Ban." *Christianity Today*. March 1, 2000. Accessed August 12, 2017. http://www.christianitytoday.com/ct/2000/marchweb-only/53.0.html

14. Westneat, Danny. "Poll Finds Americans' Growing Tolerance Stops at Atheists." *The Seattle Times*. June 21, 2014. Accessed August 12, 2017. http://www.seattletimes.com/seattle-news/poll-finds-american-srsquo-growing-tolerance-stops-at-atheists/

15. Lee, Adam. "If Peace on Earth Is Our Goal, Atheism Might Be the Means to That End." *The Guardian*. January 6, 2015. Accessed August 12, 2017. https://www.theguardian.com/commentisfree/2015/jan/06/peace-on-earth-atheism

16. Giaimo, Cara. "More Than Words: Queer, Part 1 (The Early Years)." Autostraddle. January 9, 2013. Accessed August 12, 2017. https://www.autostraddle.com/more-than-words-queer-part-1-the-early-years-153356/

17. "Queer Nation NY History." Queer Nation. Accessed August 12, 2017. http://queernationny.org/history

18. Mora, Celeste. "What Is the Singular They, and Why Should I Use It?" Grammarly. Accessed August 12, 2017. https://www.grammarly.com/blog/use-the-singular-they/

19. "Gay and Transgender Youth Homelessness by the Numbers." Center for American Progress. June 21, 2010. Accessed August 12, 2017. https://www.americanprogress.org/issues/lgbt/news/2010/06/21/7980/gay-and-transgender-youth-homelessness-by-the-numbers/

20. Talusan, Meredith. "Unerased: Counting Transgender Lives." Mic. December 8, 2016. Accessed August 12, 2017. https://mic.com/unerased

Chapter One

21. Goodnough, Abby. "Student Faces Town's Wrath in Protest Against a Prayer." *The New York Times*. January 26, 2012. Accessed July 7, 2017. http://www.nytimes.com/2012/01/27/us/rhode-island-city-enraged-over-school-prayer-lawsuit.html

22. Full disclosure: Hemant's website, *Friendly Atheist*, spearheaded the scholarship fundraising.

23. Metcalf, Andrew. "Ahlquist Inspires Two Others to Contest Prayers at Their Schools." Patch.com. June 24, 2011. Accessed July 7, 2017. https://archive.is/20120707205224/http://cranston.patch.com/articles/ahlquist-inspires-two-others-to-contest-prayers-at-their-schools.

24. "Will Phillips, 10-Year-Old, Won't Pledge Allegiance to a Country That Discriminates Against Gays (VIDEO)." *HuffPost*. May 25, 2011. Accessed July 8, 2017. http://www.huffingtonpost.com/2009/11/12/10-year-old-wont-pledge-a_n_355709.html

25. Brantley, Max. "Will Phillips to Stand for the Pledge of Allegiance Thanks to DOMA Ruling." *Arkansas Times*. June 28, 2013. Accessed

July 7, 2017. https://www.arktimes.com/ArkansasBlog/archives/2013/06/28/will-phillips-to-stand-for-the-pledge-of-allegiance-thanks-to-doma-ruling

26. Mehta, Hemant. "13-Year-Old LGBT Activist Delivers a Must-Hear Speech at Northwest Arkansas Pride Parade." Patheos. June 30, 2013. Accessed July 8, 2017. http://www.patheos.com/blogs/friendlyatheist/2013/06/30/13-year-old-lgbt-activist-will-phillips-delivers-a-must-hear-speech-at-northwest-arkansas-pride-parade

27. "The Pledge of Allegiance." USHistory.org. Independence Hall Association. Accessed July 18, 2017. http://www.ushistory.org/documents/pledge.htm

28. Inbar, Yoel, Joshua Knobe, David A. Pizarro, and Paul Bloom. "Disgust Sensitivity Predicts Intuitive Disapproval of Gays." *Emotion* vol. 9, no. 3 (2009), pp. 435-439.

29. Barthel, Michael et al. "Reddit News Users More Likely to Be Male, Young and Digital in Their News Preferences." Pew Research Center. February 25, 2016. Accessed July 7, 2017. http://www.journalism.org/2016/02/25/reddit-news-users-more-likely-to-be-male-young-and-digital-in-their-news-preferences/

30. Lipka, Michael. "10 Facts About Atheists." Pew Research Center. June 1, 2016. Accessed July 8, 2017. http://www.pewresearch.org/fact-tank/2016/06/01/10-facts-about-atheists/

31. "Request for Feedback: How Relevant Are LGBT Topics to r/atheism?" Reddit.com. August 9, 2016. https://www.reddit.com/r/atheism/comments/4wy30x/request_for_feedback_how_relevant_are_lgbt_topics

32. Stedman, Chris. "Atheism Is Not the 'New Gay Marriage' (or the New Anything Else)" Religion News Service. December 6, 2013. Accessed July 8, 2017. http://religionnews.com/2013/12/06/atheism-new-gay-marriage-new-anything-else/

33. "A Survey of LGBT Americans." Pew Research Center. June 13, 2013. Accessed July 8, 2017. http://www.pewsocialtrends.org/2013/06/13/a-survey-of-lgbt-americans/7/

34. "U.S. Public Becoming Less Religious." Pew Research Center. November 3, 2015. Accessed July 8, 2017. http://www.pewforum.org/2015/11/03/chapter-4-social-and-political-attitudes/

35. Sanchez, Ray. "Why the Onslaught of Religious Freedom Laws?" CNN.com. April 7, 2016. Accessed July 7, 2017. http://www.cnn.com/2016/04/06/us/religious-freedom-laws-why-now/

36. H.R. 1308 (103rd): Religious Freedom Restoration Act of 1993. https://www.govtrack.us/congress/bills/103/hr1308/summary

37. "Non-Discrimination Laws." Movement Advancement Project. Accessed July 7, 2017. http://www.lgbtmap.org/equality-maps/non_discrimination_laws

38. Beredjick, Camille. "Baker Rejects Customer's Birthday Cake After Learning She's Gay—From Her Facebook Profile." Patheos. July 11, 2016. Accessed July 8, 2017. http://www.patheos.com/blogs/friendlyatheist/2016/07/11/baker-rejects-customers-birthday-cake-order-after-learning-shes-gay-from-her-facebook-profile/

39. Mazza, Ed. "Pediatrician Refuses to Care for Baby With Lesbian Mothers in Michigan." *HuffPost.* February 19, 2015. Accessed July 8, 2017. http://www.huffingtonpost.com/2015/02/18/pediatrician-refuses-lesbian-mothers_n_6710128.html

40. Nazworth, Napp. "Can the US Have Both Religious Freedom and Gay Marriage? Louisiana Bill Shows Way Forward." *The Christian Post.* April 14, 2015. http://www.christianpost.com/news/can-the-us-have-both-religious-freedom-and-gay-marriage-louisiana-bill-shows-way-forward-137509

41. Applebaum, Binyamin. "What the Hobby Lobby Ruling Means for America." *The New York Times.* July 22, 2014. https://www.nytimes.com/2014/07/27/magazine/what-the-hobby-lobby-ruling-means-for-america.html

42. Liptak, Adam. "Justices to Hear Case on Religious Objections to Same-Sex Marriage." *The New York Times.* June 26, 2017. Accessed July 8, 2017. https://www.nytimes.com/2017/06/26/us/politics/supreme-court-wedding-cake-gay-couple-masterpiece-cakeshop.html

43. Ennis, Dawn. "Gavin Grimm Will Finally Have His Day in Court." LGBTQ Nation. July 5, 2017. Accessed July 8, 2017. https://www.lgbtqnation.com/2017/07/gavin-grimm-will-finally-day-court/

44. Eskridge, William N. Gaylaw. *Challenging the Apartheid of the Closet.* Cambridge, Massachusetts. Harvard University Press, 2002.

45. "Why Sodomy Laws Matter," ACLU. Accessed July 8, 2017. https://www.aclu.org/other/why-sodomy-laws-matter

46. "12 States Still Ban Sodomy a Decade After Court Ruling." *USA Today.* April 21, 2014. Accessed August 28, 2017. https://www.usatoday.com/story/news/nation/2014/04/21/12-states-ban-sodomy-a-decade-after-court-ruling/7981025/

47. Green, Emma. "Alabama's Sodomy Ban Is Unconstitutional—Finally." *The Atlantic.* June 18, 2014. Accessed July 8, 2017. http://www.theatlantic.com/national/archive/2014/06/a-man-cannot-be-raped-by-another-man-in-alabama/372973/

48. Goodstein, Laurie. "In Seven States, Atheists Push to End Largely Forgotten Ban." *The New York Times.* December 6, 2014. Accessed July 8, 2017. https://www.nytimes.com/2014/12/07/us/in-seven-states-atheists-push-to-end-largely-forgotten-ban-.html

49. Cox, Daniel, and Robert P. Jones. "America's Changing Religious Identity." PRRI. September 6, 2017. Accessed September 17, 2017. https://www.prri.org/research/american-religious-landscape-christian-religiously-unaffiliated/

50. Vincent, James. "Largest Ever Study Into the Gay Gene 'Erodes the Notion That Sexual Orientation is a Choice.'" *The Independent.* November 21, 2014. Accessed July 8, 2017. http://www.independent.co.uk/news/science/largest-ever-study-into-the-gay-gene-erodes-the-notion-that-sexual-orientation-is-a-choice-9875855.html

51. Solomon, Andrew. *Far From The Tree: Parents, Children and the Search for Identity.* New York. Scribner, 2012.

52. "Our Issue." True Colors Fund. Accessed July 8, 2017. https://truecolorsfund.org/our-issue

53. Edgell, Penny, Douglas Hartmann, Evan Stewart, and Joseph Gerteis. "Atheists and Other Cultural Outsiders: Moral Boundaries and the Non-Religious in the United States." *Social Forces* vol. 95, no. 2 (November 7, 2016), pp. 607-638.

54. Rankin, Kenrya. "STUDY: Americans Apparently Dislike Muslims Even More Than They Dislike Atheists." Colorlines. September 16, 2016. Accessed July 8, 2017. https://www.colorlines.com/articles/study-americans-apparently-dislike-muslims-even-more-they-dislike-atheists

55. Dennin, James. "Muslims Surpass Atheists as Most Hated Religious Group in America, According to New Study." Mic. September 15, 2016. Accessed July 8, 2017. https://mic.com/articles/154300/muslims-islamaphobia-atheism-religious-affiliation-trustworthiness#.CjCCXjB6m

56. Fingerhut, Hannah. "Support Steady for Same-Sex Marriage and Acceptance of Homosexuality." Pew Research Center. May 12, 2016. Accessed July 8, 2017. http://www.pewresearch.org/fact-tank/2016/05/12/support-steady-for-same-sex-marriage-and-acceptance-of-homosexuality/

57. Haas, Ann P. et al. "Suicide and Suicide Risk in Lesbian, Gay, Bisexual, and Transgender Populations: Review and Recommendations." *Journal of Homosexuality* vol. 58, no. 1 (January 4, 2011), pp. 10-51.

58. Dervic, Kanita, Maria Oquendo, Michael Grunebaum, Steve Ellis, Ainsley Burke, and J. John Mann. "Religious Affiliation and Suicide Attempt." *American Journal of Psychiatry* vol. 161, no. 12 (December 1, 2004), pp. 2303-2308. Accessed July 8, 2017.

59. Nelson, Lauren. "The Relationship Between Atheism and Suicide Is More Nuanced Than These Christians Think." Patheos. February 5, 2016. Accessed July 8, 2017. http://www.patheos.com/blogs/friendlyatheist/2016/02/05/the-relationship-between-atheism-and-suicide-is-more-nuanced-than-these-christians-think

60. Galo, Sarah, and Amanda Holpuch. "'Every Illness Is a Spiritual Problem': How Evangelical Christian Communities See Mental Health." *The Guardian.* December 22, 2014. Accessed July 8, 2017. https://www.theguardian.com/society/2014/dec/22/evangelical-christian-church-mental-illness

61. Mehta, Hemant. "The Boy Scouts Will Allow Transgender Children to Join, But Atheists Are Still Banned." Patheos. January 31, 2017. Accessed July 8, 2017. http://www.patheos.com/blogs/friendlyatheist/2017/01/31/the-boy-scouts-will-allow-transgender-children-to-join-but-atheists-are-still-banned/

62. O'Hara, Mary Emily. "Boy Scouts End Ban on Openly Gay Leaders." *The Daily Dot.* July 27, 2015. Accessed July 8, 2017. https://www.dailydot.com/irl/boy-scouts-drops-gay-adult-ban

63. Wendell, Bryan. "About the 'Belief in God' Requirement in Scouting." *Bryan on Scouting.* October 3, 2014. Accessed July 8, 2017. https://blog.scoutingmagazine.org/2014/10/03/belief-in-god-scouting

64. "Charter and Bylaws of the Boy Scouts of America." May 21, 2015. Accessed July 8, 2017. http://www.scouting.org/filestore/pdf/BSA_Charter_and_Bylaws.pdf

65. "ISIS, Many of Their Enemies Share a Homicidal Hatred of Gays." *CBS News.* June 13, 2016. Accessed July 18, 2017. http://www.cbsnews.com/news/isis-orlando-shooting-gays-execution-torture-ramadan/

66. Blake, Mariah. "Meet the American Pastor Behind Uganda's Anti-Gay Crackdown." *Mother Jones.* March 10, 2014. Accessed July 8, 2017. http://www.motherjones.com/politics/2014/03/scott-lively-anti-gay-law-uganda/

67. Gettleman, Jeffrey. "Ugandan Who Spoke Up for Gays Is Beaten to Death." *The New York Times.* January 27, 2011. Accessed July 8, 2017. http://www.nytimes.com/2011/01/28/world/africa/28uganda.html

68. "Press Release by Sexual Minorities Uganda: Brutal Murder of Gay Ugandan Human Rights Defender, David Kato." African Women's Development Fund. January 26, 2011. Accessed July 8, 2017. http://awdf.org/press-release-by-sexual-minorities-uganda-smug

69. Lively, Scott. "A Letter to the International Pro-Family Movement." Scott Lively Ministries. December 31, 2015. Accessed July 8, 2017. http://www.scottlively.net/2015/12/31/a-letter-to-the-international-pro-family-movement

70. Watson, Ivan. "Bangladeshi Al Qaeda Wing Declares War on Atheists." CNN.com. April 9, 2016. Accessed July 8, 2017. http://www.cnn.com/2016/04/09/asia/bangladesh-al-qaeda-atheists/

71. Sexual Offences Act, § 11:28 (Laws of Trinidad and Tobago 1986).

72. United States. FBI. Uniform Crime Reporting. 2015 Hate Crime Statistics. Accessed July 8, 2017. https://ucr.fbi.gov/hate-crime/2015/topic-pages/incidentsandoffenses_final

Chapter Two

73. O'Hare, Peggy. "San Antonio Sees Big Drop in Poverty Rate." *San Antonio Express-News.* September 15, 2016. Accessed July 9, 2017. http://www.expressnews.com/news/local/article/Poverty-rate-down-in-San-Antonio-but-income-9224017.php

74. Zorthian, Julia. "San Antonio's Mayor Blamed Poverty on 'People Not Being in a Relationship With Their Creator.'" Time.com. April 27, 2017. Accessed July 9, 2017. http://time.com/4757580/san-antonio-mayor-broken-people-religion-poverty/

75. Serrano, Jody. "San Antonio Passes LGBT Nondiscrimination Ordinance." *The Texas Tribune.* September 5, 2013. Accessed July 9, 2017. https://www.texastribune.org/2013/09/05/san-antonio-passes-lgbt-non-discrimination-ordinan/

76. Baugh, Josh. "Mayoral Candidates Attend Starkly Different Sunday Forums." *San Antonio Express-News.* April 19, 2015. Accessed July 9, 2017. http://www.expressnews.com/news/local/article/Mayoral-candidates-attend-starkly-different-6210356.php

77. Masci, David. "How Income Varies Among U.S. Religious Groups." Pew Research Center. October 11, 2016. Accessed July 9, 2017. http://www.pewresearch.org/fact-tank/2016/10/11/how-income-varies-among-u-s-religious-groups/

78. Crabtree, Steve. "Religiosity Highest in World's Poorest Nations." Gallup. August 31, 2010. Accessed July 9, 2017. http://www.gallup.com/poll/142727/religiosity-highest-world-poorest-nations.aspx

79. Herrera, Ivan. "Ron Nirenberg Elected Mayor of San Antonio." KSAT. com. June 10, 2017. Accessed July 9, 2017. http://www.ksat.com/news/politics/ron-nirenberg-voted-in-as-new-mayor-of-san-antonio

80. "What is Atheism?" American Atheists. Accessed July 9, 2017. https://www.atheists.org/activism/resources/about-atheism/

81. Lipka, Michael. "10 Facts About Atheists." Pew Research Center. June 1, 2016. Accessed July 9, 2017. http://www.pewresearch.org/fact-tank/2016/06/01/10-facts-about-atheists/

82. Cox, Daniel, and Robert P. Jones. "America's Changing Religious Identity." PRRI. September 6, 2017. Accessed September 17, 2017. https://www.prri.org/research/american-religious-landscape-christian-religiously-unaffiliated/

83. "Catechism of the Catholic Church." Accessed August 29, 2017. http://www.vatican.va/archive/ccc_css/archive/catechism/p3s2c2a6.htm

84. Pew Research Center. "Religious Landscape Study." 2014. Accessed September 17, 2017. http://www.pewforum.org/religious-landscape-study/

85. Leins, Casey. "Americans Are Becoming Less Religious." *U.S. News & World Report,* April 11, 2017. Accessed July 9, 2017. https://www.usnews.com/news/best-states/articles/2017-04-11/americans-are-becoming-less-religious

86. Gushee, David. "On LGBT Equality, Middle Ground Is Disappearing." Religion News Service. August 22, 2016. Accessed July 9, 2017. http://religionnews.com/2016/08/22/on-lgbt-equality-middle-ground-is-disappearing/

87. Cox, Daniel, and Robert P. Jones. "America's Changing Religious Identity." PRRI. September 6, 2017. Accessed September 17, 2017. https://www.prri.org/research/american-religious-landscape-christian-religiously-unaffiliated/

88. Jenkins, Jack. "The Mormon Church Just Announced It Won't Baptize Children Who Live With LGBT Couples." *ThinkProgress,* November 6, 2015. Accessed July 9, 2017. https://thinkprogress.org/the-mormon-church-just-announced-it-wont-baptize-children-who-live-with-lgbt-couples-43983dee90d0

89. "Exodus: Why Americans Are Leaving Religion—And Why They're Unlikely To Come Back." Public Religion Research Institute. September 22, 2016. Accessed July 9, 2017. https://www.prri.org/wp-content/uploads/2016/09/PRRI-RNS-Unaffiliated-Report.pdf

90. Healy, Jack. "Mormon Resignations Put Support for Gays Over Fealty to Faith." *The New York Times.* November 15, 2015. Accessed July 9, 2017. https://www.nytimes.com/2015/11/16/us/mormon-resignations-put-support-for-gays-over-fealty-to-faith.html

91. Tsjeng, Zing. "Teens These Days Are Queer AF, New Study Says." *Broadly.* March 10, 2016. Accessed July 9, 2017. https://broadly.vice.com/en_us/article/kb4dvz/teens-these-days-are-queer-af-new-study-says

92. Mehta, Hemant. "Kirk Cameron: When I Tell Gay People They're Going to Hell, That's Just Me Loving Them." Patheos. October 11, 2012. Accessed July 9, 2017. http://www.patheos.com/blogs/friendlyatheist/

2012/10/11/kirk-cameron-when-i-tell-gay-people-theyre-going-to-hell-thats-just-me-loving-them/

93. Martel, Frances. "Kirk Cameron Shocks Piers Morgan: Homosexuality Is 'Unnatural' And 'Destructive To . . . Civilization.'" Mediaite. March 3, 2012. Accessed July 9, 2017. http://www.mediaite.com/tv/kirk-cameron-shocks-piers-morgan-homosexuality-is-unnatural-and-destructive-to-civilization/

94. Lang, Nico. "Conservatives Are Using the Old 'Gay Friend' Trick to Try to Pacify LGBT Advocates. Don't Fall for It." *Los Angeles Times*, February 17, 2017. Accessed July 9, 2017. http://www.latimes.com/opinion/opinion-la/la-ol-gorsuch-gay-friends-republican-20170217-story.html

Chapter Three

95. Sieczkowski, Cavan. "Family Has Horrifying, Violent Reaction to Son's Coming Out as Gay." *HuffPost*. August 24, 2014. Accessed July 9, 2017. http://www.huffingtonpost.com/2014/08/28/family-son-coming-out-gay-video_n_5731462.html

96. Heffernan, Dani. "Daniel Pierce, Gay Man Disowned by Family, Joins Board of Homeless LGBT Youth Organization." GLAAD. October 30, 2014. Accessed July 9, 2017. https://www.glaad.org/blog/daniel-pierce-gay-man-disowned-family-joins-board-homeless-lgbt-youth-organization

97. *Lemon v. Kurtzman*, 403 U.S. 602 (June 28, 1971).

98. Chicago-Kent College of Law at Illinois Tech. "Lemon v. Kurtzman." *Oyez*. Accessed July 9, 2017. https://www.oyez.org/cases/1970/89

99. *Barnes Wallace v. City of San Diego* (United States Court of Appeals, Ninth Circuit, December 20, 2012).

100. Mantyla, Kyle. "Rep. Randy Weber Tearfully Begs God to Forgive America for the Sins of Legal Abortion and Marriage Equality." *Right Wing Watch*. April 27, 2017. Accessed July 9, 2017. http://www.rightwingwatch.org/post/rep-randy-weber-tearfully-begs-god-to-forgive-america-for-the-sins-of-legal-abortion-and-marriage-equality/

101. Wootson, Cleve R., Jr., and Sandhya Somashekhar. "A Lesbian Couple Got Their Marriage License—After a County Clerk Called Them an 'Abomination'." *The Washington Post*. April 19, 2017. Accessed July 9, 2017. https://www.washingtonpost.com/news/post-nation/wp/2017/04/19/a-lesbian-couple-got-their-marriage-license-after-a-w-va-clerk-called-them-an-abomination/

102. Cameron, Darla, and Bonnie Berkowitz. "The State of Gay Rights Around the World." Chart. *The Washington Post*. June 14, 2016. Accessed July 9, 2017. https://www.washingtonpost.com/graphics/world/gay-rights/

103. Chappell, Bill. "Judge Strikes Down Last Same-Sex Adoption Ban in the U.S." NPR.org. April 1, 2016. Accessed July 9, 2017. http://www.npr.org/sections/thetwo-way/2016/04/01/472667168/judge-strikes-down-last-same-sex-adoption-ban-in-the-u-s

104. "Foster and Adoption Laws." Map. Movement Advancement Project. July 7, 2017. Accessed July 9, 2017. http://www.lgbtmap.org/equality-maps/foster_and_adoption_laws

105. Stern, Mark Joseph. "The Scientific Debate Over Same-Sex Parenting Is Over." *Slate*. April 13, 2016. Accessed July 9, 2017. http://www.slate.com/blogs/outward/2016/04/13/scientific_debate_over_same_sex_parenting_is_over.html

106. Ring, Trudy. "Kentucky Judge Won't Hear Gay Parents' Adoption Cases." *The Advocate*. May 2, 2017. Accessed July 9, 2017. https://www.advocate.com/families/2017/5/02/kentucky-judge-wont-hear-gay-parents-adoption-cases

107. "Connecticut Becomes Seventh State to Ban Conversion Therapy." CBS New York, May 11, 2017. Accessed July 9, 2017. http://newyork.cbslocal.com/2017/05/11/connecticut-bans-conversion-therapy

108. "#BornPerfect: The Facts About Conversion Therapy." National Center for Lesbian Rights. Accessed July 9, 2017. http://www.nclrights.org/bornperfect-the-facts-about-conversion-therapy/

109. "SPLC Suit Forces New Jersey Group to Cease Bogus 'Conversion Therapy' Program, Pay Damages." Southern Poverty Law Center. Accessed July 9, 2017. https://www.splcenter.org/news/2015/12/18/splc-suit-forces-new-jersey-group-cease-bogus-%E2%80%98conversion-therapy%E2%80%99-program-pay-damages

110. "Pastors Sue Illinois Over Gay Conversion Therapy Ban." *Chicago Tribune*. August 11, 2016. Accessed July 9, 2017. http://www.chicagotribune.com/news/local/politics/ct-illinois-gay-conversion-therapy-ban-lawsuit-20160811-story.html

111. Boysen, Ryan. "Ill. Gay Conversion Therapy Ban Exempts Pastors, Judge Says." Law360. February 21, 2017. Accessed September 6, 2017. https://www.law360.com/articles/893579/ill-gay-conversion-therapy-ban-exempts-pastors-judge-says

112. Connley, Courtney. "Democratic Lawmakers Introduce Bill to Ban Conversion Therapy Nationwide." *ABC News*. April 28, 2017. Accessed July 9, 2017. http://abcnews.go.com/Politics/democratic-lawmakers-introduce-bill-ban-conversion-therapy-nationwide/story?id=47087995

113. United States. Department of Health and Human Services. Office of Disease Prevention and Health Promotion. Lesbian, Gay, Bisexual, and Transgender Health. Accessed July 9, 2017. https://www.healthypeople.gov/2020/topics-objectives/topic/lesbian-gay-bisexual-and-transgender-health

114. "Benitez v. North Coast Women's Care Medical Group." Lambda Legal. Accessed July 9, 2017. https://www.lambdalegal.org/in-court/cases/benitez-v-north-coast-womens-care-medical-group

115. "Benitez California Supreme Court Decision." Lambda Legal. Accessed July 9, 2017. https://www.lambdalegal.org/in-court/legal-docs/benitez_ca_20080818_decision-ca-supreme-court

116. Phillip, Abby. "Pediatrician Refuses to Treat Baby With Lesbian Parents and There's Nothing Illegal About It." *The Washington Post*, February 19, 2015. Accessed July 9, 2017. https://www.washingtonpost.com/news/morning-mix/wp/2015/02/19/pediatrician-refuses-to-treat-baby-with-lesbian-parents-and-theres-nothing-illegal-about-it/

117. Quinlan, Casey. "Trump Administration Moves to Roll Back Obamacare Protections for Trans People." *ThinkProgress*, May 3, 2017. Accessed

July 9, 2017. https://thinkprogress.org/trump-rescinds-lgbtq-protections-obamacare-3f6315b0ca52

118. James, Sandy, Jody L. Herman, Susan Rankin, Mara Keisling, Lisa Mottet, and Ma'ayan Anafi. "The Report of the 2015 U.S. Transgender Survey." National Center for Transgender Equality. 2015. Accessed July 9, 2017. http://www.transequality.org/sites/default/files/docs/usts/USTS%20Full%20Report%20-%20FINAL%201.6.17.pdf

119. Stern, Mark Joseph. "The Real Reason the Religious Right Opposes Trans Equality. (It Isn't Bathroom Predators.)" *Slate.* May 4, 2016. Accessed July 9, 2017. http://www.slate.com/blogs/outward/2016/05/04/trans_bathroom_predator_myth_is_rooted_in_religion.html

120. Terkel, Amanda. "Mike Pence's Religious Freedom Law Continues to Hang Over Indiana." *HuffPost.* September 2, 2016. Accessed July 9, 2017. http://www.huffingtonpost.com/entry/mike-pence-religious-freedom-law-indiana_us_57c839b9e4b0a22de09446d8

121. Slodysko, Brian. "Survey: Religious Objections Law Cost Indiana as Much as $60 Million." *Chicago Tribune.* January 26, 2016. Accessed July 9, 2017. http://www.chicagotribune.com/news/local/breaking/ct-survey-religious-objections-law-cost-indiana-as-much-as-60-million-20160126-story.html

122. Wilson, Nick. "Teacher Cites Bible in Letter to School Paper, Says Gay People 'Deserve to Die.'" *The Sacramento Bee.* May 11, 2017. Accessed July 9, 2017. http://www.sacbee.com/news/state/article149916022.html

123. Kosciw, Joseph G., Emily A. Greytak, Noreen M. Giga, Christian Villenas, and David J. Danischewski. "2015 National School Climate Survey." GLSEN. 2016. Accessed July 9, 2017.

124. Allen, Samantha. "Utah Says No to 'No Promo Homo' Law, But Other States Lag Behind." *The Daily Beast.* March 21, 2017. Accessed July 9, 2017. http://www.thedailybeast.com/utah-says-no-to-no-promo-homo-law-but-other-states-lag-behind

125. Ha, Thu-Huong. "The Top 10 Books Americans Tried to Ban Last Year." *Quartz,* April 10, 2017. Accessed July 9, 2017. https://qz.com/954175/banned-books-the-top-10-books-americans-tried-to-ban-in-2016/

126. Melville-Smith, Alicia. "A 6-Year-Old Was Stopped From Reading a Book About Being Transgender." *BuzzFeed.* November 29, 2015. Accessed July 9, 2017. https://www.buzzfeed.com/aliciamelvillesmith/school-cancels-reading-of-transgender-book

127. Durso, Laura E. and Gary J. Gates. "Serving Our Youth: Findings From a National Survey of Services Providers Working With Lesbian, Gay, Bisexual and Transgender Youth Who Are Homeless or at Risk of Becoming Homeless." The Williams Institute with True Colors Fund and The Palette Fund. 2012. Accessed July 9, 2017. http://williamsinstitute.law.ucla.edu/wp-content/uploads/Durso-Gates-LGBT-Homeless-Youth-Survey-July-2012.pdf

128. Morris, Alex. "The Forsaken: A Rising Number of Homeless Gay Teens Are Being Cast Out by Religious Families." *Rolling Stone.* September 3, 2014. Accessed July 9, 2017. http://www.rollingstone.com/culture/features/the-forsaken-a-rising-number-of-homeless-gay-teens-are-being-cast-out-by-religious-families-20140903

129. Drabold, Will. "Here's What Mike Pence Said on LGBT Issues Over the Years." *Time*, July 15, 2016. Accessed July 9, 2017. http://time.com/4406337/mike-pence-gay-rights-lgbt-religious-freedom/

130. Reevell, Patrick. "LGBT Activists Arrested in Moscow After Demanding Investigation of Alleged Torture of Gay Men in Chechnya." *ABC News*. May 11, 2017. Accessed July 9, 2017. http://abcnews.go.com/International/lgbt-activists-arrested-moscow-demanding-investigation-alleged-torture/story?id=47345489

Chapter Four

131. Murphy, Caryle. "Lesbian, Gay and Bisexual Americans Differ From General Public in Their Religious Affiliations." Pew Research Center. May 26, 2015. Accessed July 11, 2017. http://www.pewresearch.org/fact-tank/2015/05/26/lesbian-gay-and-bisexual-americans-differ-from-general-public-in-their-religious-affiliations/

132. Gates, Gary J. "In US, More Adults Identifying as LGBT." Gallup. January 11, 2017. Accessed July 11, 2017. http://www.gallup.com/poll/201731/lgbt-identification-rises.aspx

133. Merritt, Jonathan. "Can Atheists and Christians Work Together? An Interview With Harvard's Chris Stedman." Religion News Service, April 29, 2013. Accessed July 11, 2017. http://religionnews.com/2013/04/29/can-atheists-and-christians-work-together-an-interview-with-chris-stedman/

134. @SonofBaldwin. Tweet. August 18, 2015, 7:19 AM. https://twitter.com/SonofBaldwin/status/633644373423562753

135. Cox, Daniel, and Robert P. Jones. "America's Changing Religious Identity." PRRI. September 6, 2017. Accessed September 17, 2017. https://www.prri.org/research/american-religious-landscape-christian-religiously-unaffiliated/

136. "Affirming Church Directory." The GALIP Foundation. Accessed July 11, 2017. https://www.gaychurch.org/find_a_church/

137. Singh, Aarti Tikoo. "There Are 8 Openly Gay Imams in the World: Daayiee Abdullah." *The Times of India*, June 15, 2016. Accessed July 11, 2017. http://timesofindia.indiatimes.com/world/us/There-are-8-openly-gay-imams-in-the-world-Daayiee-Abdullah/articleshow/52754600.cms

138. Vines, Matthew. *God and the Gay Christian: The Biblical Case in Support of Same-Sex Relationships*. Convergent Books. 2014.

139. Morton, Tom. "Matthew Shepard Funeral Put Westboro Baptist Church on the Map." *Casper Star-Tribune*. March 2, 2011. Accessed July 11, 2017. http://billingsgazette.com/news/state-and-regional/wyoming/matthew-shepard-funeral-put-westboro-baptist-church-on-the-map/article_fa10936e-cb5b-5170-afd8-e7eaa0a43aa8.html

140. "About Westboro Baptist Church." Westboro Baptist Church. Accessed July 11, 2017. http://www.godhatesfags.com/wbcinfo/aboutwbc.html

141. Branson-Potts, Hailey. "Judge Strikes Down Proposed 'Sodomite Suppression Act' Calling for Killing of Gays." *Los Angeles Times*, June 23, 2015. Accessed July 11, 2017. http://www.latimes.com/local/lanow/la-me-ln-antigay-sodomite-suppression-act-struck-down-20150623-story.html

142. James, Brendan. "Who Is the Mysterious Lawyer Behind California's 'Kill All Gays' Drive?" *Talking Points Memo.* March 26, 2015. Accessed July 11, 2017. http://talkingpointsmemo.com/muckraker/matt-gregory-mclaughlin-kill-all-gays-california

143. Mehta, Hemant. "Christian Pastor: 'I Believe That the Government Should Use the Death Penalty' on Homosexuals." Patheos. July 6, 2013. Accessed July 11, 2017. http://www.patheos.com/blogs/friendlyatheist/2013/07/06/christian-pastor-i-believe-that-the-government-should-use-the-death-penalty-on-homosexuals/

144. Wright, John. "This Anti-Gay Texas Pastor Says He's Praying for Survivors of the Orlando Terror Attack to Die." The New Civil Rights Movement. Accessed July 11, 2017. http://www.thenewcivilrightsmovement.com/johnwright/pastor_calls_orlando_terror_victims_perverts_pedophiles_prays_for_survivors_to_die

145. Sieczkowski, Cavan. "Preacher Gives Shockingly Repulsive Sermon: 'Orlando Is a Little Safer.'" *HuffPost.* June 16, 2016. Accessed July 11, 2017. http://www.huffingtonpost.com/entry/baptist-preacher-praises-orlando-shooting-says-city-is-safer_us_5762b0f3e4b0df4d586f5d37

146. "Changing Attitudes on Gay Marriage." Pew Research Center. Accessed July 11, 2017. http://www.pewforum.org/fact-sheet/changing-attitudes-on-gay-marriage/

147. Towle, Andy. "Vassar College Raises More Than $100,000 for the Trevor Project in Response to Westboro Baptist Church Protest." Towleroad. February 28, 2013. Accessed July 11, 2017. http://www.towleroad.com/2013/02/vassar-college-raises-more-than-100000-for-the-trevor-project-in-response-to-westboro-baptist-church/

148. Markoe, Lauren, and Cathy Lynn Grossman. "Supreme Court Approves Sectarian Prayer at Public Meetings." *The Washington Post.* May 5, 2014. Accessed July 11, 2017. https://www.washingtonpost.com/national/religion/supreme-court-approves-sectarian-prayer-at-public-meetings/2014/05/05/62c494da-d487-11e3-8f7d-7786660fff7c_story.html

149. Winston, Kimberly. "Supreme Court Prayer Ruling May Bring Atheists, Minority Religions Together, Atheist Leader Says." *HuffPost.* May 8, 2014. Accessed July 11, 2017. http://www.huffingtonpost.com/2014/05/08/supreme-courty-prayer-ruling-atheists_n_5290425.html

150. Holley, Peter. "KKK's Official Newspaper Supports Donald Trump for President." *The Washington Post.* November 2, 2016. Accessed July 11, 2017. https://www.washingtonpost.com/news/post-politics/wp/2016/11/01/the-kkks-official-newspaper-has-endorsed-donald-trump-for-president/

151. Drabold, Will. "Here's What Mike Pence Said on LGBT Issues Over the Years." *Time.* July 15, 2016. Accessed July 11, 2017. http://time.com/4406337/mike-pence-gay-rights-lgbt-religious-freedom/

152. Blaine, Kyle, and Julia Horowitz. "How the Trump Administration Chose the 7 Countries in the Immigration Executive Order." CNN. January 30, 2017. Accessed July 11, 2017. http://edition.cnn.com/2017/01/29/politics/how-the-trump-administration-chose-the-7-countries/

153. Bearak, Max, and Darla Cameron. "Here Are the 10 Countries Where Homosexuality May Be Punished by Death." *The Washington Post.*

June 16, 2016. Accessed July 11, 2017. https://www.washingtonpost.com/news/worldviews/wp/2016/06/13/here-are-the-10-countries-where-homosexuality-may-be-punished-by-death-2/

154. Lee, Adam. "Rise of the New Atheists." *Salon*. July 30, 2012. Accessed September 9, 2017. http://www.salon.com/2012/07/30/should_atheists_make_an_alliance_with_religious_progressives/

Chapter Five

155. Fox, Fallon. "Leelah Alcorn's Suicide: Conversion Therapy Is Child Abuse." Time.com. January 8, 2015. Accessed July 19, 2017. http://time.com/3655718/leelah-alcorn-suicide-transgender-therapy/

156. Gajanan, Mahita. "Calls to Crisis Support Lines Up After Donald Trump's Victory." Time.com. November 9, 2016. Accessed July 19, 2017. http://time.com/4565274/crisis-support-line-donald-trump-election/

157. Williams, Kimberlé Crenshaw. "Mapping the Margins: Intersectionality, Identity Politics, and Violence Against Women of Color". In: Martha Albertson Fineman, Roxanne Mykitiuk, Eds. *The Public Nature of Private Violence*. (New York: Routledge, 1994), pp. 93-118.

158. Ringo, Allegra. "The Atheist Movement Needs to Disown Richard Dawkins." *Vice*. September 17, 2014. Accessed July 19, 2017. https://www.vice.com/en_us/article/jmbayk/the-atheist-movement-needs-to-disown-richard-dawkins-999

Chapter Six

159. Fernandez, Manny, and Mitch Smith. "Houston Voters Reject Broad Anti-Discrimination Ordinance." *The New York Times*. November 3, 2015. Accessed July 14, 2017. https://www.nytimes.com/2015/11/04/us/houston-voters-repeal-anti-bias-measure.html

160. Ford, Zack. "Opponents of LGBT Protections Forged Signatures or Everyone in Houston Has the Same Handwriting." *ThinkProgress*. January 13, 2015. Accessed July 14, 2017. https://thinkprogress.org/opponents-of-lgbt-protections-forged-signatures-or-everyone-in-houston-has-the-same-handwriting-dc055ce4e690

161. Balingit, Moriah. "School Board Plans to Ask U.S. Supreme Court to Hear Transgender Bathroom Case." *The Washington Post*. June 7, 2016. Accessed July 14, 2017. https://www.washingtonpost.com/local/education/school-board-plans-to-ask-us-supreme-court-to-hear-transgender-bathroom-case/2016/06/07/381c76f2-2cce-11e6-9de3-6e6e7a14000c_story.html

162. Firma, Terry. "More Republican Politicians Than Trans People Have Been Arrested for Sex Acts in Bathrooms." Patheos. April 11, 2016. Accessed July 14, 2017. http://www.patheos.com/blogs/friendlyatheist/2016/04/11/more-republican-politicians-than-trans-people-have-been-arrested-for-sex-acts-in-bathrooms/

163. Lowder, J. Bryan. "This Anti-HERO Ad Is the Definition of Transphobia." *Slate*. October 19, 2015. Accessed July 14, 2017. http://www.slate.com/blogs/outward/2015/10/19/hero_trans_bathroom_battle_campaign_for_houston_ad_is_most_transphobic_yet.html

164. "Eye on the Opposition: Enemies of Equality." Chart. *Freedom for All Americans*. Accessed July 14, 2017. http://www.freedomforallamericans.org/eye-on-the-opposition-enemies-of-equality/

165. Stern, Mark Joseph. "Why Houston's Equal Rights Ordinance Failed." *Slate.* November 4, 2015. Accessed July 14, 2017. http://www.slate.com/blogs/outward/2015/11/04/houston_hero_lgbt_ordinance_failed_because_of_transphobia.html

166. Binkovitz, Leah. "Most Houstonians Support an Equal Rights Ordinance, Survey Finds. So Why'd They Vote Against It?" *The Urban Edge.* April 25, 2016. Accessed July 14, 2017. http://urbanedge.blogs.rice.edu/2016/04/25/most-houstonians-support-an-equal-rights-ordinance-survey-finds/

167. Driessen, Katherine. "HERO Supporters Lead Opponents in New Poll." *Houston Chronicle.* October 12, 2015. Accessed July 14, 2017. http://www.houstonchronicle.com/news/houston-texas/houston/article/HERO-supporters-lead-opponents-in-new-poll-6567428.php

168. "City of Houston, Texas Ordinance No. 2014-530." May 14, 2014. Accessed July 14, 2017. https://www.houstontx.gov/equal_rights_ordinance.pdf

169. Signorile, Michelangelo. "How Houston Was Lost: Prop 8 Redux as LGBT Rights Are Put on the Ballot." *HuffPost.* November 4, 2016. Accessed July 14, 2017. http://www.huffingtonpost.com/michelangelo-signorile/how-houston-was-lost-prop_b_8471528.html

170. "Growing Support for the Houston Equal Rights Ordinance Through Faith & Hometown Pride." *Houston Unites.* Accessed July 14, 2017. http://houstonunites.org/growing-support-for-the-houston-equal-rights-ordinance-through-faith-hometown-pride/

171. Shellnutt, Kate. "Houston Atheists Present New Image." *Houston Chronicle.* October 6, 2011. Accessed July 14, 2017. http://www.chron.com/life/houston-belief/article/Freethinkers-present-new-image-2206261.php

172. "The Humanists of Houston Meetup Group." Meetup.com. Accessed July 14, 2017. https://www.meetup.com/humanism-177/

173. Lipka, Michael. "Major U.S. Metropolitan Areas Differ in Their Religious Profiles." Pew Research Center. July 29, 2015. Accessed July 14, 2017. http://www.pewresearch.org/fact-tank/2015/07/29/major-u-s-metropolitan-areas-differ-in-their-religious-profiles/

174. Stahl, Lesley. "President-Elect Trump Speaks to a Divided Country." *60 Minutes.* November 13, 2016. Accessed July 14, 2017. http://www.cbsnews.com/news/60-minutes-donald-trump-family-melania-ivanka-lesley-stahl/

175. "U.S. Public Becoming Less Religious." Pew Research Center. November 3, 2015. Accessed July 14, 2017. http://www.pewforum.org/2015/11/03/u-s-public-becoming-less-religious/

176. "2016 Democratic Party Platform." July 21, 2016. Accessed July 14, 2017. http://www.presidency.ucsb.edu/papers_pdf/117717.pdf

177. Log Cabin Republicans. "With Endorsement, Log Cabin Republicans Declare 'We Are Americans First'." News release. October 23, 2012. Log Cabin Republicans. Accessed July 18, 2017. http://www.logcabin.org/pressrelease/with-endorsement-log-cabin-republicans-declare-we-are-americans-first/

178. "Log Cabin Republicans Endorse McCain for President." GLAAD. September 3, 2008. Accessed July 18, 2017. https://www.glaad.

org/2008/09/03/log-cabin-republicans-endorse-mccain-for-president

179. Savage, Dan. "The Utter Failure of the Log Cabin Republicans." *The Stranger.* July 18, 2016. Accessed July 18, 2017. http://www.thestranger.com/slog/2016/07/18/24357871/the-utter-failure-of-the-log-cabin-republicans

180. Volsky, Igor. "Reminder: Santorum Once Linked Same-Sex Marriage To 9/11." *ThinkProgress.* January 5, 2012. Accessed July 18, 2017. https://thinkprogress.org/reminder-santorum-once-linked-same-sex-marriage-to-9-11-16e979d84730

181. Wing, Nick. "Mike Huckabee 'Ick Factor' Comments Slammed by Gay Rights Groups." *HuffPost.* June 22, 2010. Accessed July 18, 2017. http://www.huffingtonpost.com/2010/06/22/mike-huckabee-ick-factor_n_621284.html

182. Mehta, Hemant. "A Bunch of Atheists Told Me Why They Plan to Vote Republican." Patheos. March 4, 2016. Accessed September 11, 2017. http://www.patheos.com/blogs/friendlyatheist/2016/03/04/a-bunch-of-atheists-told-me-why-they-plan-to-vote-republican/

183. Beredjick, Camille. "A Descendant of the Founder of Hasidic Judaism Just Came Out as an Atheist Trans Woman." Patheos. December 7, 2015. Accessed July 18, 2017. http://www.patheos.com/blogs/friendlyatheist/2015/12/07/a-descendant-of-the-founder-of-hasidic-judaism-just-came-out-as-an-atheist-trans-woman/

184. *The Second Transition.* Accessed July 18, 2017. http://abbychavastein.com

185. Moran, Terry. "Leslie Jones' Twitter Troll Has No Regrets Over Attacking the 'Ghostbusters' Actress." *ABC News.* September 1, 2016. Accessed July 18, 2017. http://abcnews.go.com/Entertainment/leslie-jones-twitter-troll-regrets-attacking-ghostbusters-actress/story?id=41808886

186. Dolan, Eric W. "Comedian Explodes on 'Self-Loathing' Gay Conservative Who Wants to Be Straight: Face It, 'You Are Gay as F*ck!'." *Raw Story.* October 1, 2015. Accessed July 18, 2017. http://www.rawstory.com/2015/10/comedian-explodes-on-self-loathing-gay-conservative-who-wants-to-be-straight-face-it-you-are-gay-as-fck/

Chapter Seven

187. Ravitz, Jessica. "This Oklahoma Atheist Isn't Thanking the Lord." CNN. May 22, 2013. Accessed August 7, 2017. http://religion.blogs.cnn.com/2013/05/22/this-oklahoma-atheist-isnt-thanking-the-lord/

188. Ahmad, Meher. "Atheist Tornado Survivor Sparks Crazy-Juice Fueled Religious Debate." *Jezebel.* May 24, 2013. Accessed July 19, 2017. http://jezebel.com/atheist-tornado-survivor-sparks-crazy-juice-fueled-reli-509744337

189. "Atheists United." Indiegogo. https://www.indiegogo.com/projects/atheists-unite

190. "2014 U.S. Religious Landscape Study." Pew Research Center. http://www.pewforum.org/religious-landscape-study

191. "How Americans Feel About Religious Groups." Pew Research Center. July 16, 2014. Accessed July 19, 2017. http://www.pewforum.org/2014/07/16/how-americans-feel-about-religious-groups/

192. "Same-Sex Marriage, State by State." Map. Pew Research Center. June 26, 2015. http://www.pewforum.org/2015/06/26/same-sex-marriage-state-by-state/

193. Solomon, Marc. *Winning Marriage: The Inside Story of How Same-Sex Couples Took on the Politicians and Pundits—and Won.* Lebanon, New Hampshire. ForeEdge, University Press of New England, 2014.

194. "Man's Refusal to Say 'So Help Me God' Hasn't Helped Get Job as Notary Public." *Spartanburg Herald-Journal.* March 2, 1992.

195. Gellman, Susan, and Susan Looper-Friedman. "Thou Shalt Use the Equal Protection Clause for Religion Cases (Not Just the Establishment Clause)." *Journal of Constitutional Law 10,* no. 4 (May 2008). Accessed August 7, 2017.

196. Lee, Adam. "Why Is America's Most Progressive Voting Bloc Often Overlooked?" AlterNet. August 6, 2012. Accessed July 19, 2017. http://www.alternet.org/story/156452/in_fight_for_progressive_change,_staunchest_ally_is_often_overlooked%3A_atheists

197. Barker, Dan. *Godless: How an Evangelical Preacher Became One of America's Leading Atheists.* Madison, Wisconin. Ulysses Press, 2008.

198. Morales, Lymari. "Knowing Someone Gay/Lesbian Affects Views of Gay Issues." Gallup. May 29, 2009. Accessed July 19, 2017. http://www.gallup.com/poll/118931/knowing-someone-gay-lesbian-affects-views-gay-issues.aspx

199. Lipka, Michael. "Americans Are Divided Over Which Public Bathrooms Transgender People Should Use." Pew Research Center. October 3, 2016. Accessed July 19, 2017. http://www.pewresearch.org/fact-tank/2016/10/03/americans-are-divided-over-which-public-bathrooms-transgender-people-should-use/

200. "How Americans Feel About Religious Groups." Pew Research Center. July 16, 2014. Accessed July 19, 2017. http://www.pewforum.org/2014/07/16/how-americans-feel-about-religious-groups/

201. Lawrence, Jill. "'Community Organizer' Slams Attract Support for Obama." *ABC News.* September 4, 2008. Accessed July 19, 2017. http://abcnews.go.com/Politics/story?id=5731599&page=1

202. Anderson, Leigh. "How to Talk With Religious Conservatives About LGBT Rights." Lifehacker. July 13, 2017. Accessed July 17, 2017. http://lifehacker.com/how-to-talk-with-religious-conservatives-about-lgbt-rig-1796623461

Chapter Eight

203. *Cracking the Codes: The System of Racial Inequity.* Directed by Shakti Butler. Performed by Joy DeGruy. World Trust Educational Services, 2012. Clip from film. September 20, 2011. Accessed July 12, 2017. https://world-trust.org/

204. Konnikova, Maria. "I Don't Want to Be Right." *The New Yorker.* May 16, 2014. Accessed July 12, 2017. http://www.newyorker.com/science/maria-konnikova/i-dont-want-to-be-right

205. "Leviticus." *Bible Abuse Directed at Homosexuals.* Accessed July 12, 2017. https://www.stopbibleabuse.org/biblical-references/leviticus.html

206. Kearns, Shannon. "Transgender and Christian?" *Queer Theology.* Accessed July 12, 2017. https://www.queertheology.com/transgender-christian/

207. Sears, Brad, and Alan Hirsch. "No Time to Celebrate." *The Village Voice.* November 25, 2003. Accessed July 12, 2017. https://www.villagevoice.com/2003/11/25/no-time-to-celebrate/

208. Young, Cliff, and Debbie Holloway. "Is It Selfish to Not Want Children?" Crosswalk.com. August 23, 2012. Accessed July 12, 2017. http://www.crosswalk.com/family/singles/he-said-she-said/it-is-selfish-to-i-not-i-want-children.html

209. "America's Changing Religious Landscape." Pew Research Center. May 12, 2015. Accessed July 12, 2017. http://www.pewforum.org/2015/05/12/chapter-3-demographic-profiles-of-religious-groups/

210. Peck, Peggy. "Religious Belief No Barrier to Teen Pregnancy." *ABC News.* September 17, 2009. Accessed July 13, 2017. http://abcnews.go.com/Health/Sex/study-finds-teen-pregnancy-common-religious-states/story?id=8602283

211. Regnerus, Mark. "How Different Are the Adult Children of Parents Who Have Same-Sex Relationships? Findings From the New Family Structures Study." *Social Science Research* vol. 41, no. 4 (July 2012), pp. 752-770. Accessed July 13, 2017.

212. Bartlett, Tom. "Controversial Gay-Parenting Study Is Severely Flawed, Journal's Audit Finds." *The Chronicle of Higher Education.* July 26, 2012. Accessed July 13, 2017. http://www.chronicle.com/blogs/percolator/controversial-gay-parenting-study-is-severely-flawed-journals-audit-finds/30255

213. Ford, Zack. "Journal's Internal Audit Finds Flawed Gay Parenting Study to Be 'Bullshit'." *ThinkProgress.* July 27, 2012. Accessed July 13, 2017. https://thinkprogress.org/journals-internal-audit-finds-flawed-gay-parenting-study-to-be-bullshit-20b20ccf61f9

214. Rose, Scott. "University of Texas Opens Inquiry of Regnerus Study; NCRM Reporting Plays Central Role." *The New Civil Rights Movement.* Accessed July 13, 2017. http://www.thenewcivilrightsmovement.com/university_of_texas_opens_inquiry_of_regnerus_study_ncrm_reporting_plays_central_role

215. Ford, Zack. "NOM Founder Connects Dots Between Islamophobia And Homophobia." *ThinkProgress.* September 9, 2011. Accessed July 14, 2017. https://thinkprogress.org/nom-founder-connects-dots-between-islamophobia-and-homophobia-af2ac6cda66

216. Resnick, Sofia. "New Family Structures Study Intended to Sway Supreme Court On Gay Marriage, Documents Show." *HuffPost.* March 10, 2013. Accessed July 14, 2017. http://www.huffingtonpost.com/2013/03/10/supreme-court-gay-marriage_n_2850302.html

217. Ford, Zack. "Documents Reveal Anti-Gay Parenting Study Was Manipulated to Influence Supreme Court." *ThinkProgress.* March 11, 2013. Accessed July 14, 2017. https://thinkprogress.org/documents-reveal-anti-gay-parenting-study-was-manipulated-to-influence-supreme-court-1c1f4b50a216

218. Rafter, Dan. "UT Austin Denounces Mark Regnerus' Anti-Gay Study." *Human Rights Campaign Blog.* March 4, 2014. Accessed July 14, 2017.

http://www.hrc.org/blog/ut-austin-denounces-mark-regnerus-anti-gay-study

219. "Statement From the Chair Regarding Professor Regnerus." UT College of Liberal Arts. April 12, 2014. Accessed July 14, 2017. http://liberalarts.utexas.edu/sociology/news/article.php/sociology/news/7572?id=7572

220. Stern, Mark Joseph. "The Scientific Debate Over Same-Sex Parenting Is Over." *Slate,* April 13, 2016. Accessed July 14, 2017. http://www.slate.com/blogs/outward/2016/04/13/scientific_debate_over_same_sex_parenting_is_over.html

221. Conger, John J. "Proceedings of the American Psychological Association, Incorporated, for the Year 1974: Minutes of the Annual Meeting of the Council of Representatives." *American Psychologist* no. 30 (June 1, 1975). Accessed September 9, 2017. http://www.apa.org/about/policy/discrimination.aspx

222. Parry, Wynne. "Normal or Not? When One's Gender Identity Causes Distress." *Live Science.* June 3, 2013. Accessed July 14, 2017. https://www.livescience.com/37087-dsm-gender-dysphoria.html

223. DeAngelis, Tori. "New Data on Lesbian, Gay and Bisexual Mental Health." *Monitor on Psychology* no. 33 (February 2002), p. 46.

224. Russo, Francine. "Is There Something Unique About the Transgender Brain?" *Scientific American.* January 1, 2016. Accessed July 14, 2017. https://www.scientificamerican.com/article/is-there-something-unique-about-the-transgender-brain/

225. Holpuch, Amanda. "Trans Children Allowed to Express Identity 'Have Good Mental Health'." *The Guardian.* February 26, 2016. Accessed July 14, 2017. https://www.theguardian.com/society/2016/feb/26/crucial-study-transgender-children-mental-health-family-support

226. Allen, Samantha. "What Science Can Tell Us About Trans People's Brains—And What It Cannot." *The Daily Beast.* January 19, 2017. Accessed July 14, 2017. http://www.thedailybeast.com/what-science-can-tell-us-about-trans-peoples-brainsand-what-it-cannot

227. "#BornPerfect: The Facts About Conversion Therapy." National Center for Lesbian Rights. Accessed July 14, 2017. http://www.nclrights.org/bornperfect-the-facts-about-conversion-therapy/#q2

228. Title II of the Civil Rights Act (Public Accommodations). United States Department of Justice.

229. "Non-Discrimination Laws." Map. *Movement Advancement Project.* July 7, 2017. Accessed July 14, 2017. http://www.lgbtmap.org/equality-maps/non_discrimination_laws

230. "Against Nature? An Exhibition on Animal Homosexuality." UiO Naturhistorisk Museum. February 25, 2009. Accessed July 14, 2017. http://www.nhm.uio.no/besok-oss/utstillinger/skiftende/againstnature/index-eng.html

231. Mehta, Hemant. "Conservative Christians Are Flipping Out Over a Disney Cartoon With Two Gay Moms." Patheos. August 13, 2017. Accessed September 10, 2017. http://www.patheos.com/blogs/friendlyatheist/2017/08/13/conservative-christians-are-flipping-out-over-a-disney-cartoon-with-two-gay-moms/

Chapter Nine

232. "Policy and Position Statements on Conversion Therapy." *Human Rights Campaign.* Accessed July 25, 2017. http://www.hrc.org/resources/policy-and-position-statements-on-conversion-therapy

233. Miller, Hayley. "100 Anti-LGBTQ Bills Introduced in 2017." *Human Rights Campaign.* March 7, 2017. Accessed July 25, 2017. http://www.hrc.org/blog/100-anti-lgbtq-bills-introduced-in-2017

234. Holden, Dominic. "These Gay Republicans Mocked Transgender Women At A Forum In New York City." *BuzzFeed.* April 28, 2017. Accessed July 25, 2017. https://www.buzzfeed.com/dominicholden/gay-republicans-mocked-transgender-women-at-a-forum

235. Rodriguez, Mathew. "This Is What It's Like to Log Into Grindr as a Person of Color." Mic. September 18, 2015. Accessed July 25, 2017. https://mic.com/articles/125417/this-is-what-it-s-like-to-log-into-grindr-as-a-person-of-color

236. "50 States of Adoption." Family Equality Council. Accessed July 25, 2017. http://www.familyequality.org/get_informed/families_for_all/50_states_of_adoption/

237. Ford, Zack. "Allowing Transgender Youth To Transition Improves Their Mental Health, Study Finds." *ThinkProgress.* March 10, 2015. Accessed July 25, 2017. https://thinkprogress.org/allowing-transgender-youth-to-transition-improves-their-mental-health-study-finds-dd6096523375

238. Singh, Sejal, and Laura E. Durso. "Widespread Discrimination Continues to Shape LGBT People's Lives in Both Subtle and Significant Ways." Center for American Progress. May 2, 2017. Accessed July 25, 2017. https://www.americanprogress.org/issues/lgbt/news/2017/05/02/429529/widespread-discrimination-continues-shape-lgbt-peoples-lives-subtle-significant-ways/